R...

Transfo...

Other titles by Robin Greenwood:

Reclaiming the Church (Fount Original 1988)

Robin Greenwood

TRANSFORMING
PRIESTHOOD

A New Theology
of Mission and Ministry

First published in Great Britain 1994
Society for Promoting Christian Knowledge
Holy Trinity Church
Marylebone Road
London NW1 4DU

Second impression 1995

British Library Cataloguing-in-Publication Data
A catalogue record for this book is available from the
British Library.

ISBN 0-281-04761-8

Typeset by Datix International Limited, Bungay, Suffolk
Printed in Great Britain by
Redwood Books, Trowbridge, Wiltshire

To Claire, Peter, Tim, and Katherine

CONTENTS

PREFACE

This enquiry is a testimony to the courage and vision of groups of Anglicans with whom I have shared responsibility for mission and ministry for more than twenty years. For the particular stimulus to clarify my own thinking I am indebted to Professor David Ford. I also appreciate the support and encouragement of colleagues and friends in the Diocese of Gloucester, especially Kenneth Jennings, Jeremy Walsh, and John Yates. For their particular help in improving the text I thank David Brindley, Alan Dunstan, Noreen Norton, Roger Ruston, Alan Wilkinson and readers at SPCK. Enid Brinkworth has made an invaluable contribution to producing a final typescript. My warmest thanks go to my wife, Claire. My reflection on the pain and pleasure of Christian ministry has been strengthened by her insights into the dynamics of community and family living.

Robin Greenwood
Gloucester Cathedral

LIST OF ABBREVIATIONS

AA   *Apostolicam Actuositatem*, Vatican II, Decree on the Apostolate of the Laity, ET Walter Abbott, (ed.) *The Documents of Vatican II*, (London–Dublin, Geoffrey Chapman, 1966).

ABM   Advisory Board of Ministry

ACCM   Advisory Council for the Church's Ministry

ARCIC   Anglican–Roman Catholic International Commission

ASB   Alternative Service Book 1980

BCP   Book of Common Prayer 1662

BCC   British Council of Churches

BEM   *Baptism, Eucharist and Ministry*, the Lima report of the WCC Faith and Order Commission, (WCC, Geneva, 1982)

BSR   Board of Social Responsibility

CACTM   Church's Advisory Council for Training for the Ministry

CMS   Church Missionary Society

DBF   Diocesan Board of Finance

DR   Doctrine Report, 1938, Church of England.

DS   H. Denzinger and A. Schönmetzer (eds.) *Enchiridion Symbolorum*, (Freiburg im Breisgau, edition 34, 1967).

ET   English Translation

FOAG   Faith and Order Advisory Group of the Church of England Board of Mission and Unity

GS   *Gaudium et Spes*. Vatican II, Pastoral Constitution on the Church in the Modern World. (ET Abbott).

LG   *Lumen Gentium*. Vatican II, Dogmatic Constitution on the Church, (ET Abbott, 1965).

NSM   Non-Stipendiary Ministry

REB   Revised English Bible

SST   Society for the Study of Theology

WCC   World Council of Churches

INTRODUCTION

What ordained ministry does the Church of England now require? The basic question of this enquiry is, in the present context of the Church of England, how should the role of its clergy be defined? During the years 1978-86, as an Anglican priest in east Leeds, my primary aim was to make possible a Christian community in which every person could recognize his or her gifts and ministry within the Church's mission. Theologically, my passion for a new way of being church was inspired at that time by the energy and optimism generated in many parts of the world-wide Church after the Second Vatican Council. Humanly speaking, I held the conviction that within the Church the potential contribution of a whole host of people is frequently neglected and even vilified. The writers who most influenced me in their ability to be visionary about the future of the Church and to make fruitful connections between theology and the human sciences included: Avery Dulles, Hans Küng, Johann Baptist Metz, Edward Schillebeeckx, Lèon-Joseph Suenens, and others in Europe and the Third World whose writings were translated in *Concilium*.

At the end of the study, *Reclaiming the Church* (1988), in which I reflected personally on those years, I recognized that for Anglicans a key that was missing was a coherent theological statement of priesthood for today. I was working with many Christians who were searching for a way simultaneously to celebrate the ministries of clergy and laity, and for whom inherited definitions no longer seemed plausible. Throughout the country, parishes were exploring this relationship, but apart from the recapitulation of New Testament themes, the tools for making a theological statement about priesthood were not available.

In the early 1990s, there have been enormous strides

1

forward among Anglicans in the encouragement of lay ministry, with a growing emphasis on the collaborative nature of
the Church in mission and evangelism. Pragmatically and
intellectually, the argument has been won, so that the ministry
of the laity may seem to be a commonplace reality. Both
informally and in the diocesan and local structures of the
Church of England (sometimes with ecumenical cooperation),
experiments in collaborative ministry are taking place. Yet, at
the level of feelings, there remains much tension to be resolved.
I observe considerable bewilderment and anger among clergy
at the changes in the Church, and a parallel lack of courage
and confidence on the part of those laity who are eager to be
stretched in their knowledge of God, and to bring about a
new way of being church. Clergy often express a conviction
that they feel redundant because the laity have somehow
taken their place. Others have gladly given assent with their
heads to the vital role of laity in the Church, yet are held back
emotionally from sharing the power which inherited patterns
left in their hands. Equally, there are laity who feel rejected
because, despite constant reference to collaborative ministry
as an idea, the patterns of their church's life still do not give
them 'permission' to be treated as of equal value to the clergy.

The situation is increasingly aggravated by a complex
situation which includes factors such as rapid decline in the
numbers of ordinands, serving clergy, available posts, and of
money to pay stipends. There are church members who
choose to understand the move towards lay ministry purely
in terms of strategies of finance and person power. Others
have developed notions of a conspiracy among the bishops to
remove clergy and cease to look for new ordinands. The
complex truth is that the combined forces of pragmatism
and theology at the close of the twentieth century are sweep-
ing English Anglicans inexorably to a fundamentally new
concept of the parochial ministry. There remains for most of
the Church of England the commitment of a pastoral ministry to the entire population in every settlement, except for
those who choose to opt out because they hold a different
faith. What is increasingly becoming accepted is that it is no
longer plausible for ministry to be offered on the inherited
patterns, by staffing the parishes with stipendiary priests.

A growing number of dioceses are making a commitment to developing new ministerial arrangements which assume that in the future there will be a limited number of stipendiary priests and money to pay them. The new expectation is that a diminished number of clergy will be strategically deployed as members of 'local ministry teams'. The growth of local ministry teams, in which clergy and laity work together, has been one of the outstanding features of the Church of England over the past ten years. Within an overall policy for local ministry, schemes vary considerably but membership will usually include all clergy, stipendiary and non-stipendiary, readers, and an appropriate number of elected laity. There will inevitably be many problems resulting from lack of understanding, differing degrees of tolerance to change, lack of co-operation between adjacent parishes, uncertainty about the meaning of 'local', 'ministry', and 'teams', not to mention sheer human sinfulness.

However, one of the most obvious stumbling blocks in the years ahead will be the absence of a plausible and coherent theological statement of what is now meant by the expression 'parish priest'. I propose to use the term throughout this enquiry as one which I believe to be generally acknowledged in the Church of England to identify the ordained person 'in charge' of a benefice, parish, or group of parishes. There is a whole cluster of terms such as priest-in-charge, vicar, rector, which are used in specific places; 'parish priest' seems to be the most convenient way of pinpointing the category of ordained men and women who have been given responsibility by the bishop for the mission and ministry of a particular geographical territory in the Church of England.

This book has, as an underlying motive, the desire to affirm the urgent need for parish priests. Far from being redundant, in the renewed structures of English Anglicanism, clergy will have a vital task to perform. What is crucial is that the Church now requires clergy to have expectations of their role and matching skills markedly different from those of the immediate past. As a new way of being a church gradually comes to birth, an appropriate theology and role model of the parish priest is essential. The Church will not in the future be able to attract women and men to say, 'I want to serve as a parish priest' until we can say, 'this is the shape of the job; this is its theological rationale'.

This enquiry into an appropriate theology of mission and ministry for the twenty-first century does not pretend to be a front-line work of theological discovery, nor to be a practical guide on how to be a parish priest. Rather, its claim to be of value is in the attempt to focus theologically many of the fragmentary and powerful insights currently influencing the practice and informing the reflection of the Church of England. I offer these proposals in the hope that many Anglicans will recognize here a vision of priesthood which is already happening in practice. It may be objected that in this enquiry little account is taken of the fruits of the behavioural sciences. Certainly, it could have been researched from the point of view of disciplines other than theology. The specific intention has been to root the thinking in what is plausible in the contemporary Church of England, but essentially to regard the present work as a theological thesis.

In the first two-thirds of this century, claims about the identity and role of Anglican clergy had such a confident ring, that it is inevitable that pain is being experienced during the process of moving to alternative concepts. For this reason it seems essential that in the context of so much contemporary discussion and experimentation in collaborative ministry, clergy should have a new theological basis for understanding their role, with sufficient plausibility and authority to make it possible to abandon what previously seemed appropriate. The Church often seems to be late in coming to a professional recognition that if its work is to be respected, those involved in its leadership should be willing to articulate and subscribe to a publicly agreed understanding of their role.

My credentials for putting forward what I believe to be for the present moment a concept of priesthood more adequate than that bequeathed by our predecessors, lie in the particular combination of resources which have been part of my journey. Ordained priest more than two decades ago, and for the past seven years a diocesan training officer, I have kept closely in touch with the ecumenical debate about the Church and its ministry. Although I write inevitably as an Anglican, it has been my experience that members of different denominations can often see links between the Church of England's experience and their own. The first chapter of this enquiry acts as a bridge between contemporary experiences of being church and how matters were traditionally conceived. Brief reviews will be offered of the contribution to this discussion of several paradigmatic English Anglican theologians in the period 1900–70. The shelves of college libraries and second-hand bookshops contain works by clergy involved in training both ordinands and curates that remind us today of the bench-marks of the theology and practice of priesthood, which formed clergy for most of this century. Almost entirely, these came from the hands of moderate to extreme Catholics who set the Anglican agenda regarding church and ministry for much of the twentieth century. The Evangelicals of the earlier part of the century, committed to no particular theory of the Church, made little direct contribution to the development of ecclesiology or a doctrine of ministry. It will be important to identify some of the chief ingredients of the confident vision that inspired our forebears so that, facing the demands of the present, we can recognize both what remains of value, and what should now deliberately be discarded.

Chapter Two presents the next logical step in laying the foundations for an alternative concept of church and ministry. That is briefly to note the empirical context of the contemporary Church of England. Chapter Three recognizes how the 1987 *Occasional Paper 22* of the Advisory Council for the Church's Ministry entitled *Education for the Church's Ministry: the Report of the Working Party on Assessment* is fertile with ideas for a relational theology of church and ministry.

The following stage, in Chapters Four and Five, is to engage with the international ecumenical debate to discover truthful concepts for the construction of a doctrine of church (ecclesiology) and ministry. My ecclesiological vision, formed both by reflective practice and engagement with ecumenical dialogue, is determined largely by turning away from the inherited monist tendencies in thinking about God, in favour of a social trinitarianism. Rejecting the inherited understanding of all reality and the exercise of power in the Church in

Thomism + Plato/Aristotle?

terms of <u>substance,</u> and adopting one that is inherently <u>relational,</u> leads to productive concepts for describing ministerial arrangements in the Church, and priesthood in particular. An integral part of this new vision for church and priesthood is the recognition that before anything can be said of individual priests, a great deal has to be worked out regarding the being of Godself, the passionate mission of God for the salvation of the created order, and the role of the Church as a vehicle of that mission. This is why, logically, it is not until Chapter Six that proposals can be made regarding the role of the parish priest.

At the time of writing, women are assuming increasingly significant roles within the ordained ministry as pastors, missioners, educators, and members of cathedral and bishops' staffs. 1994 is the year that has witnessed the first ordinations to the priesthood of women in the Church of England. Many difficult issues exist for both men and women during this period of transition. Until it becomes normal for ordinations and appointments to be free from gender bias—confusion, anger and pain will be mixed with the pleasure that many experience now that women are accepted as priests in the Church of England. To make the language of this study as inclusive as possible (except in the historical section), I have used the male and female pronouns indiscriminately. My theological proposals about ecclesiology and priesthood take it as axiomatic that there is no legitimate gender barrier in deciding who should be ordained. It is my hope that women ordained as priests can avoid the temptation to seek for themselves that status and separation from laity that has beset ordained ministry throughout this century. Women priests will bring new life and growth to the Church of England and will hopefully help the wider Church to take new steps in understanding and developing the theology and practice of mission and ministry.

The agenda of this book, at every point, avoids being reduced to a consideration of ordination, whether of men or women, in isolation from the whole Church. In considering what kind of parish priest is required today, the Church is asking a more fundamental question about its own identity in order to fulfil its vocation as a sign and foretaste of God's desire for the salvation of all creation.

Chapter One
THEOLOGICAL INFLUENCES ON ANGLICAN PRIESTHOOD 1900–1970

Introduction

What has passed for a theology of priesthood in the Church of England this century has often been confined to a review of New Testament texts and phrases designed to endorse contemporary Anglican practice. The recurring theme of the Catholic Anglican synthesis dominant for much of the twentieth century portrays clergy as the primary representatives of the risen Christ, and through the bishops, successors to the apostles themselves. However, dissident voices constantly offered alternative visions rooted in differing approaches to the exegesis of the New Testament and the role of the institutional church in Christianity. Briefly, this opening chapter will survey several twentieth-century paradigmatic statements of a theology of church and priesthood. Together, they indicate the general character of the debate on these issues in the Church of England between 1900–70 and provide a background against which to examine the present and future.

Some Twentieth-Century Theologies of Church and Priesthood

(a) R. C. Moberly

R. C. Moberly was an Anglo-Catholic, contributor to _Lux Mundi_, and later Regius Professor of Pastoral Theology at Oxford (1892–1903). His overriding conviction was that the Church of England is authentically Catholic. The background which gave birth to Moberly's _Ministerial Priesthood_ (1886), which through many reprints remained a standard Anglican text for the first half of this century, specifically

7

identifies the following elements. First, despite the support of
the Idealist school of philosophy, Christianity was no longer
defensible to many contemporary intellectuals.[1] Second,
there was a high level of tension between those who were
loyal to what they believed to be traditional Christianity and
others who, since the time of F. D. Maurice, had been
accused of unsettling student minds with 'liberal' doctrines.[2]
In part, Moberly was directly challenging the claims of New
Testament scholars, such as Lightfoot and Hort, that the
ordained ministry was not in a literal sense divinely-given,
but merely the construction of the early Church as a practical
necessity.

   A third part of the context, and one of the specific issues
which Moberly addresses, was the Erastianism whereby the
Church was regarded as a department of State in a confidently Christian society. Moberly insisted on its separate
identity as the Catholic Church in continuity with the first
centuries and the Middle Ages.[3] A fourth tension influencing
Moberly's *Ministerial Priesthood* was his desire to distance the
Church of England from what he considered the secularizing
spirit which was diminishing the public status of the Bible
and the Established Church. He believed the Church should
be confronting the modern world with a divinely-given,
transcendent Gospel.[4] In the fifth place, despite the residual
confidence of the Church of England at the close of the
Victorian era, it was experiencing a steady decline in committed membership and, as population figures rose, a dramatic
fall in the proportion of clergy to people.[5] Sixth, there was a
growing perception of priests, who had lost much of the
prestige which Victorian clergy had enjoyed, as both separate
from society and 'not as other men'.[6] Although the hierarchy
had not recognized these facts, in 1900 urban clergy were
already lamenting a slow but steady decline in church attendance. Increasingly, at the beginning of the twentieth century,
the ministry of the Church of England was experiencing
marginalization.[7] Lastly, the impetus for Moberly's *Ministerial Priesthood* was the decisive rejection of the validity of
Anglican Orders by Leo XIII, reflecting the strident assertive-
ness of Vatican I ultramontanism.

   The Church of England's status as part of the Catholic

Church in Moberly's view, was safeguarded by the possession of a valid ordained ministry. It was Moberly's intention to prove beyond all doubt that the ordained ministry of the Church of England was not defective in its intention to ordain a sacrificing priesthood.[8] Against Rome, he asserts that the Church of England has a claim to exist, quite literally, in full continuity with the ancient Catholic Church because it has a divinely-given understanding of ordained ministry that portrays bishop and priest as God's immediate representatives. It was generally speaking Moberly's Prayer Book Catholicism, rather than the kind that looked to Rome for normative standards, that was to become 'middle of the road' to 'high Anglicanism' as the twentieth century progressed.

Moberly denounces the explanation of the origins of Christian ministry represented in Edwin Hatch's *Bampton Lectures* (1880), while applauding Charles Gore's *The Church and the Ministry* (1889). The former, he believes, presented the institutional unity of the Church as though it were achieved through the mere chance of human ingenuity; the latter showed how it was truly nothing less than God's detailed plan. He appeals to Scripture as proof that the Church's unity as a 'kingdom' with enrolled membership, organized with 'officers, discipline, and government' was not a secondary human development of Christian life. Rather, from the beginning, it was essentially and divinely-given, 'direct and complete'.[9] Constantly referring to Scripture and the early fathers, Moberly insists that despite the failings of the Church and her ministers, the Holy Spirit always works through divinely ordained 'methods'.[10]

His interpretation of the New Testament letters suggests that all Christians belong to a single Body in which ordained ministers are certainly not intermediaries, but 'organs of the Body through which the life inherent in the total Body expresses itself in particular functions of detail'.[11] Moberly insists that all Christians share in the gifts and responsibilities of membership of Christ's Body, but that, just as a human body needs a point of practical effectiveness, so, 'the ministry is the instrument as well as the symbol of the church's unity, and no man can share her fellowship except in acceptance of

its offices'.[12] On the one hand, he wishes to stress the significance of all church members, but on the other, precisely
because his ecclesiology finds its validation in the ministerial
priesthood itself, he is bound so to over-emphasize the role of
clergy as the divinely-appointed and separate means by
which Christ's priesthood is made effective to the Church,
that he diminishes the significance of all who are not ordained. He emphasizes that priest and layman are certainly
equal 'as far as their personal prerogatives of spiritual life are
concerned', but are inevitably distinct because of the different
specific authority given to them.[13]

The result, is a dual form of representation of Christ in the
Church, a hierarchy of the clerical and the lay. Moberly
stresses that priests are no closer to God than laity. Ordination, however, gives them a different interior character or
status and a responsibility for tasks which do not belong to
laity. His hope is that it may be possible to speak, on the one
hand, of the separate status of priesthood, and on the other,
to deny that ordination brings an automatic closeness to God
or that the priesthood should be conceived of as working
with God vicariously on behalf of all. He places the blame
for misunderstandings and resultant clerical dependency on
a reduction of standards in lay Christianity, and on a widespread misrepresentation of the word 'layman' as meaning
negatively, 'not an expert', rather than positively, 'a member
of the People of God'.[14]

In facing up to the nature of the distinction between clergy
and laity, Moberly asserts that Scripture is clear (with the
support of the BCP Ordinal) that ordination depends essentially on the call of God to the individual above and beyond
baptism. This could be particularly demonstrated in the
phrases: 'Even so I send you' and 'Receive ye the Holy
Ghost'.[15] To relate the vocation of the individual and that of
the whole Church, Moberly turns to the notion of apostolic
succession. He recalls the principle that in the Church's
tradition, beginning with the first century letter of Clement of
Rome, ministerial office is primarily an outward and orderly
institution. It is dependent for its validity upon tactile transmission, continuous and authorized, from the Apostles, whose
own commission was direct from Jesus Christ.[16]

In summary, Moberly's view was that, unlike Protestants, Anglicans belong to the episcopalian, Catholic church in which the incarnational spirit is pivotal, and in which there is an ordained ministry, a group superior to the body of baptized Christians, individually and divinely commissioned. The ordained ministry of the Church of England may be said to be inherited linearly from the apostolate of the earliest days of the Church. The priest of the Church of England is assured of being Christ's representative, exercizing a ministry which is a blend of practical efficiency and faithfulness in liturgy and pastoralia, and the love of the Good Shepherd spoken of in John 10.

Despite his constant efforts to emphasize the spiritual equality of all Christians, the lasting effect of Moberly's work was to encourage and support a vision of ordained ministry as essentially individualistic, superordinate and separate from the laity. He believed, also that the ministerial priest for whom he offers the rationale was both secure from the criticisms of Rome, and of a totally different character from the ministry of the Protestant Free Churches. Moberly's theological statement is of ordained priests set over against laity, and of a Church of England set over against other traditions. He represents for a significant strand within the Church of England's understanding and practice of ordained ministry that indeed is far from extinct today, though increasingly to be found in a defensive and idiosyncratic position.[17]

(b) W. H. Griffith Thomas

The evidence is sparse for a reasoned critique of this approach to ordained ministry in the early years of the century. However, a contrasting view is certainly offered in the theology implicit in the manual of instruction for church members written by the Evangelical cleric and academic W. H. Griffith Thomas. A distinguished preacher in London, Thomas later became principal of Wycliffe Hall, Oxford. Through his prolific writing, conference speeches, and personal ministry his influence was strong among Evangelical clergy. His emphasis was upon the importance of the Reformation settlement in which the Book of Common Prayer and the Articles of the Church of England enshrined pure unadulterated Christianity. He found this faith upheld by the early fathers as well as post-Reformation writers such as Lancelot Andrews and John Cosin. It was the Tractarians, he believed, who were attempting to steer the Church of England off course.[18] Griffith Thomas believed that ordained ministry was to be regarded as merely a special means by which the church 'expresses and perpetuates its life and witness'. In other words, ordained ministry was a human development of the New Testament ministry which should be regarded as a practical evolution in response to need, rather than as a divine commission. He does not recognize a distinct order of bishops. Ordination, for Thomas, creates no special class of person because Christianity, comprising the spiritual gifts of everyone, is 'a religion which is a priesthood and not one that has a priesthood'. He regards priests neither as mediators or representatives of Christ, nor as the Church's rulers, for clergy and laity share this responsibility. Apostolic succession is not 'a historical connection with the times of the Apostles by laying on of hands', but is a succession of faithfulness to the reality and spirit of apostolic doctrine and life.[19]

The unquestionable verdict of history is that it was Moberly's powerful paradigm, rather than that articulated by Thomas, that received general acceptance. The Church of England in the main, for the first half of the twentieth century, became committed to emphasizing above all things a historically rooted validation of its authority in which clergy, as the primary representatives of Christ, were regarded as the divinely appointed hierarchy.

(c) Roland Allen

An almost romantic figure first made a significantly different contribution to the Anglican debate about church and ministry in the years after World War I. Roland Allen's important insights were largely overlooked in his day, but were republished and reassessed fifty years later, largely through the influence of David Paton. Slowly but unquestionably, the vision of Roland Allen has continued to raise questions regarding the accepted assumptions about vocation to ordained ministry understood in individualistic terms. A moderate High Church missionary, with experience in North China, Allen used the language of 'apostolic succession' in a way that contrasted sharply with the accepted Anglo-Catholic doctrine of his day.[20] Although his proposals for reform were aimed primarily at the mission situation in which he worked, they contained implications for the doctrine and polity of the Church in general.

Allen, with reference to Paul's missionary methods, criticizes the assumption that authority in the Church should be the prerogative of a tiny minority. He questions the accepted wisdom of selecting and training only those young men who can satisfy examiners in stringent academic tests. The ministry of the Church, he claims, needs a wide range of people and abilities. So often, those who can succeed academically are unable to communicate with the majority of society or to relate to regular church members. Allen's own phrases speak for themselves: 'They come, as it were, from outside'; 'The natural leaders are silenced'; 'There is no opportunity for the church to find its prophets . . . Nor for the prophets to find themselves.' He maintains that the better way lies in a combination of both local and professionally trained church leaders.[21] The 1930 Lambeth Conference gave the notion of local voluntary clergy a muted welcome, laying down certain guidelines, but on the whole saw the obstacles rather than the potential.[22]

still true

Allen's observation that the Church in every situation should take as its model the clear diversity of practice of the early Church is an indicator of why he went largely unheard within the prevailing atmosphere of the Church of his day. He was searching for an open Church that could offer a compelling gospel of hope to a post-war Britain. However, the Moberly paradigm of a clerically validated Church remained dominant. It may be fairly claimed that Allen's work has still to be recognized as a major pointer for the reshaping of the ministry of episcopalian churches.[23]

View of Author?

(d) Doctrine Report 1938 *Temple*

It is possible to glimpse something of a change in mood, and in a moderately Catholic direction, in the sections on the

Church and the sacraments in *Doctrine in the Church of England*,
the Report of the Commission on Christian Doctrine appointed by the Archbishops of Canterbury and York (1922,
published in 1938) and presided over mostly by William
Temple.

The section on the Church emphasizes that the experience
of redemption is both individual and corporate, and should
be seen as both personal and institutional.[24] Although the
Church's inherent unity is not destroyed by divisions in the
outward organization, Christians need to reconcile past history and present needs through new and appropriate forms
of worship and ministerial organization.[25] The idea of the
catholicity of the Church should not be used to foster divisions and distinctions. Rather, catholicity should be understood as a way of recognizing that the many separate
churches have partially what the entire Church possesses
more fully, and that God desires an end to doctrinal and
sacramental divisions. Ministry (like the Scriptures, creeds
and sacraments) is an 'institutional safeguard' for the
Church's continuity in fellowship and witness', based on
Christ's commissioning of the Twelve (Mark 3.14).[26]

The Report describes clergy as the 'organ for the performance of certain distinctive and characteristic acts' of the
Church. Ministry is to be regarded as an original and
essential element in the whole Church understood as the
Body of Christ, in which, 'every member has his place and
share according to his different capabilities and calling'.[27]
Ordained ministry can only properly be understood as distinctive from the laity, yet always understood in close relationship
with the Body and never at the expense of God's gifts to the
Church of prophecy, evangelism, and teaching. Ministerial
authority (for preaching, leadership in worship, teaching,
and pastoral care) is handed on by those who hold it already,
but it derives essentially from the 'Risen, Reigning, and
Present Lord Himself'.[28]

The Commission members believed it essential to detach
themselves from the tradition of using the myth of a single
New Testament form of ministry to justify one present-day
church order to the exclusion of another: 'We no longer
regard precedents, as such, as decisive for all time.'[29] A vital

strand within the doctrine of ministry was that the ordained
are effective instruments of unity and continuity in that they
possess the authority of the wider Church. The Report links
the present work of clergy to the original commission given
by Christ to the Apostles and continuously transmitted, but
with the important caution that occasions arise when the
official ministry becomes so distorted that it is legitimate to
revolt against it.

In summary, the Report concludes that a merely mechanical or historical ministerial succession alone cannot guarantee
the continuity of the essence of the Church. Endorsing the
Lambeth Conference conclusions of 1920, the Report emphasizes the role of the historic episcopate as the uniquely
recognized organ of continuity, though not necessarily in one
particular form.[30] It views the functions of bishops, priests
and deacons as traceable 'in principle' to the New Testament
Church, but also open to necessary adaption in a changing
world.

In a section devoted specifically to priesthood, the Report
emphasizes the corporate priesthood of the whole Church,
within which the ordained are commissioned representatives
of the Body of Christ. Within the Church's ministry, priests
share in the work of the episcopate, and in a way that is not
given to the laity, have a particular authorization to pro-
nounce absolution, and to be the formal focus for the celebration of the Eucharist. Wary of the misunderstandings surrounding the issue of sacrifice as related to priesthood, the
Report emphasizes that the Christian priest represents the
whole Church and derives his authority from the revelation
of God in the crucified Christ.[31]

(e) Michael Ramsey

Theologian and successively Archbishop of York and Canterbury, Ramsey was a keystone figure in Anglican development
this century, standing himself in the moderate Catholic position. Regarding our present theme, in studying the origins of
the Church, Ramsey deliberately moves the emphasis away
from the Church considered primarily as an institution
founded by Christ. Instead he focuses on the Apostles knowing

the Lord's death and the resurrection of which the Body of the Church, with its life and order, is the expression.[32] The question of the reunion of the churches also hinges on Christ's passion. Reconciliation is only possible by churches dying to themselves and rising with Christ. Ramsey identifies the Catholic and Evangelical impasse on the matters of order, continuity, ministry, and sacraments: 'the one emphasizing historic structure and the other God's Word and justification by faith'.[33] His ecclesiology, focussed on the gospel and the cross, moves away from legalistic and institutional language.

In the light of Old Testament references to God's blessing on sacrificial suffering, fulfilled by Jesus ultimately in his death and resurrection, Ramsey shows how the Church created by his death takes on the characteristics of the old Israel. For Christians, Christ's passion is not a stumbling block but rather, 'the centre of its existence, of its worship and of the way of unity which it offers to mankind'.[34] Here was a theology of church that was new in that it did not ignore the fruits of biblical scholarship in attempting to make connections between modern church order and the Church of the apostles.[35]

His ecclesiology embraces every baptized Christian rather than asserting the priority of a commissioned leadership élite. Baptism into a new relation with Christ and his Body is the primary significant fact about Christianity. Welcoming the fruits of biblical scholarship that point to the recognition of a great diversity of forms of ministry in the early Church, he moves away from concentrating on episcopacy as the linch-pin. He replaces it with an ecclesiology based on the relationship between the development of ministries and 'the Body and the Gospel of God'.[36] His conclusion is, that in the context of the baptism into Christ of all members of his Church, the episcopate is the expression of the unity of the body.[37] Like Oliver Quick, the moderate Anglo-Catholic, he believed that all sections of a divided Church are incomplete and those who possess episcopacy need to do so in humility.[38] Ramsey explores the character of the Eucharist particularly as drawing together the whole of human life into the sacrifice of Christ. He argues persuasively that it may be understood in sacrificial terms, provided that abuses are corrected that lead to an over-emphasis on the death of Christ to the exclusion of the resurrection and ascension, and his heavenly priesthood. Such abuses occur when the work of the Father and of Christ are conceived to be separate, and when it is forgotten that ministerial priesthood 'is the priesthood of the one Body focused in certain organs which act for the Lord and for the Body'.[39]

In harmony with New Testament and liturgical scholars, Ramsey makes available the ecclesiological *raison d'être* of the Parish Communion movement that was becoming already the instrument that would rapidly combine many strands of Catholic Anglicanism with the main body of the Church of England.[40] He provides the theology which enables the Church of England to begin to move away from the idea of the Eucharist as an occasional act of personal piety, and to see it instead as the focal point and source of life for a 'Christian sociology'.

(f) John A. T. Robinson

John Robinson, bishop and New Testament scholar, in his study in Pauline theology, *The Body* (reprinted three times in the five years after its publication in 1952), wrote in the double conviction that it was urgent for humankind to work collectively, and that the New Testament vision of solidarity has profound contemporary implication and relevance. Robinson knits together European and British biblical scholarship to transcend previous attempts to define church authority in terms of authority delegated from the apostles. In harmony with Ramsey's *The Gospel and the Catholic Church*, he emphasizes that Christians are corporate because they are 'in Christ'. He shows how Paul uses the analogy of the human body to describe how the Church is to be identified with Christ's risen body, 'in all its concrete reality'.[41] He constantly urged the Church of England to move away from internal agendas towards being 'the leaven of the new creation'.[42]

The working out of this doctrine liturgically was a passionate concern for Robinson, so that what is done in worship accurately reflects the people's theology of church. If laity took an active part in the eucharistic liturgy, Robinson was convinced they would simultaneously be empowered for mission as the Church in the world. The way to bring home to the laity that they are the Church, rather than the passive objects of clerical ministry, was to make plain the full implications of the eucharistic liturgy. He was also convinced that the internal ordering of church buildings had a profound effect on the expectation laity might receive of themselves as apostles.[43]

Another vital strand of Robinson's ecclesiological contribution was his insistence that the Church's worship should not create in the popular mind an image of a sacred world set against the secular. He invites the Church to offer a vision of the sacredness of the secular in which the Eucharist is the clue to the Christian renewal of the social order. As the Eucharist is the pattern of the Church's mission, so the internal life of the Church is the pattern for the whole of redeemed society.[44] Although he recalled that the essence of the God of mainstream Christian worship and understanding is known as three Persons, he did not develop the significance for church and ministry of the interaction of Father, Son, and Holy Spirit.[45]

This powerful and exciting challenge to the Church to be incarnated in society whilst also being the salt of the earth, was to remain a common theme of prophets through the rest of the century, and yet perversely the reality has been extremely slow in coming to birth. Generally speaking, parish churches have either failed to become collaborative and attractive communities celebrating communion in the crucified and risen Christ, or they have so defended their boundaries that most of the relationship between faith and everyday life has been eroded.[46]

(g) F. R. Barry

The Bishop of Southwell, F. R. Barry, passionately concerned that the Church might be instrumental in the process of revival after World War II, takes up Paul's theme (Eph. 4.11,12) that the body of the Church is called to ministry. The Church is composed of many lay ministers commissioned by confirmation for work in society. The proper work of professional clergy is to call and train the laity for prophecy, evangelism, and apostolic tasks.[47] His persistent contribution was significant in the process of moving the Church of England away from a concern about clerical validity and historical pedigree. Instead, he offered a vision of a national Church with a predominantly lay character though led by varied styles of ministry, unconstrained by parish boundaries.[48]

In preparation for the 1958 Lambeth Conference, Barry attempted to provide an understanding of the nature and function of the ordained ministry with an urgent plea for an increase in clergy numbers for the sake of the Church's mission. His statistics reminded the Church of England that ordinations (below 600 a year) were not keeping pace with deaths and retirements; the average age of the clergy was then given as approximately 52–55; there was a growing tendency towards ordaining older men, with a shorter ministerial working life (of the 496 ordained in 1956, 25 per cent were over forty years old). His ecclesiology arises from the Church's increasing marginalization and detachment from society, and the rising strength of the other world religions. While he acknowledges that the Church of England as an institution was stronger and more aware of itself as a Church than it had been in the 1920s, what he questions is its sense of direction. Barry feared the practice of adversarial denominationalism as a contradiction of the gospel: 'The paramount summons to the Church today is to move out into the community, to make more Christians and leaven the whole lump'.[49] In particular he calls for the reclaiming to a living faith of those who are only nominally Church of England. He echoes Guy Mayfield who in the same year wrote, 'It is now possible to be a layman to a greater or lesser degree'.[50]

In particular, he asks whether it is any longer possible to discuss the provision and the structure of the ordained ministry without a far more thorough investigation of what is meant by the ministry of the laity and its place in the life of the Church and the Christian mission.[51] The new influence of the French Catholic theologian, Yves Congar, whose *Lay People in the Church* had been published in English the previous year, leads Barry to state confidently that the primary question in a book about ordained ministry must be 'What is a layman?' He laments that in *Vocation and Ministry* he was not able to reveal more of the supportive confidence given to him by Congar. However, he judges correctly that Congar, while recognizing that there are implications for the role of the clergy in remoulding the Church's understanding of the laity, does not advance the argument for some Anglicans. So the laity remain dependent on the clergy.[52]

Vocation, for Barry, is for every person to give to God what he asks in all areas of human living. For Christians, in particular, this is to respond to God's call to be 'saints', responding in faith, penitence, and thanksgiving to that love revealed in the gospel. All Christians are called to worship and to receive 'those means of grace by which we are brought into fellowship with God through the mediation of Jesus Christ'.[53] Accepting that the world does seem hostile to religion, Barry, with reference to F. D. Maurice and Herbert Kelly, stresses that it is an impoverished Christianity that concerns itself only about the Church, rather than the entire order of creation. He looks to the end of a long era of Christianity that, in effect, encouraged two tiers of commitment, clerical and lay. Referring to Paul's letters, Barry urges an emphasis on Christian vocation understood as every person pursuing his or her daily life. The Church's mission does not consist of merely 'churchy' things but in the redeeming of society—its art, its science, its industry and politics, its homes, its schools, its work, and its recreation—recognizing in them God's hope for the world and baptizing them into Christ.[54] In this context Barry locates the ordained ministry. Emphasizing the individual's inner call, Barry also assumes the influence of family, friends, books, clergy, colleges, schools in the process of fostering vocations, before it is ratified by ordination at the hands of the bishop on behalf of the Church. It is vital then to be clear about the nature and function of the Church. For Barry, this far exceeds concerns about apostolic succession and validity of orders. He portrays the Church as always at the service of the Kingdom of God, and often against the odds, consisting of its total membership co-operating for the reconciling of the

world to God's will. There are close links here with the
Parish and People Movement and with John Robinson, as
Barry celebrates the achievement of the English Reformers,
who believed themselves in worship and ministry to be 'the
congregation of Christ's flock'. The Anglican Eucharist is
only properly offered, he insists, by the Church—not by a
hierarchy at a distant altar.[55]
Barry longs for humble, clear-sighted, courageous,
masculine-tempered, clergy to minister to laity in their vital
but distinct calling, and to be themselves on the frontier of
mission in the local community. The Church of England has
taken a long time to respond to Barry's vision of clergy as
those who encourage and support the laity in their mission.[56]
He believed that a purposeful Church will recruit those it
needs for professional leadership. Certainly, he recognizes
that ordinands must respond to God's inner call, but also
that the Church as a matter of course must take positive
action to choose for ordained ministry men from a wider
range of cultures than previously.[57] Raising the profile of
Roland Allen, Barry encourages the assembled bishops at
Lambeth 1958 to explore the possibilities of a supplementary
ministry, not merely as an expedient in the face of clergy
shortage, but because it would make a positive contribution
to the understanding of the Church's nature and life.[58] His
awareness of the problems and dangers of local and 'part-
time' clergy, need to be heeded in the 1990s with as much
care as the positive elements of his vision.

(h) A. T. Hanson

Professor A. T. Hanson challenges the understanding of
apostolic succession advocated by Kirk and his fellow essay-
ists in *The Apostolic Ministry* (1946). He argues that the
doctrine of the apostolic succession favoured by Kirk is
flawed partly because it could not be proved that a *shaliach*,
(a key rabbinic term translated 'servant' or 'witness') was
empowered to appoint a successor. Further, Hanson regarded
it as impossible to make a secure link of succession between
the twelve apostles and the first bishops.[59] Hanson concludes
against the Anglican Catholic ecclesiology, that there is no

proof that any of the Twelve was responsible for a particular succession of bishops, or that the particular succession which, according to the Pastorals was commissioned by Paul, can be traced to modern times.

Hanson exposes the tendency in previous attempts at theologies of ministry for writers to read their own theories into the evidence from the early Church.[60] He criticises the influential but a priori methods of Gore, Moberly, and Kirk for beginning by considering the position of the apostles as reflected in the Synoptics, and then leaping straight to some period in the second century, and only then considering the Epistles. Hanson demonstrates that the New Testament was not capable of offering a single doctrine of ordained ministry which can be used to test the validity or non-validity of others. What is of primary importance for Hanson, is the fundamentally inseparable link between ministry and church, rather than the question of ministerial succession. He appeals for discussion to be focused more on a theology of ministry and less on its historical pedigree.[61]

Influential Clerical Role Models

The importance of role models is widely recognized today. It seems likely that integrated with theological teaching, the influence of college staff and especially principals has been an important contributory factor in the formation of clergy. This was plainly recognized by the choices ordinands made in putting themselves in the hands of a particular college. Bishop Headlam of Gloucester reveals in correspondence with Principal Graham of Cuddesdon his suspicion that the colleges were stereotyping clergy, and that training in parishes was preferable.[62] To enhance the examination of the theological themes outlined above, there follows here brief mention of the chief characteristics of the thought and style of three significant figures who, for approximately fifteen years each, were theological college principals in the formative years of this period. Those to be discussed here are: J. B. Seaton, Principal of Cuddesdon, 1913–28, B. K. Cunningham, Principal of Westcott House, 1919–34, and Eric Graham, Principal of Cuddesdon, 1929–43. Holtby passes on Garbett's comment that, 'B. K. Cunningham and 'Jimmy' Seaton had had a greater influence on the Church in his time than any other two men'.[63] Whilst other members of staff changed with frequency, the influence on the ordinands of a long-staying principal was immense, especially with relatively small numbers in the college.[64]

(a) Social Background and Leadership Style

Seaton, son of a Leeds surgeon, was brought up in a devout household and educated at Leeds Grammar School, and Christ Church, Oxford. His career as a priest, teacher, and bishop was that of one whose talent and ability to meet enormously different challenges was always recognized.

Cunningham came from a wealthy Scottish family, from an early age was instructed in an evangelical Christianity, and was educated at Marlborough and Trinity, Cambridge. He has been described as a staunch supporter of the public school system, and at Westcott was proud to be 'preparing English gentlemen for Holy Orders'. Good manners and courtesy were primary requisites for those whom he trained to be priests. He placed great store by the virtues of continuity and stability. His insistence on formal dinner each night in term, at which students were expected to wear 'boiled shirts' gives a clear message concerning the kind of clergy he had in mind.[65] He also displayed the natural reticence towards women who were confidently feminine that characterized many who, through segregated education, had little experience of close relationships with the opposite sex. By contrast, some of his relationships with 'his boys' through several generations were warm and close.[66]

Graham was described by Owen Chadwick as having many natural talents combined with humility and self-restraint.[67] He was brought up an Evangelical, the son of an archdeacon, educated at Cheltenham and Oriel College, Oxford. It was characteristic of his style that he showed a dislike of modern administration and left his successor no written records. In contrast, his up-dating of his intercessions list was said to be punctilious. Unlike Cunningham, he accepted few invitations to speak beyond the college and only in exceptional circumstances would allow himself to be away overnight during term.

(b) Intellectual Discipline

Although Cunningham, known to his friends as 'the professor', had a love of academic excellence and insisted that sound learning was the hallmark of a good English clergyman, he himself found such concentration on study uncongenial.[68] He was constantly in demand, however, as a speaker and, even on holiday, was often overstretched in balancing commitments between preaching, speaking, and correspondence.

Seaton attracted students from Oxford and Cambridge, but also from the newer universities. He was not a creative scholar. He remained faithful to his original inspiration found in *Lux Mundi*, never finding reason to dissent from the doctrine of the Church of England as expressed by Gore, and also as presented in *Sacrament of Sacrifice*, by Dr Parsons, Bishop of Southwark.[69]

1st Past.

2nd Doctrine

Graham was quickly recognized as possessing scholarly gifts, so that after a first curacy he became in 1914 Vice-Principal of Salisbury Theological College. He fostered academically able students. A College inspection report of 1932 reveals that of forty six men at Cuddesdon, with one exception, the students were all graduates of Oxford or Cambridge.[70] However, Graham chose not to become intellectually excellent in a specialist field, and could be accused of failing to develop his own theological thinking from that which he had adopted in his own earlier training. In this way he gave to the ordinands a powerful message that doctrine took second place to the pastoral work of the priest.

(c) Attitude to the Priesthood

Cunningham insisted that he was training clergy who, as 'sons of God and English gentlemen', would not lose their links with their lay peers.[71] Priests were to be natural and human rather than a professional clerical coterie. He himself modelled the combination of holiness and humanity, sacramental friendliness and humour that he desired for his students. The active pursuit of sport was regarded as *de rigueur* in this human portrait, not least because it built up the sense of common life.

Seaton was opposed to clericalism, and regarded Cuddesdon as the place for preparation for a busy ministry among all kinds of people in the world.

Correspondence to Graham from bishops in England and throughout the Anglican Communion reveal how much Cuddesdon-trained priests were admired and sought after. Henson of Durham, for example, describes them as 'just the kind of men I should desire to ordain'.[72] Graham had a tough fight with CACTM to make the case for 'detached' colleges that were remote from universities, and even despite his efforts, some of these colleges subsequently were closed. The Church of England was ambivalent regarding how far it wished its ordinands in study, prayer, and life to embrace society, and how far to avoid contact with it. Graham, by contrast, had a clear vision of offering to ordinands a period of disciplined preparation for priesthood, away from the normal pressures of life.[73] The closed, corporate life of the college was to encourage a sense of the discipline that was clearly his ideal of the dedicated parish priest, so that he was able to say with confidence: 'It should not be difficult to distinguish between a theological College and a country club, but as there would appear to be some confusion among us at present, let me try to differentiate.'[74]

(d) Churchmanship

Cunningham had no party concerns, and looked for a comprehensive Church where there could be breadth of vision and 'freedom in God'. He was happiest when the students in college themselves displayed the range of churchmanship, from post-Tractarian to Presbyterian, to which he himself owed a debt.[75] His preference was for simplicity and intimacy in the corporate worship.

Graham (together with Bishop Strong of Oxford) expressed a clear preference for simplicity in worship, and wished the college to retain 'broad lines . . . very definitely

Church of England.' Graham discouraged the recurring suggestion among some students that the 'Roman' or 'Western'
liturgical insights should be taken exclusively in arrangements for Catholic ceremonial.

(e) Spirituality

Cunningham taught priests the need to be close to God and
to live constantly in his presence. Although the only two
rules of college were attendance at morning prayer and
formal dinner, he fostered a sense of corporateness by himself
living in college and being constantly available to 'his boys'.[76]
The drinking of the cup of sacrifice and the servanthood of
Christ were key New Testament images for Cunningham's
brand of priesthood. These inspired in his students that sense
of service to humanity, at whatever personal cost, which has
been a prevailing characteristic of the upper middle class
Christian-inspired ethic for much of the twentieth century.

Seaton gave a great deal of energy to fostering a sense of
community, he was a centre of good spirits and took care to
be 'one with his students'.[77]

At Cuddesdon under Graham, the spiritual life was focused in the corporate discipline of worshipping together at
set times each day, followed by a rule of silence after com-
pline. The Cuddesdon Office Book, revised over a lengthy
period in the 1930s by Eric Milner-White at Graham's
invitation, offers a paradigm of Anglican spirituality of the
time that paid meticulous attention to historical and literary
detail.[78] Despite considerable criticism from respected senior
clergy, concerned about losing the old atmosphere, or about
apparent extravagance on a worship space, Graham's courageous decision to press ahead with the re-ordering of the
College chapel has many reverberations with similar decisions throughout this century. Graham was clearly giving
encouragement to the view that worship, being central to
the Church's life, requires an appropriate and worthy setting.
Against Bishop Barnes of Birmingham, Graham was prepared to defend the moderate catholicism of the doctrine of
the real presence in the Eucharist.[79] Graham offered his
students the model of a priest who took service and interces-

sion as the centre of his dedication. However, it is also said of him that although he expected self-discipline, he discouraged over-scrupulosity, displayed a sense of humour, and made goodness seem attractive.[80]

(f) Pastoral Care

Cunningham exalted as the greatest task possible, the everyday pastoral care of the parish priest. He encouraged his students to take posts in the working class northern towns, assuming that the country living was for the later years when energy might be flagging. He himself set a high standard in after-care, principally through an Embertide leaflet and hand-written correspondence with former students, advising them on many matters regarding their careers and personal lives. He was extremely reluctant, however, to offer overt help on 'spiritual' matters, typified perhaps by his rather coded expression 'But you know, dear boy, you have my prayer'.[81]

Seaton, from the earliest days of his ministry as a priest, had been recognized as one with 'a distinctive facility for influencing younger men . . . guiding them through their perplexities and endowing them with something of his own resolute and cheerful faith'.[82] He was famous for taking students on country walks for such exchanges. He also modelled the faithful parish priest in the village parish for which the Principal of Cuddesdon had responsibility besides the College. Graham made a significant and lasting impression on his students as a wise and sympathetic counsellor available to those with personal difficulties.

In conclusion: the overwhelming power of these personalities, who placed highest priority on caring for their students over long periods and in great detail, made its mark on the Church of England in this period. They were men of great confidence in a sense of what was right, appropriate, and necessary for clergy to be faithful to their calling. They demonstrated and fostered an understanding of vocation that was highly personal and demanding.

Although culture and intelligence were prized, a deep concern for theological reflection was not regarded as a

priority or even as essential in a college principal and therefore, by example, in a clergyman. Despite the unanimous
protest against clericalism of the three principals, their own
idiosyncratic behaviour and natural energetic leadership offered a message that ministry is something offered to the
weak and the many by the strong and the few. The sense of
companionship which was encouraged in the colleges did its
work in fostering in student clergy a sense of common identity
over against their future parishioners. Further, the emphasis
on the disciplined life and way of prayer for clergy encouraged the opposite view of the role of the laity. In two
respects especially, the principals' hopes were often subsequently frustrated: namely, with regard to churchmanship
and professionalism. The first, opposed by the principals, has
remained throughout this century both as enriching the
diversity as well as opposing the effectiveness of the Church
of England. The second, also suspected, has been a form of
protection and an element in the style of most clergy. Yet
there has been a reluctance among clergy to become overpro-
fessional in the sense of not wishing to adopt in their fulness
secular models of management and education.

The great gift of warm pastoral care that the students
were offered was very likely to instill into them the priority
of this above all else. It should be no surprise that throughout
the period under consideration, parish clergy took it for
granted that the chief call on their time was to offer pastoral
care, mainly to church members, but also to the entire
neighbourhood. From a separate and confident position of
authority, clergy entered into a kind of unwritten contract
with parishioners, which resonates clearly with the relationship they had with their college principals. Clergy for their
part, were constantly available to all church members for the
Sacraments, the Word, and care and advice in trouble. On
their part, laity were expected only to be faithful in worship,
loyal to the Church, and to be recipients of the pastoral care
of the clergy. Although the parallel is far from an exact
match, there are intriguing likenesses between the role of
principal and student as illustrated from the brief review
undertaken here.

Conclusion

The chief direct influences on a theology of church and priesthood have been identified, and in particular two closely linked dilemmas. First, there was the question of how to speak adequately of the roles of clergy and laity as representatives of Christ, and second, how to discover an appropriate balance between the Church's internal and external relationships. The conclusion may be drawn that despite many valiant attempts, neither was finally successfully achieved. One of the chief reasons for this was that throughout the period, for a large part of the Church, concern to validate Church of England ecclesiology historically through the ministerial priesthood remained the primary agenda. However, not to oversimplify naively, it must also be said that the literature surveyed does reveal a wide variety of overlapping beliefs and practices. The authors reviewed were entirely English Anglicans, but it was the case that gradually a head of pressure was built up by the influence of the ecumenical movement. Authors such as Bonhoeffer, Brunner, Küng, Rahner, Tillich, as well as the Second Vatican Council and the World Council of Churches, enlarged the vision of those who engaged with them.

The evidence leads to the conclusion that, certainly until the early seventies, a 'middle-of-the-road' Anglicanism was established among the majority of Church of England clergymen and parishes. Even though few took much trouble to articulate such a theology of ministry, in a time of ecclesiastical recession, it proved highly congenial. Moderate catholicism, notably as epitomised in Michael Ramsey, was implicit in behaviour and relationships both inside and outside the Church of England.

There are three strands to this conclusion: a summary of the essence of the understanding that was dominant in the period, an indication of early signs of a renewed understanding of ecclesiology, and a note of important elements of priesthood that should be carried through the present transitional period.

a) The Influence of the Catholic Movement

The chief underlying strands of the Anglican understanding of ordained ministry dominating the first half of the twentieth century (and still lingering through the ministries of those trained at the end of that era) may be summarized as follows.

(i) *Foundational Myth*

The argument that won the day presented a theology of the Church which emphasized its nature as a divinely-established institution founded in prescriptive detail by Christ. This was given added impetus by stressing the divinity and transcendence of Christ to the exclusion of his humanity. Generally ignoring or rejecting the emerging fruits of critical scholarship, the view was taken that a single development of ministerial order was discernible throughout the New Testament and early Church period which exactly supported Anglican polity. The commission given by Christ to the Twelve was passed on in a linear fashion through the first bishops to the validly consecrated bishops and ordained clergy of the Catholic Church of the present century.

In his shrewd and substantial analysis of Anglo-Catholicism, Pickering, with the experience of twenty years lecturing in sociology, comments that, in an oversimplified form it could be said that the matter rested on whether or not the institution of the Church was the invention of man or whether it was made by God. For Protestants and liberals, there were no special criteria for speaking about the Church's organization other than would be true for any social institution. Like any organization, its form evolved to suit the needs of the times. A consequence of this view was that church order was not permanently fixed but able to react to changing needs and contexts. Pickering shows how those who adopt a Protestant ecclesiology often presume that a single model of church order can be read out of the New Testament. On this basis Protestants have often taken as their guide for any overall organization of the Church, a gathered community pattern in which members adhere to certain beliefs about Jesus Christ. Pickering's analysis is that for Protestants, whatever structure a church adopts, it will be a modification of an early Church pattern determined by pragmatic reasons.[83]

For two reasons in particular, the foundation for Anglo-Catholic or Protestant monistic understandings of church and ministry must now be regarded as discredited. First, the inherited pattern was based on the attempt to synthesize what scholars now perceive as early Christian experiments, into the foundation myth of an ordered and unchanging tradition, imposing a preselected pattern upon its flux.[84] Second, the priority of that agenda severely handicapped the Church of England's attempt to reach an appropriate and publicly accepted ecclesiology that could take account of the significance of all the members of the Church as well as of the clergy, and could articulate the role of the Church in the world.

A significant agenda in this ecclesiology, through emphasising its early provenance and divinely-given pedigree, was deliberately to make a clear statement of the Church's autonomy with regard to the State. The emphasis on orthodoxy, defending the faith of the past, and a sense of orderly unity, to be found in an uncritical approach to Ephesians and Pastoral Letters, made these documents particularly significant as a defence of the early twentieth-century explanation of the origins and nature of the ministry of the Church, especially in an intellectual climate unsympathetic to Christian faith. In matters of doctrine, liturgy, ethics, and administration, generally speaking, Church of England laity were allowed limited responsibility under the firm control and domination of the clergy. Despite many changes in perception and practice through the decades, 1900–70, towards a more open style of church government, clerical control remained a powerful factor.

One of the results was to hasten the movement towards a marginalized Church in which clergy confined themselves to so-called 'spiritual' over against 'secular' matters. The emphasis on the divinely commissioned separateness of the priest coincided with a decline in the public status of clergy and indeed, a continual decline in membership and in the influence of the whole Church in the networks of community and national life.

(ii) Ministry the Preserve of the Clergy

Two corollaries of the foundational myth were first, the restriction of ministry to those ordained by a validly ordained bishop, and the relegation of laity to a passive role as individual recipients of the separate ministry of the ordained. Although it was frequently emphasized that the ministry of laity was 'in the world', there was no real vision for drawing it out and supporting it. Second, the clerical role often created a mutually agreed distance between priest and people, so that they rarely encountered each other personally in worship, parish life or human relations.

Although a recurrent theme in the manuals was the role of laity in assisting clergy in their work, one of the chief strands of the Church of England's self-consciousness in this period was to identify the incumbent, together with the parish church building itself, not only as the representative focus, but as synonymous with the life and work of the Church itself. Whatever was attempted by way of enhancing the role of the whole Church, there persisted to varying degrees, the notion that clergy were in the end representatives of Christ in a distinctive and separate category.

Typically, worship was regarded as the area of professional clerical responsibility. Whereas there was a high expectation of the growth in spiritual maturity of the clergy, laity on the whole did not have high expectations of themselves. One of the supposed benefits of residential training in theological colleges was for clergy to be given a vision and a method for the basis of a prayer-life that would see them through the trials of ordained life, even though the wisdom has increasingly been questioned of offering to secular married clergy a semi-monastic pattern of spirituality.

The possession of an indelible priestly character was an underlying assumption for many clergy in this era. As the early Church was understood to hold its authority through the reception of apostolic power, it was concluded that no one could ever be accepted as a minister unless he had unquestionably received commissioned authority from Christ through the apostles and bishops. The Church had no authority to add to, or make changes to, the givenness of the transmission of the apostolic charge.

(iii) Opposition to Church Unity

This commitment to a single understanding of the nature and development of ordained ministry fuelled the polemic of confessional conflict and placed severe obstacles in the path of church unity. Despite the frequent adulation of Roman liturgical practice and ministerial discipline, it was central to the Anglo-Catholic ministerial theology to be opposed both to the authority claims of Roman Catholic ultramontanism and also to Protestant ecclesiological suspicion. The claim of the Catholic Anglican foundational myth was to have preserved pure apostolic order, untainted by aggressively proclaimed Roman exclusivism and by Protestant indifference to the historical preservation of apostolic succession.

The sticking point was the prevailing understanding that the New Testament provided clear support for the Anglo-Catholic understanding of clerical authority. What was required as a defence of the very life of the Church of England, both against Roman Catholics and other Protestant churches, was in itself creating a disastrous distortion of the proper relationship between clergy and laity, as well as raising enormous barriers against the general population. A Church of England that was primarily concerned with demonstrating its historical credentials was not in a position to communicate the Gospel to the general public.

(b) Signs of a New Ecclesiology

As the period progressed, a number of fundamental issues coming together were eventually convincing the Church of England to move to another understanding of itself and its ministry. Defensiveness over against Roman Catholicism and the Free churches began to break down, leaving room for a more honest and less confessional stance. So it was possible to begin to hear, often remarkably through scholars of other denominations, a plea for the fruits of historical and textual criticism to be allowed to contribute to ecclesiology.

The area where, as yet, there was little hope was the matter of clerical independence. For so many decades, the colleges had produced clergy with the expectation of one day being in charge of their own parish, such that their theology, spirituality and ministerial strategies were not yet open to a corporate approach.

(c) Positive Attributes of Clerical Ministry

Ecclesiology is permanently in transition. It would be facile to reject everything in a previous paradigm in favour of what is new. Although in the period 1900-70 the Church's perception of its mission and ministry was limited by the overemphasis on the role of the parish priest, there were significant positive factors, some of which should be encouraged in the present and the future.

First, there is material for thanksgiving in that, as ministers of word and sacrament, many parish priests followed their vocation with faithfulness, vision, and effectiveness. Often in spite of obscurity, poverty, eccentricity, and even a sense of failure, people and communities were brought closer to a knowledge of God through such significant priestly ministry.

Second, despite the general judgement of sociologists and journalists, particular clergy in their locality were on the whole regarded with affection and respect as perhaps the only local public figures who were interested in the welfare of the entire neighbourhood. Often they served as chairmen of school governing bodies and sometimes on local councils. They also had their place in the administration of hospitals, charities, and social clubs. It was often the clergy who praised and encouraged small groups who were giving valuable service to the neighbourhood. Essential to this model of clerical ministry was the belief that God was as much present in and concerned for the neighbourhood as for the community of faith. It has to be said, however, that a significant contributory factor was the willingness of church members, clerical and lay, as well as the wider community, to accept patterns of immature dependency.

Third, and especially before pastoral re-organization began to take its toll, clergy were available to the sick, the mentally ill, those in need, the very young and the elderly. This was a period when although numbers were in decline, the occasional offices of the Church were still required by the public for the celebration of birth (churching and baptism), puberty (confirmation), marriage (the wedding ceremony), and death (burial). A folk memory lingers of many parish priests who were hard-working and prided themselves on being widely available for many hours in the week. There was a confidence among clergy in knowing what to do each day that was mirrored and nurtured by the stable rythms of the lectionary, calendar, and language of the Book of Common Prayer.

Fourth, the colleges had given their students a commitment to prayer, discipline and, to some extent, biblical and theological study. Church of England clergy were characterized, as well as caricatured in the public eye, for their separateness and godliness. Positively, it must be said that the sheer sense of God that the Church of England carried and portrayed during this period must not be forgotten. This concentration of the divine lay at the heart of its life. The negative side was that holiness was often associated with a semi-monastic state, unsuitable for the married priest ministering alone, and demanding too little from the laity.

Fifth, many clergy worked hard to build a congregation of worshipping and faithful Christian people.

Sixth, through the rapidly changing society of the twentieth century, the Church of England offered to many communities and individuals a vital sense of stability and moral integrity. Although its leaders were often gently mocked in public for their eccentricities, at an inter-personal level their ministry was often valued far beyond the boundaries of the worshipping community.

As we move on now to search for appropriate ways of defining the role of clergy in the present time, there is no sense in which this represents a criticism of the traditional ministry of Church of England parish priests as we have explored it in this chapter. Rather, it will be a matter of recognizing how what was distinctively healthy and valuable in the clerical ministry of the past can not only be carried forward, but positively shared and developed within the ministries of all church members.

Chapter Two
THE DEMANDS OF
THE PRESENT

Introduction

We have seen how, earlier in the twentieth century, prophetic figures were pointing the way towards a new basis for understanding the Church and its ministry. Within English Anglican circles such voices were frequently muted by powerful forces maintaining the status quo. In this chapter, I shall briefly outline what is inevitably a very personal judgement—though one which I believe to be widely shared—of the Church of England's present character and needs. I recognize that some English Anglicans believe that the articulation of a distinctive and integrated ecclesiology is either inappropriate or an enterprise doomed to failure.[1] Many who in 1992 opposed the right or ability of the Church of England Synod to decide on the eligibility of women to become priests, stated that they regarded Anglicans as having no doctrine or authority other than that granted by membership of the wider Catholic and Orthodox churches. The ideas to be discussed in this book have arisen through my own dialogue with theologians who offer truthful concepts from varying Christian traditions: English and European Protestants, Orthodox, Roman Catholic, as well as Anglican. My presupposition is that the ecclesiology of any church will be partly distinctive and related to its particular history, and partly open at any one time to receiving challenge and inspiration from sister churches across the world. Anglicans in England can expect, therefore, both to receive from the breadth of Christian reflective experience, and contribute from the uniquely comprehensive characteristics and varying gifts that are the outcome of a continuing struggle for integrity within a highly complex context.[2]

The historically focused stance of the Church of England

which underlay the period portrayed in Chapter One, though far from monochrome and not without its critics, was presented as essentially the embodiment of New Testament Christianity, in Archbishop Laud's phrase, 'that faith which was once (and but once for all) delivered to the saints'. At the end of the modern period, despairing that the Church of England has lost its sense of coherence, the group is sizeable that continues to lobby for the retention of much of that earlier picture. Further, in the way that complex organizations have of being resistant to change, the Church of England has largely attracted to its membership and leadership those who like it as it is. It often seems to be that the reasons for this conservativism, rather than being theological, are more to be located in the understandable need to find an anchor of stability in a confusing and turbulent world.

However, for those Anglicans who do not want the Church to serve them as a safe haven but as an instrument of God's mission, there is increasing stress and frustration. In their impatience and pain, some have abandoned the worship and institutional life of a Church that only constrains rather than empowers their Christian faith.

The Church of England's life is both enriched and complicated by the Anglican commitment to the concept of dispersed authority.[3] There has been a long expectation, at national, diocesan, deanery and parish levels, that everyone is entitled to have their own understanding of the Church and its ministry, saluting all developments, rejecting only what is plainly corrupt or insane. I recognize, therefore, that in making the suggestion that the Church of England should clarify its understanding of ecclesiology in order to meet the demands of the present, there could be stiff opposition from those who foresee the erosion of cherished freedoms. My own hope is that a doctrine of Church and of ministry can be shaped in which it will be possible for English Anglicans to maintain the tradition of a rich local diversity, but in combination with a movement towards an articulated agreed ecclesiology. This would mean excluding, in the present human context, certain interpretations of church and ministry as inadequate, unorthodox or inappropriate, while making space for local variations and interpretations of the essential idea.[4] The perennial question as to whether or not it would be possible to hold a set of beliefs which would automatically exclude one from membership of the Church of England, is one which still raises temperatures, not least in the context of a Decade of Evangelism.[5] A despondent view of the state of the Church of England has been well articulated by Stephen Sykes in the following terms:

> Has not the Church of England become a church without a structure of authority capable of speaking with authority, and worse, a church without a vision, a church which has ceased to believe that its corporate decisions could be guided by the Holy Spirit?[6]

It is supportive to my argument that Sykes has moved away from this, his earlier judgement. As this enquiry continues, I hope to demonstrate how it is possible for the Church of England to be united by an ecclesiological vision that need not be equated with uniformity of expression. The question of 'membership' of the Church of England is clearly a crucial one to be discussed as the first item in this brief overview of the situation and demands of the present.

1. Membership

I am indebted to the theory of John Milbank suggesting that all theology should be reconceived as a kind of 'Christian sociology', 'the explication of a socio-linguistic practice, or as the constant renarration of this practice as it has historically developed'.[7] Such a closely woven ecclesiology is not at present possessed by the Church of England but I am encouraged by Bishop Stephen Sykes' own re-evaluation, after twenty five years, of that which constitutes the genius of Anglicanism.[8] He used to be downcast in the face of the complexity and diversification of the Church of England's life and message. On reflection he now celebrates the often broken but courageous pluriform Anglican testimony to the knowledge and praise of God, who is the creator and saviour of a pluralistic world.

So far as membership of the Church of England is concerned, there are many indications of a rich and diverse core of church life identifiable within those parishes and institutions that, generally speaking, choose to accept and work with the liturgical, social and missionary context envisaged in the 1980 Alternative Service Book. In this connection I would define 'membership' in a more precise way than was common among Anglicans even ten years ago, without I trust becoming sectarian. There is a literal sense in which all baptized and confirmed persons have a right to think of themselves as 'members' of the Church. Such membership has often been explained on the analogy of layers of an onion, with church people permitted to take up whichever position suited them at a particular stage of their lives.

Another approach is to propose that primarily there are those Anglican Christians for whom eucharistic worship focusses their sense of belonging and purpose. I recognize there are many Evangelicals and others who frequent the Eucharist deliberately and devoutly on a regular but infrequent basis. Frequency of sharing in the Eucharist is not a guide to measuring its importance for those concerned. Earlier this century it was common for laity to be taught in confirmation classes to attend the Eucharist once a month and mattins or evensong on other Sundays. The Church of England, having struggled over many decades to re-establish the centrality of the Eucharist, is slowly recognizing that a eucharistically-based church does not need to prove this constantly by restricting public worship to celebrations of Holy Communion. Instead, there are growing opportunities both for varying our experiences of eucharistic celebration and for recognizing its connections with every other part of Christian discipleship.

Observation in parishes reveals a core group of those 'members' who worship regularly together, and who are known to each other. Clergy surveying a congregation over a period of a month recognize who is presently a member, who is on the way to becoming a core member, who is an occasional attender, and who is a visitor.[9] This does not exclude those members who are now prevented by infirmity from making the journey to the church building. Those who are on the way to core membership, in theory includes all the baptized and confirmed, but practically will include a wide variety of the parents of children who are members, those who attend study groups, those who attend church social events or have confidential conversations about Christian faith with trusted church members. The assumption that all baptized or confirmed people who live in the neighbourhood are to be regarded as members of the Church is, I believe, anachronistic and unrealistic. This is not intended as a criticism—the local church may not for example make any space for them to be members—nor as a judgement about their relationship to God's Kingdom. It is simply a recognition that, while initiation ceremonies are important starting points on a journey, the next stage may be postponed, often indefinitely.

When I use the word 'member' in this book, therefore, I am referring to that particular group of Anglicans who to varying degrees are recognizably travelling with a particular local church. That is to say, they are to be identified as those who worship publicly on a regular basis and recognize that this has some implication for their involvement in the Church's internal and external activities. There are, of course, many members who are children, as well as adults, whose effective membership may be almost totally limited to public worship.

The membership of the Church of England is predominantly suburban, white-European, middle-aged-to-elderly, articulate and middle class. The status of age, wealth, and class are often linked with an implicit expectation among some categories of membership that they will have what others, e.g., young parents, perceive as a disproportionate degree of power in determining policies. Such domination of one group by another within the Church often points to the absence of the challenge for every Christian to pursue a personal spiritual maturity. Despite many new challenges in recent years, the majority of lay Christians still do not receive 'permission' to take themselves seriously as praying, thinking, and witnessing members of the Body of Christ.

The Church's baptized and confirmed and regular church-going membership, in numerical decline, varies considerably in its understanding of commitment, mission, and evangelism.[10] The critique of its established position needs to be sustained and penetrating. In the light of so much genuine interchange between denominations today, and also such facts as that the Roman Catholic Church now has a greater number of regular communicants than the Church of England, the question of the right of the latter to regard itself as the 'established' Church is one to be faced with all seriousness.[11] Further, although random surveys have shown that as many as 70 per cent of the population believe in 'God', they do not find it easy to make the connection between their experience and the institutional Church. An underlying condescension among clergy is evident when they overlook the capacity of the general public to think complex thoughts about God and to experience deep insights regarding the mysteries of life and death. There are many church leaders who, in the language of the bishops of the West Indian Province (1988), would judge quite unequivocally of Britain, 'Many still live without the reality of the knowledge, love and redeeming power of Jesus Christ' or, 'Clergy and laity alike, in large measure, are not excited about what mission is all about, and their concerns are often confined to balancing the budget.'[12]

A cluster of networks or interlocking circles of adherence for the most part remain an essential feature of 'membership' of the Church of England. Obvious exceptions include the inner-city Catholic or Evangelical church with a demanding membership formula, or the suburban congregation defined by a particular theological and spiritual stance. In the next twenty years the future of the Church of England could be much more influenced by the house church or Peoples' Church movement.[13] The survival long into the twenty-first century of the Church of England may in fact partly depend on a willingness to learn from the house churches to recognize the potential of every member, to give dignity to everyone's contribution to understanding the faith, to abandon its old habits of condescension towards other groups, to become versatile and responsive to local culture and, above all, ecumenical. To take on some of these characteristics would not necessarily threaten the Church of England's ability to be part of the Catholic Church available for the building up of the life of each person in a particular neighbourhood.

The Church of England's membership is predominantly female.[14] Its leadership by contrast is largely male. Ecumenically, the urgent need for the Church to hear and respond to the voices of the women's movement has notably been channelled through the works of such authors as Rosemary Radford Reuther, Phyllis Trible, Monica Furlong, Elizabeth Moltmann-Wendel, Catharina Halkes, and Elizabeth Schüssler Fiorenza. The latter, in discussing the eucharistic life of all churches has asked, in the light of ingrained ecclesial sexism, 'How can women or anyone for that matter consciously participate in the perpetuation and celebration of structural sin?'[15] The pressing need for the Church of England to work for the co-operation and involvement of women and for inclusive language is reflected in a growing body of literature, groups, and conferences.[16] In particular there should be the hope that women's contribution to ecclesiology will challenge the way the Church's ministerial life is arranged, and the structures of its decision-making processes. Experience of womens' voices together with those of men in liturgy, at the altar, in preaching, pastoral care, administration and leadership, increasingly draws out a wholeness and gentleness which is already showing signs of enhancing the Church's ability to communicate with a wide spectrum of people.[17]

2. Women and Men in Ordained Ministry

Others have traced in the history of the past three decades the details of progress towards the removal of all barriers to women's ordination, culminating in the General Synod vote on 11 November 1992.[18] It was at Lambeth 1978 that the Anglican Communion pronounced on the legal autonomy of each province to decide on the admission of women to Holy Orders.[19] Now it is possible to look forward to the Church of England's leadership offering a focus of all male and female collaboration for the Kingdom of God. This is not to deny the fear, anger, harassment and humiliation experienced by some women in orders. Naturally, the decision to ordain women priests has increased the stress of those clergy and parishes fundamentally opposed, but in an increasing number of parishes, there is an affirmation and recognition of the rightness and value of womens' ministry, and a trusting expectancy prevails.

Generally, there is already a recognition of the new and positive fruits of collaboration between women and men in the cause of the kingdom. But we should be foolish not to expect acute anxiety and stress arising from the renewed understanding of women's authority in a Church where men have for so long assumed the right to govern alone and where women have been largely defined as helpers and supporters. Some of the issues that a new status for women in ministry will raise include: challenging exclusive liturgical language, male and female stereotyping, and expectations of the balance of time given to ministry, family, friendships, and personal development. Positively, women in ministry will have resources to promote within the Church the search for a contemporary theology of priesthood: in modelling good practice for team-work and shared ministry; in making more open and honest connections between eucharistic celebration and human concerns; in understanding and communicating with those whom the Church often marginalizes; in allowing rationality to be better balanced by the recognition of feelings; in deepening the spiritual and liturgical life of congregations; and in furthering the local church's capability of offering pastoral care to the neighbourhood.[20]

3. Forms of Public Worship

I argued above that despite variations in frequency of celebration, the word and sacrament of the Eucharist focuses, defines, and nurtures English Anglican spirituality. However, largely through ecumenical theological debate, motivation for mission, and a decline in the number of clergy available, other forms and styles of worship are gradually but cautiously being explored. The influence of the Pentecostalist movement on the Church of England should not be underestimated.[21] In the 1970s Ramsey, Terwilliger, and Allchin together in a broadcast testified to the value of the charismatic movement for all Christians:

The most powerful force within the church at this moment is the 'charismatic movement'. It is a great surge of awareness of the Holy Spirit, sometimes pentecostal in form, always an intense revival of vital prayer and the awareness of God's working . . . It is possible to sense that in all of this we are in the grip of a divine action to which we must respond, alive and alert to its meaning. Christ is being made known to us by the Spirit; the Charismatic Christ is being revealed in the mind and heart of the church. This is theology in its deepest sense; this is the knowledge of God. Come Holy Spirit![22]

In the Church of England nationally, publications such as *Promise of his Glory* and *Lent, Holy Week and Easter* have fostered a greater balance between formality and spontaneity. On the whole the vision and material of the ASB 1980 and subsequent moves towards a revision in 2000, is accepted and put to use. In Chapter One, I concluded that the Church of England had been constantly held back from a deep level of communication with the public at large by a preoccupation with an internal Catholic agenda about identity. In 1978, in a manual for revising the presentation of the Eucharist, Michael Perham offered release from a single Anglican liturgical tradition that could be called 'Catholic', to new and varied traditions that were no less 'Catholic'.[23] The Church of England Liturgical Commission published its own commentary on the ASB 1980; Lionel Dakers (Director of the Royal School of Church Music) offered a practical guide to the use of the ASB 1980; in 1981, Colin Buchanan editor of *News of Liturgy*, a significant monthly paper for reflective practitioners, claimed that liturgy must be an event in which, in God's presence, Christians relate to each other. It was unusually sensitive and pastorally helpful that a children's illustrated version of Rite 'A' Holy Communion from ASB was published in 1981; a valuable and accessible illustrated guide to the ASB, commended by the Archbishop of Canterbury, was produced by Buchanan, Lloyd and Miller in 1980. Alan Dunstan, in the annual Bible School of St Giles in the Fields, Holborn in 1984, made connections between a Christian understanding of God and contemporary liturgical revision; Robin Green in 1987 connected prayer and worship with recent psychological discoveries in the pursuit of pastorally sensitive liturgy.

In the 1990s, there is increasing evidence of groups of laity (predominantly female and particularly in extensive rural benefices) creating and presenting 'family' or 'village' services with help from clergy and published material. George Guiver's *Company of Voices* (1988) has provided a new vision leading to many parishes examining the possibilities for lay-led offices of varying degrees of formality, to be held on several occasions a week in the buildings on which so much care and money is lavished. Imaginative local churches are demonstrating how the maturity of the congregation and opportunities for evangelism are developed, by celebrating the Eucharist in a variety of ways on different occasions, and also through the presentation of a wide spectrum of other forms of worship.

The Archbishops' Commission on Rural Areas Report, in the chapter on 'Spirituality and Worship', recalled that a high percentage of rural people interviewed claimed to have attended church recently. Many of these would be in my category of 'on the way to membership', though many would have an infrequent pattern of regular attendance at worship, which for them constitutes membership, while others regard membership as the birthright of English people. The commissioners noted that many of these country dwellers had stated their preference for clergy who would pray with, rather than separately from, local people. They also asked that the Church, remembering that God is concerned with the whole creation, would respect those who came to worship at one-off events such as Remembrance Sunday and Harvest Thanksgiving. Paragraph 9.22 of the report articulates a longing which embraces a wide range of people's cultures, linking them to the kaleidoscopic worship of the country church. Notably, the report encourages bell-ringing and musical involvement, Sunday services at regular times, preferably in the middle of the morning, attentive to local needs; it encourages genuine ecumenical planning of worship that sometimes concentrates on breaking the Word when a priest is not available, using new material such as *Patterns for Worship*, 1991; it maintains that family services and other simple and imaginative acts of worship for small groups should be available whether clergy can be present or not: 'Liturgy is an activity for 24 hours a day because it cannot stop at the door of the church.'[24]

4. Re-ordering Church Buildings

In many ways the emphasis of Hebert, Robinson, and others in the earlier part of this century on the corporate and open-to-the-world aspect of ecclesiology is only now finding a thorough expression in the Church of England. Theory and practice among Anglicans, despite the emphasis on individualism in society, exhibits signs of a new balance developing between an individualistic and a corporate view of Christian discipleship. It is common to hear clergy teaching and preaching on the New Testament themes of the People of God, the Body of Christ and the royal priesthood of believers. This movement is being given expression in liturgies that draw out the themes of the year, and the complex needs of differing occasions.

However, rigidity in the deployment of liturgical space can be one of the greatest opponents to this development. In-built conservatism seems to come to the surface in particular regarding the interior design of churches. There are those who have come to understand the relationship between the deployment of space and concepts of relationship in schools, the theatre, management training, and catering. They are among those who recognize that the style of furniture and the arrangements of various groups of people within the church building makes a powerful statement about the community's self-awareness. What may appear on the surface to be a dispute about the movement of a row of pews can at one level also be the expression of a deep anxiety about moving from a known and safe ecclesiology to another.

Frustration is created because of a frequent fear in church councils of making necessary changes in the furnishings. An overwhelming sense of responsibility matched by a lack of historical awareness can prevent church people from recognizing that present arrangements were designed perhaps only a few generations ago and then simply because of their fore-

bears' perceptions of what was required for the public worship of God. Others have been seduced by doctrinaire conser-
vationism born of lack of confidence in late twentieth-century
architecture, of a lack of engagement with theology and
spirituality, and of a growing distance between those who
regard church buildings as places of worship and those who
regard them as places of historical continuity. It has to be
admitted too that some disastrous re-orderings have been the
result of superficial thinking, or achieved against professional
advice. However, in some places a revolution in ecclesiology
has been made possible through re-ordering the worship
space, incorporating a wide variety of musical culture, discovering a multitude of ways of appreciating the meanings of
Scripture, relating worship to the rest of life in ways that
nourish both Church and society, and creating a more re-
laxed atmosphere which includes all ages and temperaments.
At the heart of this debate lies the question of a church
community's wide range of beliefs about God and his manner
of relating to it.

5. Lack of Finance

The constant reduction in the support given to parishes by
the Church Commissioners, together with the effects of infla-
tion and rising costs, mean that with few exceptions financial
constraints increasingly dominate strategic planning. The
fact that the greater proportion of giving now falls on the
committed congregation, rather than on the whole community, has implications for the perception of the Church no
longer as a public institution to be taken for granted, but as
a more precarious voluntary body in danger of reducing its
vision to that of a mere sect. Giving thoughtfully is a subject
addressed with increasing honesty and earnestness by bishops
and stewardship officers, yet there is a residual culture within
the Church of England which is resistant to making a realistic
contribution towards the cost of ordained ministry. Further,
in this climate of financial stringency clear links are being
made between expectations of accountability and staff development in secular agencies, and parallel situations amongst
paid clergy in parish and specialist ministries. Alongside this,

is the un-Catholic notion of those parishes that are more
well-off being uncomfortable at subsidizing others with fewer
resources. This factor, in combination with the decreasing
numbers of ordained clergy, is a highly significant element in
Church of England strategic planning. It is not uncommon
to hear senior Anglican clergy musing on just what the base
line will be in the twenty-first century. What is the lowest
ratio of stipendiary clergy to the rest of the Church that is
workable? One of the keys to the future vitality of the
Church of England is precisely the subject of this book.

Unless there is a clear identification among Anglicans of
the nature of the Church and its professional ministry, there
will be no role models to follow nor confident church life
that takes the significance of lay ministry as axiomatic.
Without role models it is difficult to see how a sufficient
stream of new clergy will be maintained. Without a confident
ecclesiology, church life will feel uneasy and lacking in confidence. In both cases, essential finance will not be forthcom-
ing. If a new ecclesiology is adopted and made to work, in
time clergy vocations, collaborative ministry and finances
may come right. In the short-term the outlook is by no
means good. The worst possible route would be for wealthy
parishes to mirror the individualism of contemporary society
by declaring independence and leaving others to their fate.
There is every reason to assume that, supported by God's
grace, the Church of England will have to descend to the
depths of its confidence and only out of that brokenness rise
in a very different and chastened form.

6. Collaborative Ministry

Lay people who have travelled with the Church of England
through the recent decades of reform, or who become members without a previous church background, do expect a
certain degree of interdependence between clergy and laity,
and a controlled involvement in agreeing matters of doctrine,
and decision-taking processes, and the planning and leading
of worship. The literature on the new understanding of the
laity is vast, standing under the names of internationally
recognized scholars such as Congar, Doohan, Faivre, Küng,

Metz, Schillebeeckx, Suenens, and a vast number of interpreters and reflective practitioners. Undergirded by biblical imagery (notably 1 Cor. 12.4ff), most parishes today express an understanding of the sharing of God's gifts throughout the entire People of God, within which gifts of leadership should be recognized and exercised. However, as we shall see later, difficulties arise over the most appropriate ways of bringing to birth this new way of being church.

In the official language of the Church of England we read:

> The proper relationship between the ministry of the whole people of God and that of the ordained ministry joined in the service of God's activity in the world, has proved difficult for the church to maintain, not least at present. There have been constant tendencies for the tasks of one to subsume those of the other, so that in theory it is treated as 'the' ministry, whereas the two are actually *interdependent*, the health of each depending on that of the other. Both together do what neither can do alone.[25]

In the First Statement on Authority in ARCIC I, there is an emphasis on 'mutual responsibility and interdependence' on the part of those with ministerial authority, and the recognition that ordained ministers commissioned to discern 'God's will' and 'give authoritative expression' to it, are 'part of the community, sharing its quest for understanding the Gospel in obedience to Christ and receptive to the needs and concerns of all'.[26] Consequent restatements of the theology and role of ordained ministry as inter-dependent members of one body draw on ecumenical scholarship and reflective practice.[27] A renewed understanding of baptism as a significant key to mission and ministry rather than ordination alone, is proving influential as well as controversial.[28]

However, there remains, for a complex variety of reasons, a disproportionate emphasis on the role of the clergy to the detriment of the whole body of the church. With unexpectedly glorious exceptions, it is still the case that the majority of parishes regard the presence of a priest, preferably male and stipendiary, to be the major requirement and resource for the church to flourish and engage in its work. This can be demonstrated from the current Church of England debate in the dioceses on the appropriateness of local non-stipendiary ministry (in association with parish or benefice teams which include readers and laity) as the way forward in the face of the continuing sharp decline in the numbers of stipendiary clergy and of money to pay them. The argument for such schemes of local ministry takes account of both the *Faith in the Countryside* commissioners' perception of 'a clergy-shaped hole' in the heart of each parish as well as the appropriateness of a new collaboration between clergy and laity.[29] There are three essential principles contained in the vision for local ministry. First, it is a highly effective way to release for lay people their prayer authority to make the church happen locally. Through systematic training, their calling from God through the local community to a demanding ministry is made effective. Second, local ministry schemes give lay people authority from the bishop. The diocese invites a team to be the corporate ministry in the local neighbourhood. The authority of local choice is properly balanced by the catholic overseeing of the bishop and his officers. Third, group-related training, which is theological reflection on life and ministry, transforms the members into a coherent local ministry team. Such teams are not the transient helpers of stipendiary clergy, but a strong development of the mission of the whole Church, called by God through the local community.

In response to these changes, some clergy and laity respond that for over twenty years they have looked forward and worked towards local ministry. In particular, some parishes relish the idea of a locally selected and trained clergy. Nevertheless, there are responsible parish clergy and lay officers, in favour of increased lay-clerical co-operation, who fear that plans for local ministry and for radical pastoral reorganisation are in some way a diocesan conspiracy to reduce the numbers of stipendiary clergy. So, in discussion, I have heard pleas for new ministerial strategies to be introduced in parallel with the inherited parish structures. The recognition that the traditional parish staffing arrangements cannot continue into the future (rather than being in temporary recession) may be accepted only reluctantly and gradually in many places.

In the face of the inherited tendency in the Church of

England for clergy to work alone, separate from other clergy, readers, and laity, the bishops' guidelines on local ministry insist that locally ordained priests must operate within the context of a lay team.[30]

I believe progress is gradually being made from a self-awareness of the Church as a haphazard assembling of passive individuals led by clergy, to one of a corporate missionary agency in which the ministries of the whole Church and the ordained are bound to each other. But this agenda has a long way still to run. In particular, the Church of England has a long history of finding it difficult to trust working class parishioners with pastoral, liturgical and administrative responsibilities.[31] The experience of many diocesan officers, for example, would indicate that the recent definition of the Church's task to serve God's mission in the world holds meaning for only a minority of Church of England members, but that slowly perceptions are changing.[32]

The model persists of a benign priesthood shepherding a passive flock. However in the ecumenical Decade of Evangelism (evangelization) there are increasing calls for every Church member to make connections between initiation into the Church and a shared responsibility for mission. The Catechumenate Movement offers a particularly significant vision in which clergy and laity together work out the implications of Christian allegiance with candidates, so that the corporate dimension of the Church and personal freedom of exploration are predominant.

Within the Roman Catholic context of catechesis in Germany, Italy, and Africa, variations occur of an experiential-educational project offered by a team consisting of laity, clergy, and religious. The move is away from clergy alone passing on the faith, towards a group who together represent the Church and help candidates for initiation make their own connections between their life experience and Christianity. It operates on the basis that within the whole life of a liturgical community, small mutually supportive groups of Christians, in collaboration with clergy, provide a vital basis for religious formation.[33] The movement places significance on welcoming new members and encouraging enquirers. It stimulates people to support each other, offers to meet particular needs, helps people to understand and engage in personal and liturgical prayer, and provides an environment for conversion. Its methods include creative use of Scripture, of Sunday worship, and the integration of newcomers into community life and service. There is an emphasis on spiritual guidance, retreats, and on witness and liturgical symbolism. The cycle of the year brings its special points, such as Pentecost, for commissioning to ministries before the parish.

The Church should have an expectation that all who enter on such ministries responsibly will, for the sake of those among whom they minister, take up the offer of spiritual and educational development and support.[34]

7. Service and Witness

One of the most pressing problems for life in the Church of England is how to encourage all the members to equip themselves better to make connections between the worship and internal energy of the people of God, and the opportunities and frustrations of the world.[35] Diocesan specialist ministers testify to the rarity of local churches taking with seriousness the support of the laity in their secular tasks. At its best, though usually through the input of a minority, the Church in a spirit of service and witness engages with issues of poverty and famine overseas and, through a process of appraisal, begins to take seriously the needs and concerns of the locality in which the parish church is set. Despite the availability of literature from Liberation Theologians, Church of England practice has a restrained character in social matters.[36] Bishop David Sheppard has assessed this accurately:

> We live in a polarized society. In the same city people have widely different experiences, and see the same events through very different eyes. The church is one of the few bridges which can reach across to different sides of that polarized society. It is part of our reconciling task to help different groups to listen to what others perceive to be happening.[37]

8. Centralism and Locality

At the level of feelings, dioceses have a constant difficulty because many clergy and parishes claim to be marginalized. Those who live on the edge of diocesan boundaries, or simply away from the main centres of population often say that no one knows that they are doing. Despite logical arguments suggesting that a diocese has many gathering points and networks—and despite hard evidence of the visits by bishops and archdeacons, this mood persists.

The situation is compounded by the inherited sense of freedom in Anglicanism which has encouraged the maverick priest or the idiosyncratic parish. Without wishing to impose a uniform model of mission and ministry, there are moves in some dioceses towards diocesan staff inviting everyone to recognize that at particular moments of the Church's development, the wisdom seems to be that some styles of ministry are appropriate whilst others are not. For example, in the Diocese of Gloucester a series of meetings entitled 'Joining' are arranged among groups of new parish priests, the Bishop's staff and specialist ministers. Clergy are invited to reflect together as part of the joining process on where the diocese (and their group of parishes) is at this moment on a number of key issues in order to detect more precisely what their own personal experience and insights will contribute. The question here is whether it is possible in the Church of England for a publicly owned statement of mission and ministry (in the world wide ecumenical and Anglican context) to be fused with local interpretations.[38]

9. A Theologically Uneducated Church

Although the Church of England finds its membership largely within the educated classes, with the exception of parishes where this has become a basic element of strategy, biblical and theological expertise are undeveloped. However, the same energy that is motivating lay involvement can be discerned also as instrumental in revolutionizing expectations of lay education and training, and also of widening the possibilities for spiritual deepening and stretching.[39] The movement towards local ministry teams, which is bringing about a quiet revolution in the approach to the parochial ministry in several dioceses, includes a strong commitment to a way of learning, which assures an interactive process between clergy and laity, between the local and the wider church, between faith and the local context, and between intellectual rationality and experiences of feeling, prayer, and human maturing. There is an increasing commitment also to in-service clergy education and training.

These ecclesial elements, found to greater and lesser degrees in parishes of the Church of England, constitute the positive and negative aspects of the social reality within which this book will articulate a theology of church and of the parish priest. Although my final concern here will be to search for ways of understanding the role of the parish priest, it is already becoming clear that in the context we have just surveyed, the days have gone when such a ministry could be defined in isolation.

Chapter Three
THE DAWNING OF A
NEW ERA

In the search for an alternative theological statement of priesthood, suitable for the Church of England today, a productive start can be made by examining the recent work of The General Synod's Advisory Board for Ministry. In a typically unsung English Anglican manner, over the past decade, the bishops, General Synod, and their advisors have initiated a quiet but effective revolution. Through the slow and detailed route of committees, reports, debates, and the construction of policy documents, the Church of England has been preparing for the dramatic change which is now coming about in the manner in which ministry is offered both to church members and to the wider community. I therefore begin the process of exploring a theology of the parish priest by enthusiastically recognizing the potentiality of this process.

The Advisory Board of Ministry (ABM) and the Theological Colleges and Courses together have engaged in an extensive and demanding process of discovering new concepts of ordained ministry and correspondingly appropriate patterns of education. The ABM, previously known as the Advisory Council for the Church's Ministry, (ACCM), in its *Occasional Paper 22*, entitled 'Education for the Church's Ministry: The Report of the Working Party on Assessment' (January 1987) set out guide-lines requiring the response of all theological colleges and courses. Never before has the Church of England officially asked itself the questions, 'what kind of church are we?' and therefore, 'what quality of ordained ministry is required, and how should the training take place?' *ACCM Occasional Paper 22* proposes that it will be impossible to equip people properly for ordination until a clearer understanding of the nature of ordained ministry can be agreed:

The time has come to grasp the nettle. The rationale of theological education in the Church of England has never been made fully explicit. Will we ever be able to equip people to exercise ordained ministry properly in the Church of England until we have come to a clearer understanding of the sort of ordained ministry the Church of England requires?[1]

What Ordained Ministry Does the Church of England Require?

With a view to devolving to the colleges and courses the responsibility for creating programmes of training and assessment (though with national supervision and monitoring), *ACCM 22* sets out general principles concerning the nature of ordained ministry as an invitation to each college and course to respond in more detail. The process was aimed at improving the standards and efficiency of education and assessment for the ordained ministry of the Church of England.

Paragraph 26 of the document boldly turns on its head much previous understanding of ordination expressed in terms of the individual. Rather, it states that it is the nature of the Church itself that determines the nature of its ministry. It emphasizes that ordained ministry should be discussed only in the context of ecclesiology, in that all ministry should be referred to the ministry of Christ in the Church. Training for ministry should have in mind the needs of the Church as a whole, rather than considering primarily the particular minister in differing situations. Equally the former responsibilities, backgrounds and experiences of ordinands in training should be seen as secondary to the task of training for ordained ministry within the whole Church. Although particular colleges and courses may consider the actual diversity of ministerial situations, as a whole, 'the Church must manifest its own nature in its ministry, and determine to train its ministry accordingly'.

In *paragraph 27* the emphasis is on the Church's task,

corporately, to serve the mission of God in the world. In diverse contexts, the Church's task is twofold. First, it has to proclaim the creative activity of God. The Church announces that the world is constituted in its proper nature by God and affirms it where it reflects that nature. Second, it has to proclaim the redemptive activity of God by which the world is once again given its proper being and fulfilled according to God's purposes. The Church is said to follow, and attempt to be conformed to, the work of God in Jesus Christ through the Holy Spirit, in and for the world, so to bring the world to its intended salvation through relatedness to God. It is emphasized that this is not simply a matter of interpreting the world and its future in God's promises, but of realizing their consequences by working to conform the Church and the world to the purposes of God.

Speaking of the corporate and ordained ministry in the service of the mission of God in the world, *paragraph 28* indicates that the Church of England is now fully committed to an understanding of the corporate ministry of the People of God and, within its life and task, to a distinctive ordained ministry.

Paragraph 29 speaks of these two kinds of ministry (the ministry of the whole people and that of the ordained) as bound to each other, and animating each other, in the corporate task of proclaiming and realising the creative and redemptive activity of God in the world. In the Church's task, ministry is by nature corporate, but ordained ministry has the responsibility for recognizing the activity of God in and for this corporate ministry, representing it to the members of the Church. The key concept offered by ABM is that ordained ministry has the task of focusing and collecting the corporate ministry in a co-ordinated pattern, as well as of distributing it in the service of God's work in the world.[2] On their part, the members of the community of the Church are called to trust and sustain in the faith the ordained in their particular task. In other words, laity and clergy properly animate each other, focusing the activity of God in each other, so bringing each other to be in sharing God's mission. The Church is to be interanimative in its performance and, therefore, in its being.

This concept of interanimation is developed in *paragraph 30*, as revealed in particular ministries within the entire mission of God in the world. Emerging tasks, vocations, and capacities are each a means of focusing the ministry of the whole Church. Like these, ordained ministry focuses the entire ministry of the Church, but is charged also to do so by recognizing, coordinating and distributing the ministry of others. ABM emphasizes that this is not to be limited by being understood in purely managerial or leadership analogies.[3] The ordained ministry is to be seen as seeking to bring the creative and redemptive work of God to fruition within the ministries of others in the world.

Paragraph 31 acknowledges that the proper relationship between the ministry of the whole People of God and that of the ordained ministry, joined together in the service of God's activity in the world, has proved difficult to maintain. It speaks of the danger of one ministry subsuming the other and becoming in effect the only ministry. The vision to be achieved, and the one on which the health of each is based, is one in which these ministries are interdependent. Together they can do what neither can do alone.

Consequently, *paragraph 32* states that college and course training should be of such a kind as to produce an interdependency within the one ministry of the Church. Further, *paragraph 33* indicates that ministry is not to be regarded as an end in itself nor to be concerned only with traditional parish tasks. Its purpose is to serve the mission of God in the world, and its proper nature can only be achieved insofar as it promotes engagement in God's creative and redemptive activity. The training in theological colleges and courses should, therefore, be able to reflect this requirement.

Paragraph 34 looks for co-operation in ministry between churches and within secular institutions as the proper situation for the Church and its ordained ministry to fulfil, in the widest terms, their allotted task. There is also a need for discernment of the whole Church's proper engagement with God's mission in the world and of how, through the focusing and distribution of the ordained, everyone should be helped to realize their ministry.

At the heart of this discerning process, suggests *paragraph*

35, lies the need for the Church to understand its nature and task within God's mission, and to recognize the differing responsibilities of particular members. Theological, spiritual, and practical skills are required to exercise such discrimination. *Paragraph 36* looks for the Church to ordain those who are committed to and trained for the interdependent ministry of the whole people of God, serving God's mission in the world.

Avoiding individualistic preparation, says *paragraph 37*, the colleges and courses must develop in persons to be ordained intellectual, spiritual and practical qualities to enable the ordained ministry to create the whole Church as an interdependent ministerial body called to collaborate with God's creative and redemptive activity in the world.

Paragraph 38 identifies three qualities for the ordained ministry. First, there are those qualities by which the minister participates in the creative and redemptive activity of God through personal commitment to Christ and in a life of disciplined faith. Second, qualities are required by which the minister lives and works within and builds up the ministry of the entire Church. Third, the ministry requires qualities for identifying situations to which the Church must address itself within the complexities of the world, and to discern how, in an interdependent manner, the whole ministry of the Church may best be deployed to that end.

Within what are necessarily carefully formulated and jargon-ridden paragraphs, the Church of England here officially declared its hand and opened up an imaginative and exciting agenda. In turn the colleges and courses each made their response as to how they see themselves implementing educational and training strategies to bring to reality a new vision for church and ministry. This vision represents a very significant milestone in the process of the debates of this century on church and ministry within the Church of England and more recently on an ecumenical basis.

Continuity and Discontinuity between
ACCM Occasional Paper 22 *and the Period*
1900–1970

Although in both cases, beneath the summaries lie varieties of emphasis and expression arising from churchmanship as well as theological assumptions, certain essential themes can be clearly identified. To save repetition of words, I shall refer to the theology of ordained ministry generally to be found in the period 1900–70 as 'received' and that of *ACCM 22* as 'contemporary'.

(a) Context

The authors discussed in Chapter One illustrated English Anglican debate about the Church. In a world of wars and social and moral upheaval the Church of England appears with hindsight to have been more concerned for the purity of its pedigree and the assurance of its internal relations, than for maintaining its credibility in society and proclaiming the Gospel to the world. Paradoxically, the historical agenda of proving beyond doubt, through the theory of apostolic succession, the validity of the Church depended on a denial that historical and social context had any significance. The historically focused ministerial oligarchy, confidently separate from the everyday world and unaccountable to anyone but God, was able to regard itself as the permanent subject of all relationships. To have spoken of a dialogue or an interaction with the Church's context would have appeared faithless, or at least to throw doubt on the divine commission directly given for all time by Christ.

By contrast, the contemporary theology of *ACCM 22* and the college responses, to differing degrees, deliberately face context as an issue and as a resource.[4] The chief question to which colleges were responding was: 'What Ordained Ministry does the Church of England Require?' This question implies that a choice is possible in dialogue with the present situation. Such a question would have made no sense to Anglican theologians such as Moberly, Frere, Gore, or Kirk, for whom ordained ministry was to a great extent identified with a direct and individual commission to represent Christ to the non-ordained (and vice versa), within an institution whose shape was divinely predetermined for all time. The received theology was also conditioned by its era to regard the world through a British or Empire perspective. In contrast, contemporary ecclesiology takes in the broad sweep of world and cosmic affairs. It recognizes that in a 'global village' the Church has to commend its gospel in dialogue and to work on its own vision of faith in Christ in collaboration with others in all faiths and of none.

(b) The Nature of God

The received theology was trinitarian in name and certainly in the formal expressions of liturgical life, but was in effect monist in character. The emphasis was on God's lordship and transcendence, as subject to the object that was his creation, rather than on his present personal interaction, and relatedness. This was proclaimed in a particular emphasis on the Father's past work in sending the Son in history. Applied to ecclesiology, the monist and monarchical understanding of God led to a belief in a highly authoritarian changeless institution which, assured in its own rightness, aspired to reflecting the divine transcendence.

In marked contrast, contemporary theology generally speaks of a God who engages vulnerably with the world. Consequently, an imperfect Church shares in the brokenness of human society, and interacts with its context to strengthen, rather than deny its relatedness. Certainly this God who is the creator and redeemer of all, has sent his Son in history, but he comes also in the present and in the future. Through the Spirit, worshippers are drawn into communion with the trinitarian life, and God is known as one who interacts openly with the world in its sinfulness. This God is known in vulnerability and ambiguity as much as in certainty and clarity. The contemporary ecclesiology of the college responses expects the Church to wrestle with the dilemma of being in but not of the world, and to live with compromise between the present reality of the Church of England and the future hope of perfection. The future reference of God's creative and redemptive work in Christ through the Spirit is seldom mentioned in the responses. However, there is enough of it to signal a change from the received theology, which was totally grounded in the historical mission of the Son.

(c) The Church as Community

The overwhelming emphasis of much of the received position laid stress on the individual Christian. Apostolic succession depended on a bishop being commissioned by an apostle and then bishop following after bishop through history. Here was guaranteed, (especially through the presence of several bishops at a consecration) a linear validation of ministerial authority from Christ. Consequently, and naturally in the post-enlightenment social and philosophical environment, it was the individual Christian and the individual Christian priest that was paramount, to the detriment of the sense of community.

Many of the clergy handbooks of the period 1900–70 spoke in terms of the personal possession and awesome solo responsibility of priesthood. Only gradually from the 1930s, the beginnings of a concern for the Church's corporate nature were traced through a renewed understanding of liturgy and an appreciation of the 'body' and 'people' language of Paul. The empirical evidence, however, indicates that to a great extent this proceeded in parallel with a tradition of clerical responsibility and power.

In the twentieth century, decades of ecumenical theology have gradually established the notion of the Church as a community. Against a social and political climate that favours individualism, the contemporary theology begins from a sense of the People of God having a corporate share in God's mission. However, there are sufficient reminders of a longing to identify the Church primarily in terms of the authority and roles of the clergy, to suggest that there is still some way to go before the Church of England might agree on a theology of ordained ministry that takes trinitarian relations and the future hope of the Church seriously.

In the college responses, all ministry belongs essentially to

Christ and is never the possession of any human being. Although it certainly bears an authority, this is characterized more by service than power, and more by influential presence than by legal authority. Knowledge of God and the ability to serve his purposes arise within and through the praise, collaboration and shared ministry of the whole Church.

(d) An Integrated Ministry

It follows that the contemporary approach to ministry significantly distances itself from the received position, in which the Church was largely defined through the individual priest being set apart from the majority of church members. The contemporary understanding resists the assumption that clergy are permanently fixed in a position of superordination. Frequently this century, efforts have been made to suggest that in spiritual terms there is no difference in degree between Christians, ordained or not. The effect of claiming greater responsibility for the ordained has been coupled with the expectation that somehow they would be the recipients of a matching sense of holiness, wisdom, and sense of vocation. Although this was often formally denied, there is every indication that it was (and to a great extent remains) an essential part of the clerical myth.

The contemporary theology of the college responses places emphasis on the identity of all Christians in sharing through the Spirit the undifferentiated ministry of Christ. The notion of priestly character, classically formulated by Aquinas, which was mostly assumed (in an unspecified way) in the received Anglican theology of ordained ministry, is subsumed into the theology of a primary common baptismal character within which all Christians are rooted into the life of God and discover his purposes and gifts.

To a high degree, the automatic bias against or omission of mention of women in the received theology is missing from the college responses. The Anglo-Catholic colleges contain those who make no secret of their opposition to the ordination of women as priests but their position is by no means unchallenged.

Essentially, instead of a theology that implied a passive

laity dependent on a commissioned, skilled and isolated clergy, the responses assume that all ministry is properly collaborative. The distinctive tasks of the ordained, in word, sacrament, and service, particularly concerning community leadership, are not related to personal status or to a share in God's mission isolated from that of any other, ordained or lay.

(e) A Desire for Unity

The received theology contained a strong element of defensiveness. At the heart of the self-definition of that particular form of Anglicanism, focused on the role of bishops, priests and deacons, which dominated the Church of England over much of the first half of this century, was the assumption that the others were simply wrong. The authoritarian, historically pure, unchangeable institution of Christ could only have one form, the episcopalian. The inadequacy of this monist approach is now starkly exposed, particularly in the light of a renewed appreciation of trinitarian theology. The contemporary ecclesiology assumes that God is at work in the ministerial arrangements of other churches and that this implies no diminishment in the significance of the Church of England.

The Inspiration Offered in the Response to ACCM 22 *for a Theology of Church and Ministry*

(a) The Church in the Purposes of God

The 1990 ACCM Working Party, chaired by Canon Professor Rowan Williams, making an initial comment on the responses of the colleges to *ACCM 22*, declares itself somewhat disappointed at the overall lack of emphasis given to understanding the world and society as the context of the Church's mission and ministry. My own development of an Anglican theology of church and ministry will attempt to respond to that criticism by emphasizing that the Church should only define its existence and purpose within the environment of society, the world, and the cosmos as the locus of God's creative and redemptive activity. The Church's calling to be the present sign and first-fruits of God's final purposes that all things through the Spirit should find their unity in Christ, will be the base-line of my own ecclesiological proposals.

In the four responses which I have had opportunity to consider, the context of the Church's ministry within the complexities of society in Britain, in a world setting, is certainly assumed. There is reference to mission as well as to ministry. What is required is an ecclesiology that understands how to be both challenging and consoling to society, and also knows how to receive challenge and consolation from society.

The necessary confidence that the Church requires in order to model and preach redeemed human relationships, must be one based on dialogue rather than on the kind of domination that comes from a belief in its own perfection. The Church may be a sign and a foretaste of the Kingdom, but as yet, by grace, it has made only a fragmentary beginning. What may be discovered in the college responses regarding the style of church community most appropriate to this task? There are references to a pilgrim Church on a journey, where the goal is nothing less than God's kingdom embracing all nations and all creation under Christ. This Church must reveal the reality of life in Christ in the search for peace, justice, love, reconciliation, and kindness. The expectation is expressed that the Church out of its experience in worship will choose to be responsible for a share in God's concern for the world. This responsibility includes caring for and confronting groups and institutions, inside and beyond the Church, through evangelism, pastoral care, social and political concern, supporting the weak and opposing injustice and bringing help to those in need.

However, none of the responses gives sufficient space to a concept of the Church serving God's mission as the most appropriate basis for understanding ordained ministry. There is still evidence of a concentration of energy on the individual ordained person, and where the corporate ministry of the Church is mentioned, it is often related back historically to the ministry of Christ, to the exclusion of an eschatological dimension. There is a reluctance to move away from the tradition of placing confidence for salvation simply in membership of the Church of the present, where the past life of Jesus is made a reality. However, there is some evidence of seeking a Church that has a concern for the future as well as for the past and present. One of the responses believes in a Church called by God to work with him for the consummation of all things; while another locates the Church's present work in the period between Christ's incarnation, and God's final saving act—that recalls that the Church's constant prayer is, 'Your kingdom come'. Much greater theological emphasis could have been given to the insight that the Church is not merely limited by its past, nor confined to the concepts of the present, but is open to God's future. As we shall later explore in this book, we can learn from Jürgen Moltmann to read history back from its consummation in Christ. This will help us realize possibilities for a theology of the Church, otherwise undreamed of, yet keep us from making the short-cut of attributing to the Church in the present the protection of infallibility or even indefectibility.

I shall take care to avoid proposing an ecclesiology which is idealist and remote from the realities of the contemporary Church of England. No ecclesiology can in itself combat the distortions in human relationships that members bring to the Church through wilfulness and lack of an energizing vision for the future. The Church of England's present critical circumstances, however, illustrate all too clearly the results of attempting to live pragmatically with no publicly defined vision of church and ministry.

According to the comments of Rowan Williams' working party, the responses I was able to consider were not untypical of those of all the colleges and courses. The responses pay little attention to the institutional nature of the Church of England. Nevertheless the 1990 Working Party Report, *Ordination and the Church's Ministry: A Theological Evaluation*, suggests that the very fact that students are living within the ecclesiastical institutions of theological colleges provides material for reflection.[5] One of the key points here is that institutions are complex by nature and can only operate successfully through the delicate interaction of the participants. Rather than being ordered by a single powerful or dominating individual or group, the strategy and quality of life of the college should be created by collaboration, accountability, discussion, and guiding influences. This is of the utmost significance for a trinitarian understanding of the structures of the whole of the Church of England. A college that is too unified in its theological outlook and the ordering of its life, and is too isolated from the tensions in the world and the wider Church, can hardly be a fitting experience for ministry within the mainstream of the Church of England.

Only in two of the responses which I read was it mentioned, briefly, that the colleges are preparing students for ordination into the real rather than an invisible or ideal church. One of them believes ordinands should have a realistic readiness to work within the structures of the church-as-institution, and another expresses the need to train for ministry people who can live with the reality of ministry as it is in the Church of England at the moment, and in the way it is developing, in what they see as its strengths and its weaknesses. Two give no overt hint of the ambiguities of working as an ordained minister within the Church of England. However, there is some recognition of the capacity of corporate college life to provide a challenge, as well as a refuge for learning about the nature of all Christian communities.

The conclusion is that although, generally speaking, the colleges recognize the importance of social and historical context for ecclesiology, and have some investment in recognizing the Church as a sign and foretaste of the Kingdom, there would be great benefits in further developing these concepts. My own proposals, by contrast, will insist that a fundamentally eschatological approach to a doctrine of the Church is of vital significance for the following reasons.

First, the Church and its ministry has only one purpose: it shares with the triune God his passionate concern for the final ordering of the universe in peace. Second, the Church will, therefore, be concerned about its own internal life to the extent that it is ordered in such a way as best to serve its overall task of sharing in the divine mission. Third, the shape and destiny of the Church will be influenced not only by the historical events and prototypical significance of the career of Jesus Christ, but also by reading back from God's final act, when Christ through the Spirit and to the glory of the Father, will draw all things into harmony. Fourth, there will be both discouragement and hope for the institutional church that has a self-awareness of living out its vocation in the period between Christ's victory on the cross and the final *shalom* of God's desire. Lastly, all attempts by churches to denigrate the apostolicity of others or the validity of their ministries, are revealed as archaic in that they are based on a purely historical and Christological account of Church origins. The doctrine of the free gift of God's spirit to the churches that is the result of a thoroughgoing eschatology reveals the inadequacy of all purely confessional attempts to ratify the existence of one church at the expense of others.

(b) Participating in the Trinity

According to the 1990 ACCM review, a variety of treatments of the Trinity come through in the college and course responses. This is reflected in the four responses I considered. One alludes to the overflowing of trinitarian life as the inspiration and the shape of God's mission which is centred and realized in Jesus Christ. One has no trinitarian input, speaking of the Creator God and Christ, but not once of the Spirit in relation to the Church. Another states significantly, though without development, that ministry exercised between people of equal status by grace, should be seen as reflecting the life of the trinitarian Persons, equal in divinity and dignity, but differentiated in person and order. Yet another makes a brief statement that God, through Christ in the Spirit, draws human beings into the communion of the divine love and with one another.

The unity of the trinitarian Persons in love is stated by one to be a compelling model for ecumenism and also as a mystery to be studied, but other than this there is no attempt to draw out the significance of the doctrine of the Trinity for ecclesiology. Again, one response speaks of the Church's mission springing out of God's love for the world articulated supremely in the sending of Christ, and realized through the work of the Holy Spirit. Although the college is glad to include within its life members representing many divergent theological stances, this is not specifically related to trinitarian thinking.

It must be openly admitted that the four college responses selected reveal a low level of commitment to trinitarian thinking, certainly in comparison, apparently, with some of the other responses analyzed in ACCM. The 1990 appraisal chaired by Rowan Williams, in Chapter 3 'Participating in the Trinity', notes a variety of trinitarian stances, not without anxiety that in some cases they reinforce hierarchy and individualism. The Report is concerned that 'An insecure or ill-founded doctrine of the Trinity would weaken the theological foundations of how the Church and its ministry are conceived'.[6] However, in many respects the four colleges chosen represent a broad cross section of respected training institutions within the Church of England, and the absence of evidence of a developed trinitarian doctrine in their submissions makes its own point.

The sparse references to the Trinity in the four college responses leads me to develop the ecclesiological line of thinking first hinted at in *ACCM 22*. Through a rigorous dialogue with recent trinitarian proposals of four contemporary theologians—Leonardo Boff, Colin Gunton, Jürgen Moltmann, and John Zizioulas,—I believe it is possible to develop a powerful ecclesiology for the contemporary English Anglican context. My own ecclesiological proposals will focus on the following points:

1. The relational trinitarianism which represents Christian orthodoxy, allows the Church to recognize and work with the complexity of God's activity in the world, avoiding inappropriate polarizations and dichotomies, notably between Church and world and between ordained and non-ordained.

2. A thoroughgoing trinitarianism roots the life of the world and the mission of the Church into the communion of praise which is the life of God. Through worship, and in particular the Eucharist, the Church with all its own clusters of interrelations, is drawn into the loving mutuality that is God's being.

3. Because God's being is essentially relational, as a social trinitarianism reveals, the shape of God's ultimate intention for the universe should be so described. The Church, therefore, in sharing in the divine mission, is invited not only to work for, but actually to be (albeit imperfectly) a first draft of a trinitarian-shaped community of love, which is a model for all human relationships.

4. It follows, as will be examined in the following chapters, that as a relational trinitarianism offers the most profound clues to the concrete relationships that are most appropriate to the life and task of the Church, there are particular implications for the development and interdependence of the orders of ministry, which in their uniqueness constitute the Church in its unity.

In these principal areas, despite the emphases on collaboration in ministry, the four college responses revealed the early stages of their own development of a thoroughly trinitarian ecclesiology.

(c) Ordained Ministry and the Church as Communion

The statements of the four colleges reveal a concern to promote the unity in difference of ministries, and indeed the companionship of the Church with the world at the service of God's hope.

One response centres the Church's ministry on the twofold ministry of Christ into which, through baptism, every Christian is received: a proclamation to the world of men and women, and service of God. Each member of the Church has unique and varied gifts and opportunities, skills and character, for exercising a ministry. As the text of that submission reveals, its principal thrust speaks of the interconnectedness of ministry through seeking greater wholeness in Christ. Openness and a spirit of listening, the breaking down of cultural and social barriers, are essential elements in the ecumenical context envisaged. However, the cameos of ministry provided in the response seem on the whole weighted towards the roles and skills of the clergy over against, rather than in companionship with, the laity.

Another submission begins from the point that salvation comes by incorporation in that community whose life is shaped by the life of the crucified Christ, the paradigm of God's intention for all humanity. The emphasis on ordained ministry (especially in the role of the presbyters as the ministerial priesthood) tends to make the ordained the subject in relation to the object (laity) who are to be overseen, taught, and their needs cared for. However, there is a denial that the hierarchy of the three orders whose ministry reflects the threefold role of Christ in mediation, proclamation and service confers special status over against lay persons. Indeed, here the vocation of all the baptized is affirmed, within which the ministry of clergy is to be understood as providing for the whole an emphasis and direction. Their relationship is seen in the context of collaboration, mutual responsibility and interdependence within a Church whose character represents Christ and therefore the holiness of God. However, despite the response echoing back familiar phrases about interaction between ordained and non-ordained, to be found in the *ACCM 22* document that challenged the colleges to respond, one of the responses still seemed heavily weighted towards a traditional clerical ministry.

In another response, the expectation of the interrelation between ministries is both explicated and assumed at some length. As a model, the emphasis is placed on the collaborative process between staff, student representatives and governors by which the response was drafted. It decries the commonly observed model of omnicompetent and solo clerical ministry, commending team and group ministry to include accredited laity. Ministry belongs to the whole Church. The ministry of overseeing in the Church, with moral rather than legal authority,[7] is provided to co-ordinate different skills and gifts which Christ through the Spirit distributes. Warnings are issued against allowing such a ministry to be exercised except in mutuality and humility, and with consent and the constraints of mutual correction. Leadership is said to be about helping the whole Church to respond to Christ's commissioning and sending out; it involves sharing between clergy and with laity; and it assumes a helping ministry of healing and social work. It assumes a dialectic between

institutional and charismatic ministry, which is partly held
in unity through being discovered together within a single
person. When this person is partly itinerant, it allows for a
proper critical spirit to be contained within the Church's life.
As both minister and ministered to, giving responsibility and
being responsible, saved and yet a sinner, the leader must
hold the balance of dialogue between his or her own ministry
and that of others. Particularly in liturgy, the leader reveals
what should be true of the whole community in terms of
maturing in Christ. Bishops and priests never act in isolation
within their own denomination and with others. All those
selected and trained for public ministry in the Church are
required to have an understanding of what it means to share
with others in communion in Christ. Although the response
is commendable for the overall mood which it sets, it does
not offer a theological model of how this collaboration might
become a realizable objective.

In one of the responses it is acknowledged that the Church
is a community of those who have varied ministries and the
gifts to perform them. Those in holy orders will often be
expected to provide a serving quality of leadership within
this context. Although it is recognized that ordained ministry
has often disenfranchised other ministries, the response insists
on the unique characteristics of this ministry. All ministry
stems from Christ and is corporate, belonging to the Church
rather than individual. The ordained, by their special
concentration on and life-long commitment to exploring
faith and discipleship, should be empowered to help others
follow their own paths in these areas. In practical terms the
college looks for strenuous attempts to seek collaboration,
though not without hints of unintended patronization
glimpsed in a phrase such as 'readiness to work with the laity
is an attitude of mind'. A theological model of mutuality
would counterbalance the tendency to regard the ministry as
essentially fragments and individuals who must be summoned
to work from their diversity together.

Chapter Four
A RELATIONAL THEOLOGY OF MISSION AND MINISTRY

Introduction

In the opening chapters of this study I have argued the case for an urgent new approach to the doctrine of the Church and its ordained ministry, especially as focused in the role of the parish priest in the Church of England. Support remains strong for the repetition of inherited concepts of church and ministry, especially, it often seems, among those who show little evidence of having given time to investigating contemporary alternatives. However, it seems more likely now than an adequate basis for a doctrine of ministry can be found in a three-way unfolding conversation between the scriptural and patristic accounts of the Church's historical roots, an analysis of the needs of the present time, and contemporary concepts, both theological and scientific, of the nature of God and of all reality.[1] However, for any proposals to bear the stamp of authenticity or to be received by the parishes of the Church of England, it is important, rather than looking entirely for points of differentiation, also to be aware of areas of transition and continuity.[2] Changes in patterns of authority are often more fragmentary than fully-fledged definition maintains, and competing models are not usually utterly incompatible. In the process of the Church of England adopting radically new ministerial arrangements, there are likely to be deep points of continuity.

To take with utter seriousness the contemporary intellectual climate is not to be identified, as some would claim, merely with an accommodation to the dominant values of the present culture.[3] Churches at the end of the twentieth century are tending to emphasize that God and world should not be considered simply as two opposed realities like transcendence and immanence, eternity and time, Creator and creature. To represent the world in these terms is too static an interpretation. However, the present intellectual climate presses for the introduction of such categories as history, process, freedom, which make room for concepts of dynamism, interrelatedness, mutuality, and inclusiveness. Such tendencies propose a view of the world not defined as a mere otherness from God, but as the locus of God's self-communication.

2. Reconsidering Trinitarianism

Against the prevailing background of naturalistic humanism which finds belief in God to be anachronistic and credulous, a number of significant theological writers of the twentieth century have given energy both to considering the validity of the concept of God as well as to the task of reformulating the concept in ways that hold contemporary meaning and relevance. For contemporary secular humanists, it is not so much the nature or character of God that is in question as the plausibility or even relevance of the divine.[4] A contemporary Christian apologetic needs to hold in tension an understanding of God as the source of all being, and the relationship between God and humanity, together with the whole of creation. It is within this context, in close association with the twentieth-century upsurge in exploration of the nature of God as triune, that new possibilities emerge for giving a satisfactory account of the relation between creator and creature.

Throughout the Christian era, contrasting views have existed on the significance of the trinitarian doctrine of God. While some have perceived the Trinity as intrinsic to the biblical revelation and to religious experience, others have claimed that such a doctrine should have only the status of speculation.[5] The latter group have been suspicious of claims to convey indispensable truths about the nature or being of God.[6] Although it is wise to be cautious regarding any human claims to the knowledge of God, I shall take it as axiomatic that at the heart of all Christian theology lies the perennial question of what God must be like if he is to be at one and the same time true to his inner nature and yet also able to relate to humanity and be active in creation.[7]

There may now be observed a growing movement among theologians, towards an emphasis less on the unity, transcendence, immovability, and independence of God, and more on his dynamic, related, and even vulnerable aspects. In particular, there is a concern to continue developing the long-neglected concept of the trinitarian theology of God against the background of late twentieth-century thought. In 1980 Moltmann, as a prelude to his own creative thinking on the Trinity, provided a helpful overview of earlier trinitarianism, noting that trinitarian doctrine has a low profile in modern apologetic writings.[8] The doctrine of the Trinity declined from its central place in Christian theology in the late Middle Ages when the mystery was considered to be of importance only in matters of worship and prayer. After the period of the Enlightenment the doctrine of the Trinity was finally marginalized. For the first half of the twentieth century, theological thought considered the Trinity as of interest merely as a passing phase in historical development. The works on the Church of England and its ministry discussed in Chapter One of this book did not treat trinitarian thought as occupying central place, or as a first principle in questions of Anglican ecclesiology.[9]

The Church of England has contributed to and taken note of the resurgence of trinitarian theology in the Doctrine Commission Report *We believe in the Holy Spirit* (1991) and in its contribution to the British Council of Churches' working party report *The Forgotten Trinity* (1989). In the writing of an English Anglican doctrine of church and ministry, the position of trinitarian theology may, therefore, be considered as central to dogmatic thought.

There is strong support for locating the revival of trinitarianism this century in Karl Barth's desire to show that the Trinity, rather than 'God' in general terms, is essential to Christian belief. Robert Jenson, for example, finds that Barth, in line with the classic Christian tradition, attempts to speak of God under rigorous obedience to a rule:

> God is in himself precisely what he is in the history between the man Jesus Christ and the One he called 'Father' and us in their Spirit. It is, indeed, from Barth

that twentieth-century theology has learned that the doctrine of Trinity has explanatory and interpretative *use* for the whole of theology; it is by him that the current vigorous revival of trinitarian reflection was enabled.[10]

For Barth, the doctrine of the Trinity explains the Christian revelation. An uncompromising trinitarian theology, which he presented in the first volume of his *Church Dogmatics*, was the centre around which he incorporated the whole of his doctrine of being.[11] In marked reaction against the monarchic emphasis of Friedrich Schleiermacher, Barth emphasized the triune nature of the God who chooses to be identified by revealing himself to humanity in Jesus Christ. It was consistent for Schleiermacher to put the doctrine of the Trinity at the end of his doctrine of faith, as he understood Christianity to be primarily and essentially a 'monotheistic mode of belief'.[12] In contrast with inherited theoretizing, which had tended to express belief in God through the analogy of substance, and therefore explained revelation as God's *action* towards humanity, Barth considered God more in terms of 'occurrence' or of 'appearance'. Hill has summarized that for Barth, 'God for us is still God . . . it is part of revelation that what God is for us he is in himself . . . God *is* revelation' and again, 'Revelation is trinitarian, in other words. And since the revelation-event *is* God, God is himself Trinity.'[13] Barth himself wrote of the trinitarian revelation of God: 'Indeed, this God will and can make Himself manifest in no other way than in the That and How of this revelation. He is completely Himself in this That and How.' Barth's own formula, equivalent to the New Testament symbols Father, Son and Holy Spirit, was 'God is Revealer, Revelation, and Revealedness'.[14]

The Trinity, for Barth, is not merely an inference from revelation, but intrinsic to the earliest Christian faith and understanding, calling for continual reappropriation in contemporary language. 'It belongs to the Church. It is a *theologoumenon*. It is a Dogma.'[15] For Barth the Church's doctrine of the Trinity is the correct interpretation of the revelation of God. Despite tendencies towards modalism, with Barth there was revitalized as a fundamental strand of the contemporary theological process, a highly significant redevelopment of the Christian understanding of God as triune.[16]

If Barth is recognized as a point of new departure in the development of trinitarian thought, it would be wrong to proceed without noting representatives of widely differing Christian traditions, who as the twentieth century has progressed, have added their weight to this process. A significant number of theologians from the major traditions have been responsible for advancing the Christian understanding of God and his activity in the world in trinitarian terms. Among them they can be numbered A. M. Allchin (Anglican), Marie-Dominique Chenu (Roman Catholic), Bernard Lonergan (Roman Catholic), Vladimir Lossky (Orthodox), Donald M. MacKinnon (Anglican), John Macquarrie (Anglican), Lesslie Newbigin (United Reformed), Wolfhart Pannenberg (German Protestant), Karl Rahner (Roman Catholic), T. F. Torrance (Presbyterian), and A. W. Wainwright (Anglican). I mention this comprehensive list of trinitarian theologians as the background against which to select a particular approach to trinitarian theorizing for the sake of my ecclesiological proposals.

Recent research has brought me into dialogue with a canon of four writers of different traditions who in distinctive ways share an understanding of God as a relational triune being. It is my proposal that the theologians who can help us particularly regarding the theme of this study are Professor Leonardo Boff (Roman Catholic, liberation theologian), Professor Colin Gunton (United Reformed Church), Professor Jürgen Moltmann (Reformed), and Metropolitan John Zizioulas (Orthodox). Although there are significant differences between the trinitarian beliefs of these four, their ability to inspire a doctrine of the Church based on the Trinity lies in their insights into the analogy between the relational nature of God, and the relational understanding of society and the world.

3. The Triune God

In a unique way, Christians engaged in personal prayer and public worship recognize that they are brought into relationship with the triune God and with one another through the action of the Son and the Spirit. A vital strand of Christian theology speaks of knowing God precisely through his personal self-revelation in Jesus and in the continuing life and worship of the church. Despite the inadequacies and failure of our experiences of church and liturgy, Christians are constituted in the faith by the mediating role of the Son and the inspiration of the Spirit. The Methodist hymnologist, Dr Tripp is right to suggest that Christian worship is always trinitarian in character because the Church itself, in all its being and activity, in sin and failure, 'springs from the trinitarian love which is the divine essence'.[17] The period 1900–70 briefly reviewed earlier showed Anglicans basing ecclesiology and a doctrine of ministry on Christology, with little reference to the work of the Spirit. Clergy were successors of apostles, themselves appointed by Christ. English Anglicans frequently pressed the case for the universalizing of their own understanding of the Church to the detriment of ecumenical relations, and the denial of indigenous cultures in England and elsewhere in the world where missionaries established new churches. There are strong arguments today for an integration of pneumatology with Christology. This offers the double effect of reducing the inherited emphasis on the Church as a universal and self-justifying institution inaugurated in every detail by Christ, and of re-emphasizing the role of the Spirit in constituting the Church in variety and vulnerability.[18]

Although God is accessible through the Son and in the Spirit to all humanity, the particular gift of Christian faith is to recognize and respond to the truth and potential of that relationship between the triune God and all creation. Human sin consists in the wilful breaking of this relationship with God and neighbour to which God's response, in the atonement through his Son, is to restore the fragmented relationship. This redemption is truly 'a ransom for many' in that the Son's taking flesh and dying and rising renews, and, most importantly for the argument of this enquiry, re-orders and redirects the creation towards the hope of God's final peace. God's closeness to humanity, even in times of harrowing pain, has led Moltmann to speak of the death of Jesus as an event in the life of the Trinity. He demonstrates from the writings of the Anglican, C. E. Rolt (1913), how central to Anglican theology is the bringing together of the cross of Christ and God's eternal nature as Trinity.[19] Such trinitarian theology finds support in the triadic formulas of the New Testament which indicate how baptized believers slowly came to recognize in the person and career of Jesus Christ the Saviour, the presence of the God who is creator of heaven and earth. The carpenter is also the cosmic creator-redeemer and the one who uniquely focuses and demonstrates the healing presence of the Lord of all.[20]

However, there has been a tendency within Christianity so to emphasize the person and work of Jesus, described classically in the metaphors of victory, justification and sacrifice, as an event in past history, that the connection between Jesus and the inner life of the God who has a passionate concern for the final ordering of the universe is diminished. A significant correction of balance is achieved by taking note of that element within the Christian tradition which takes as a starting point the Creator's wisdom of a future perfection. In this way there can be demonstrated a continuity in the presence and action of God from the work of Creation, through the work of Jesus Christ, and forward to eternity.[21] In particular, Moltmann's emphasis on the history of Christ in future perspective draws out the meaning of the Father's glorification in the Son, and the life of the Christian, as both sharing in Christ's crucifixion and glorification. He illuminates the Christian understanding of a new creation by expressing it in terms of the future goal of the trinitarian history of God's dealings with creation.[22] The one raised in glory is the one who was crucified.

To make the intellectual connection between Jesus of Nazareth and the Christ, the eternal Word, early Christians developed the theology of the *homoousion*, the Son who is 'of one being' with the Father, the one on whose lips John could place the saying, 'I and the Father are One'.[23] Within the intricate disputes that surrounded this term, its essential purpose may be discerned as indicating that, ontologically, there is the possibility of a sharing in 'being' itself. The Council of Nicaea (325), against the Arian heresy, declared that the Son is not a creature but as fully and equally God as the Father. The Council Fathers solemnly declared that Jesus Christ, Son of God is, 'from the being (*ousia*) of the Father, God from Light, Light from Light, true God from true God, one in being (*homoousios*) with the Father, through whom all things were made, those in heaven and those on earth'.[24] Although there remained questions to be answered, this definition committed orthodox Christians to an understanding of God as inherently relational in his being.[25] From this point for the Christian Church, *to be* and *to be in relation* become identical. All being derives from God's own being. Therefore, simultaneously, for someone or something to *be*, two things are necessary: being itself (*hypostasis*) and being in relation (i.e., being a person).

Taking this a stage further, the Cappadocian Fathers, Basil the Great, bishop of Caesarea (329–79), his blood brother Gregory of Nyssa (c. 335–94) and his friend Gregory of Nazianzus (329–90), were decisively influential in the formulation of the doctrine of the Trinity. Although today we recognize their seminal contribution, especially because of the emphasis they made on the place and status of the Holy Spirit, they were generally uneasy about all human attempts to use words to illustrate the relations of the Trinity to each other.[26] Through the maze of scholarly debate regarding the precise contribution of the Cappadocians, it is possible to distil the new Christian insight that *communion* lies at the heart of God's being.[27] So, for example, for Gregory of Nazianzus, thought about God needs to include both unity and plurality: 'No sooner do I conceive of the One, than I am illuminated by the splendour of the Three; no sooner do I distinguish them than I am carried back to the One.'[28]

The work of the Cappadocian theologians can be summarized under three points. First, against their Greek intellectual background, they recognized that they were deliberately being innovative concerning the being of the Trinity as 'a new and paradoxical conception of a united separation or a separated unity'.[29] In deliberate opposition to Arius, they developed a new vocabulary for the divine unity, not in terms of mathematics, nor of subordination, but as the inseparable relation of the particular persons of the Godhead, Father, the Son and the Spirit as three *hypostases*.[30]

Second, the Cappadocians were offering a markedly new perception of the theology of the nature of God. Their concept of the Trinity, in contrast to that of the dogmatic manuals of the West and those of the East in modern times, is that Father, Son, and Spirit, as an inseparable communion of mutual love, are nothing other than a single being.[31] God is communion, a loving dynamism of three Persons in relation. To speak of Christ, therefore, always means referring at the same time to the Father and the Spirit. The incarnation is formed by the work of the Spirit and is the expression and realization of the will of the Father. This insight offers a radically different basis for understanding the Church from that which characterized English Anglicanism in the period 1900–70. The Church is born, not just in relation to the Son of God, but to the entire Trinity. Given power and life by the Spirit, the Church is characterised as *koinonia* (2 Cor. 13.13). Such a Church is not limited by attempting to protect its homogeneity, but knows itself to be a differentiated unity, simultaneously one and many. Avoiding merely abstract speculation about the immanent Trinity, the Cappadocians reflect on the analogy of human reproduction to speak of the co-inherence of the Father and the Son. The Father shares his being with the Son and the Spirit, and so can be said to 'cause' them. So Gregory of Nyssa speaks of 'one and the same Person (*prosopon*) of the Father out of whom the Son is "begotten" and the Spirit proceeds'.[32]

To explain how the one substance can be simultaneously present in the three Persons, the Cappadocians appeal to the analogy of a universal and its particulars. Of the relation of the Father to the Spirit they use the analogies of breathing or procession.[33] This may appear to place an imbalance of power in the generative work of the Father (the *fons et origo Trinitatis*). However, it is seen not to be the case precisely because the ontology of God is the relationship of the unique Persons co-existing in mutual love. Therefore, the three Persons constitute one another and exist within each other as the being of God through an interdependent giving and receiving. As Boff expresses this relationship: 'They are what they are because of their intrinsic, essential communion.'[34] Nothing, therefore, remains of God apart from this being in relation to one another of the particular Persons. The Cappadocian thesis of the Father as 'cause' implies that the ultimate ontological category which creates being, is neither an impersonal and incommunicable substance, nor a structure of communion, but a *person*.[35]

Third, the Cappadocian theology of the triune God gave to Christianity new potential for speaking of the ordering or conceptualizing of persons in relation, difference, and freedom. Personal relations are recognized as belonging to the structure of creation itself. 'Person' from here onwards takes on a distinction from what is understood by the term 'individual'. Whilst the latter is defined in terms of separation, the former is essentially recognizable in relations with others.

The work of the Cappadocians is not an end in itself but a significant turning point. Overlooked for too many centuries, they provide a springboard for continued reflection on the triune nature of God which the core group of dialogue partners for this enquiry, Boff, Gunton, Moltmann and Zizioulas have recognized. God is to be recognized only as a communion of Persons, each with distinctive and particular ways of being. The relation of the trinitarian Persons is what constitutes them mutually in their uniqueness as Father, Son, and Spirit. The individual *hypostases*, or identities of the Persons, are formed through the others, and through the ways in which the others relate to them.

The Persons of the Trinity are unique and distinct, yet at the same time interdependent in a process of mutual love. Their identity and individuality, therefore, are neither asocial nor presocial, but arise out of their relations and co-inherence. Each of the Persons is a social unity with specific characteristics uniquely theirs and yet simultaneously in community. In a relationship of *perichoresis* the persons exist only as they exist for others, not merely as they exist in and for themselves. The fourth-century Greek trinitarian theologians coined the term *perichoresis* (Latin, *circumincessio*—interpenetration) to express the communion that *is* God's Being. *Perichoresis* means that each Person of the Godhead contains the other two, each, by invitation, penetrating the others and being penetrated by them. 'Penetration' could be misunderstood as a harsh or unwelcome intrustion or invasion of territory. What has to be remembered is the sense of mutual invitation implied in *perichoresis*. Other English expressions that might be offered to unpack the meaning are 'mutual indwelling' and 'living within each other'. There is scriptural support for the choice of *perichoresis* as a key to understanding the Trinity as reciprocal communion without any denial of differentiation, in John 10.30, 'The Father and I are one', and v. 38, 'the Father is in me, and I in him'. The Greek *hen* emphasizes organic union. There never was a time when the three existed in isolation.

Nor is the perichoretic relationship of communion of the Persons of the Trinity closed in on to itself, but rather is opened in a centrifugal movement. The three Persons of God invite into unity with themselves humanity and the whole created order. In the Trinity, the Persons each live beyond their own borders in relation with the others. To have being is, therefore, to be in the other so as to understand oneself and the other from the perspective of the other. As Boff expresses the life of the Trinity,

> There is a complete circulation of life and a perfect coequality between the Persons, without any anteriority or superiority of one over another. Everything in them is common and communicated one to another, except what cannot be communicated: what distinguishes one from the others. The Father is fully in the Son and the Holy Spirit; the Son is fully in the Father and the Holy Spirit; the Holy Spirit is fully in the Father and the Son. This is the source of the utopia of equality—with due respect for differences—full communion and just relationships in society and history.[36]

Profound interrelatedness and mutual interpenetration, yet always within a spirit of freedom, lie at the heart of the triune life.

The trinitarian relationship is indeed constituted in freedom or mutual courtesy and this freedom characterizes its way of being, externally as well as internally. The quality of life within the triune being of God, which is given and created in the dialogue and interrelationship between the

Persons, overflows as God's externally directed communication in the processes of creation and redemption. In this work as Creator, God relates to what is other in such a way as to guarantee its independence and uniqueness, but also to call it into free relation with himself and the whole of creation.

Through the Son and the Spirit, God's gift of freedom, springing from his own inner being, comes to humanity. Can such a gift of freedom also have meaning for the non-personal part of creation? Perhaps what it could mean for the non-personal world to be free would better be conveyed by the term 'contingent'. Moltmann writes of the freedom of God in creating, that he 'loves the world with the very same love as he himself *is*'.[37]

Following Plato, Boethius, many Greek Fathers, and later artists and theologians, in an essay, *The Triune God as Artist*, Jeremy Begbie has explored the extent to which analogies of artistic creativity are helpful in elucidating the trinitarian character of the creation of the cosmos. Regarding contingency, he reminds us that in parallel with artist, picture, and appreciator, the inhabitant of the universe is at liberty to enjoy its fruits without acknowledging their author. To avoid pantheism and deism, Begbie focuses not on the relation between God and the cosmos but on the continuing relationship of creativity which, strictly speaking, extends the bounds of the analogy between artist and painting. The analogy could be developed in terms of a whole lifetime of artistry. He revives the contribution of Dorothy Sayers to emphasize the inbuilt respect for the integrity of the artistic medium which well illustrates the nature of contingency in the relationship between God and the universe. Sayers insisted on the importance of an artist respecting the integrity of the chosen medium. She sees here an analogy with God's self-limitation in creation. Once the artist has selected paint, pigment, words, sound, metre, a character in a play, a theme, or whatever, there is implied a measure of limitation on the artist's development of the work. The medium possesses an integrity to be 'honoured and developed, not abused'. Vanstone's enquiry into the character of the creator God also emphasized the immense respect of the chosen kenotic, self-limiting love of God towards creation. Begbie prefers in the end, to move away from the analogy of a single artist (in a clearer parellel with the trinitarian concept) to focus on the mutual exchange taking place between the artist, less as communicator of his idea, and more in a relationship of exchange with the physical medium as well as with artistry past and present.[38]

The triune God (whose being is perichoretic communion) can have no need to create a world in order to have that with which to communicate. There is no necessity or self-fulfilment implied in the creation of the universe, in order to enter into relationship. It follows that the world of nature is the product of a free generosity of the triune God who is himself relational. As a communion of difference, God the Trinity reaches out in openness for a relationship of love with creation.[39] The likeness of God to his non-personal creation needs to be expressed with immense caution. However, in terms of something approaching a conceptual parallel, it is reasonable to claim that the inner freedom of the Trinity is to some degree reflected in the freedom with which he enters into relation with that which is other than himself, the world.[40] All creation may, therefore, be conceived of as bearing the stamp of its Creator in the image of God as the Scriptures attribute to humankind the gift of the image of God.

Within the fabric of Western Christian thought, there has been a long tradition of expressing the divine image in humanity in terms of an internal attribute such as reason or consciousness. Human beings have been conceived of as related to God primarily through their individuality. The result has often appeared as static and internal, denying a sense of inherent relationship with others as part of the construct of being. If, however, a trinitarian understanding of the divine as a perichoretic community of Persons in relation is adopted, it offers the opportunity to understand the unique and saving work of God in humanity in thoroughly relational terms.

The social trinitarian concept has a significant bearing on the nature of all relationality whether personal or impersonal. If it is accepted that the conceptualizing of God himself and the ordering of the world of time and space is most truly informed by the trinitarian paradigm, it follows that theological discourse has the potential to provide the most truthful description of all reality as life-in-relationship.[41] Gunton has well expressed the relationship between the trinitarian God, humanity and creation in these words:

> The triune God has created humankind as finite persons-in-relation who are called to acknowledge his creation by becoming the persons they are and by enabling the rest of the creation to make its due response of praise.[42]

This enquiry will propose that there are significant links between the elaboration of the Christian theology of the trinitarian Creator and Redeemer, and the dynamic ordering of the world and its inhabitants. In conclusion, therefore, it is a distinctive focus of Christian belief that, despite the brokenness of sin and evil, all of creation is summoned to echo or mirror the trinitarian relationships.[43] Consequently the Christian Church, in communion with the Son and through the Spirit, has in its own life the most appropriate tools for making proposals for the right ordering of society now and in the future.

4. The Trinitarian Roots of Ecclesiology

I have come to recognize that the quest to find trustworthy concepts to describe the Church and its ministry is intimately connected with the knowledge that God's own revealed life imparts concerning the ordering of all relations: between God and humanity, people and each other in society, and humanity and the universe. An ecclesiology for a Church which is a sign and a foretaste of God's final ordering of all things in Christ, will be informed and nurtured by a social trinitarianism.[44]

The Christian West has been impoverished in its ecclesiological understanding to the extent that a social trinitarianism has been almost entirely disregarded and certainly not brought into the doctrine of Church and ministry.[45]

Chapter One of this book demonstrated the consequences of developing ecclesiology predominantly on a Christological basis, with regard both to the historical shape and direction of the life of Jesus and also its dogmatic significance. Many theologians have now come to question the validity of the inherited tradition of a casual effect in the history of the Church between events in the life of Jesus and contemporary ministerial arrangements, whether resulting largely in a community reflecting the new Israel (as in Schleiermacher) or in a clerically defined church. In itself, the Church is nothing. It can only be true to its calling when it is clearly filled with the life of the Spirit, revealing God active in history.[46]

The Church called into existence by the triune God, however faintly, may be said to have the potential in Christ and through the Spirit, to model or be a sign of that *communion* which is the being of Godself and the shape of his desire for the ultimate ordering of the entire Creation. So far, I have reached three important conclusions which resonate with Gunton's statement that in the light of the Trinity everything looks different. First, God's being is most accurately understood by Christians as Trinity: a communion of Father, Son and Holy Spirit. Second, it is essential to God's purpose for the universe that all relationships should be understood as echoing the trinitarian pattern. Third, the Church, having a particular task to prepare the way for godly relationships in society and creation, must allow its ministerial arrangements to echo the trinitarian relationships of loving communion.

Zizioulas, who advocates the significance for today of the patristic belief in the existence of a deep bond between the being of humanity, of the world, and of God, agrees with Moltmann that the Church as part of creation should reflect God's being in humility, contingency and the rejection of the way of domination. He begins from the divine givenness of a communion relationship between the world, its people, and God which must dictate to the Church the ordering of its own internal life. Indispensable to understanding the work of Zizioulas are an awareness of these two patristic keys: (a) There is no true being without communion. Nothing exists as an individual conceivable in itself. Communion is an ontological category; and (b) Communion which does not come from a 'hypostasis', a concrete and free person, and which does not lead to 'hypostases', concrete and free persons, is not an 'image' of the being of God. Every form of so-called communion, therefore, which denies or suppresses the freedom of the person is inadmissible.[47] A triune God whose inner life may be expressed in terms of perichoretic being, implies a Church in which there are no permanent structures of subordination but rather, overlapping patterns of mutual relationship. The same person or group of persons will be sometimes subordinate and at other times superordinate, according to the gifts and graces being exercized appropriate to the occasion.

To belong to the Church means that, by growing in communion with the Trinity, we accept a shared responsibility for a regeneration of relations within society generally, and also between the human race and its global environment. The Scriptures indicate that God sees the destiny of humanity as bound up with that of the entire cosmos.[48]

A deist theology makes no proper recognition of the interrelatedness of God, his people and their cosmic environment. A trinitarian ontology that understands the creator God as a communion of love offers more hope of a theory of the world's proper ordering than does a tendency towards static, undifferentiated monotheism. As a divinely inspired alternative to the wisdom of secular reason embodied as individualism or collectivism, a theological insight rooted in a thoroughly social trinitarianism proposes an alternative ordering.[49] A world-view that adopts unity and separate identity to make fundamental sense of things, will have particular difficulty in living with differences. They can hardly be tolerated. But Christian belief in the Trinity means that differences must be accepted for what they are. The Church is possessed by a vision of God and the created order as open and engaged in a life-process. Unity is not to be equated with the denial of difference or the reduction of them all to one, but speaks of the mutual intercommunion and interpenetration of elements of difference.

How far contemporary Britain is from such a vision may be observed, for example, in terms of public architecture. We are surrounded by supermarkets, shopping malls, tourist information centres, schools, petrol stations, and restaurants

more notable for their identity than their imaginative difference. The unmet needs for hospital patients, prisoners, clients
of the social services, and tenants, to be treated as both
unique and mutually related, hangs like a cloud of depression
especially over the relatively powerless in our society.[50]
The Church in this light can model and prescribe a society
formed by mutually constitutive relations.[51] Individualism
denies our need of human relationships at all, except in
urgent matters of economic usage. Collectivism reduces all
members of human society to the status of disposable cogs in
the machine of a corporate enterprise. Both lack a profound
sense of reciprocity, so that power groups may arise and
dispossess or make redundant relatively powerless persons in
the name of progress or in the pursuit of economic theory.
Neither social system, collectivism nor individualism, allow
for the reciprocal freedom and the proper relational existence
of the constituent persons.[52] The inspiration of a thoroughgoing trinitarianism, by contrast, refuses to treat any person
or group either as totally isolated or as a mere unit in a
collective game.[53] Zizioulas shows how the highest or true
understanding of personhood, based on an accurate vision of
God as community, is the Church's unique contribution to
the human quest for meaning and wholeness. 'If God does
not exist, the person does not exist.'[54] As the Father, the Son
and the Spirit are mutually constituted in their unique
being, precisely through their free otherness-in-relation, so
the Church has the mission to show society how, in a healthy
culture, each particular person is both unique and yet mutually related to the being of the whole.[55]
The pursuit of a theological vision for the right ordering of
creation should take as a starting point the double belief that
human beings are intended and destined to be in mutual
relation with others, after the image of the trinitarian God.
People become their unique selves through the quality of
their relationships. So it becomes possible to make connections between the freedom to be ascribed to the persons of
God and the human autonomy of free responsibility.[56]
The idea of and the human struggle towards freedom runs
deep in the history of humanity and was never more sharply
focused than at the present time.[57] We are daily called upon

to wrestle with the right of each person to full development, with its accompanying dangers of individualism and narcissism, the human ability to influence the development of ecosystems, to pollute rivers and yet to desire pure drinking water, the right to procreate without control and to develop methods of artificial insemination, and yet to eat without limit. We are faced with the contrasting claims of all to be gainfully employed, and for shareholders to reap high profits, and company directors to live in luxury. It becomes immediately apparent that society is largely defined by the conflict of 'freedoms' rather than a vision of differentiated relationship.

Nothing can be worthy of the name 'salvation', 'liberation', or 'freedom'—terms which have many points of convergence—that represents freedom (salvation or liberation) for some, at the expense of, or through the exclusion, of others. This could easily be demonstrated at the level of international politics or food aid. Christianity is notorious for saying 'no' to human pleasures whilst in its own disciplines and structures often oppressing and repressing persons on grounds of race, culture or gender.

In what sense can our knowledge of the freedom of God help to refine the notion of human relatedness, especially in the area of deliberately chosen self-restraint for the promotion of the freedom of others? Moltmann, who is notable for his courageous efforts to articulate the dialogue between God and humanity in the search for justice and peace on the global scale, maintains that the orthodox Christian tradition, despite all appearances to the contrary, does have a message of hope for humanity. He stresses that the triune God is not a lonely Lord in heaven, beyond feelings, who puts everyone under his heavy rule. Rather, the Christian God is a community of loving relationship. This is what John means when he writes, 'I am in the Father and the Father is in me'.

To be the subject of one's own destiny (within the constants of political and ideological powers, violence and wickedness) is deliberately to mirror the image of God by being externally orientated in creativity and reconciliation and choosing to align one's intentions with those of God. Dialogue here means that, on God's side at least, there is respect for freedom and independence and an absence of overdetermination. In the mystery of God's grace human beings are addressed as God's dialogue partners. They are therefore free to make what response they will, and all that they do and make of themselves is in fact a response to God—though that may take the form of conscious or unconscious rejection.[58]

Just as Godself is free and not bound to create or enter into relation with anyone or anything, God who initiates dialogue with humanity, also gives to his creation the freedom for co-operation to be withheld. True sociality arises for humanity through lives of thankful recognition of the redemption brought about in Jesus Christ. In his free choice to be orientated towards God and others in the spirit of God's peace, undistorted human response is exemplified. This response of humanity to God's invitation reveals the quality of divine love as a given within creation, yet never demanded as obedience, always as a free invitation to choose.[59] To respond in freedom to Christ's call is to be willing to be true to God and to contribute to the creation of redeemed sociality. 'Being-in-gratitude' is the human personal mirror image response to the triune God's gracious movement towards his creation. A relationship with this God is part of all existence; the shape of that relationship is reflected in the acceptance or rejection of God's being and creative intention.[60]

5. A Relational Understanding of All Reality

To sum up the argument so far: my conclusion is that the search for an adequate ecclesiology and doctrine of ministry lies within the context of the service of the triune God's ultimate purposes for the entire creation. The Church may only be regarded as acting authentically when it makes itself available, through a critical correlation between New Testament Christianity, the living tradition of faith and the demands of the present, to make a distinctive contribution to the right ordering of the world in the present and the future. God's final purposes are revealed both in his gift of Jesus Christ, and through the Spirit, the present and future task in which God provokes the involvement of humanity.[61] An ecclesiology, therefore, is required which can fuse together the Church's role as agent of God's ultimate intention for all creation with a renewed appreciation of a social trinitarian understanding of God.

The life of the Church, as sign and foretaste of the salvation of all things, should be seen as totally bound up with that of the whole creation which is its context. There is a weight of theological opinion that would recognize the trinitarian character of God, not only in terms of direct revelation, but also as a reading of human and natural life, when interpreted truly, in relational terms. An essential part of the present context is also the significant trend of contemporary thought that advocates an interdisciplinary approach to any part of the search for truth.[62] Religious understandings which fail to engage with other disciplines have limited conceptions, appear increasingly marginalized and irrelevant, and by merely following their own isolated trajectory become 'dysfunctional'.[63] In every generation, Christian theology has been in dialogue with contemporary philosophy and culture. The early fathers related their theology to the ideas of Platonism, the Church of the Middle Ages to neo-Aristotelianism, and that of post-war Europe to the existentialist comment on society. There is always the danger of allowing the dialogue to become distorted, so that either faith or culture dominate each other. However, in the late twentieth century the exciting possibility arises for a renewed trinitarian theology to engage with the relationality being explored in the disciplines of cosmology, anthropology, physics or psychology.[64]

Increasingly, interpreters of modern scientific theories are informing the educated public that, as modern scientific work continues, the classical mechanistic, predictable, timeless mode of nature familiar to Western thought is losing credibility.[65] I can make few intellectual claims to understand the detail of the argument, but I sense the truth of a fundamental shift as it has, for example, been described by John L. Casti:

> The age of absolutes, if it ever really existed, is now definitely and permanently passé. Einstein's work buried once and for all the concepts of absolute space and time,

while Heisenberg shot down the belief in absolutely precise measurement. Gödel, of course, stamped paid to the quaint and curious ideas of absolute proof and truth. Even more recently, we find sociobiologists trying valiantly (and with some measure of success) to terminate with extreme prejudice the incomprehensible notion of absolute free will. Moreover, chaos theorists have been making a tidy living of late telling us that even if we did know the mechanism, we still wouldn't know the phenomena. Taken as a whole, modern science has redrawn the map of human knowledge so that it now shows potholes and detours not only along every side street and back alley, but on all the major highways and byways as well.[66]

As alternative perceptions of reality are articulated among scientists, it is becoming sharply apparent that a new awareness of·context requires a markedly different response from theologians and the Christian community. Among some contributors, work on the interface between science and religion is moving beyond the inherited antagonisms.

A doctrine of the Church that takes account of God's final purposes for the world, and is based on a sound doctrine of the Trinity, rather than being governed merely by historical precedent, requires a multi-disciplinary approach. However, extreme caution is required on the part of the theologian presuming to make observations based on scientific theories on the nature of complexity and change which are themselves in transition and come to him second-hand. It is perhaps as well to remember that there exists an appropriate scepticism among both scientists and theologians regarding ideologically weighted theses concerning too naive an interaction between science and religion.[67] However, the emerging contemporary imaginative sense of the universe may recognize in a relational trinitarian concept a version of ultimate reality which cannot immediately be dismissed as irrelevant, and which should rightly be diagnosed as a vital constituent in a dynamic and complex understanding of reality.

This is in marked contrast with the attempt by Don Cupitt to explain the Christian God to a secular society. Instead of offering to the world a concept of God who is a relational being promoting freedom in diversity, Cupitt has dismissed the God of Christian faith as one of 'pernicious heteronomy', the enemy of liberation. Cupitt speaks of the *creatio ex nihilo* God rejected by Marx as unacceptable to a modern understanding of the world in which changes occur slowly and continuously in line with the development of knowledge.[68] Gunton responds to this by commending the typology of the nineteenth-century philosopher poet S. T. Coleridge, who recognized that a vital issue for Christian apologetics lay in the affirmation of freedom, particularity, and difference within the relationships between God and creation, and between individuals and the world. He accuses Cupitt of allowing only such meaning to the world as human beings at any one time can name.[69] For Coleridge the Trinity, a given rather than a construct, was the *idea idearum*, 'the one substrative truth which is the form, manner, and involvement of all truths'.[70] Coleridge takes as axiomatic the phrase 'the limits of your language are the limits of your world'. Gunton and Cupitt in an important way reach the same conclusion that the impersonal, spectator God of theism will no longer satisfy. In the company of many others, I acknowledge Cupitt's contribution towards a contextual theology and one which speaks to many on the edge of Christian belief, but press on with more optimism to rediscover in the tension between the Church's tradition so far, and the urgent needs of the world today, inspiration for an ever deeper engagement with and understanding of the relational and saving triune God. For Christian theologians, recognizing the limitations of even the most inspired of human insights, there is the reasonable expectation of a coherent link between the nature of God as a triune relational being and the reality of all created matter.

(a) Some Modern Scientific Conceptions of Non-Personal Reality

There exists a growing consensus that the present point in scientific understanding, named variously, a 'turning point' (Fritjof Capra) or a 'paradigm shift' (Thomas Kuhn), places humanity in a new interpretative situation. Theologians, recognizing a new context and a new task, are reminding the Church of its own particular insight into the marks of the created order, and invite further theological development of the Trinitarian concept:

> Unsettlement there surely is, but there is too the joy of recognition. The tradition of a Trinitarian manner of conceiving of ultimate reality with an emphasis on the relational, the processive, the communal, unity in distinction can find many points of convergence with the new paradigm of reality as it has been described.[71]

It would be impossible to do justice to a rapidly growing and often vertiginous scientific perspective on the nature of reality within the limits of this enquiry. However, an ecclesiology that intends to relate to and contribute to reconceiving its widest context, needs to take note of recent developments in the conceptualizing of the non-personal world. There is a compelling wealth of evidence in some recent scientific writing for an understanding of the ordering of the world in dynamic terms. During the past fifty years the preoccupations of the sciences have begun to move away from the mechanistic approach of natural philosophy that evolved in the wake of the dualism of pure mind and mechanical body classically associated with the name of Descartes.[72] Stephen Toulmin in *Cosmopolis* has shown how Descartes, in the face of the breakdown of the powerful medieval synthesis, was attempting to find a new philosophical and social coherence. Descartes was instrumental in the formation in his generation of a culture centred on an interior world in which the self alone becomes the ultimate point of reference. Such a world view is still prevalent but beginning to give place to another. Now especially since the turn of this present century, some pioneering scientists have distanced themselves from a mechanical understanding of reality conceived as merely formal systems based on abstract rational theory.[73] As we learn to abandon a perspective of knowledge concentrated only in severely compartmentalized and rationalist discourse, our theories about the world can no longer be appropriately expressed in terms of universal, deterministic, immutable and timeless systems.[74] In general terms, classical physics operated with the assumption, widely influential until very recently, that the universe had a clear rationale, so that even those currently problematical areas would eventually yield their secrets. For much of the modern era matter could be identified with four characteristics, indicated by the expressions: determinism, classical realism, infinite subdivisibility of energy, and separability.[75] Such confidence in the predictability of the natural world is now recognized to be far from secure.

Current trends in leading theories in fundamental physics, cosmology, and computing sciences concentrate on a holistic approach to theorizing about the ordering of matter rather than the traditional reductionist assumption that various scientific disciplines in isolation from each other, can explain everything. Hardy, pioneering from a Christian theologians' perspective a multi-disciplinary approach between theology, cosmology, and world history, notes with dissatisfaction the tendency to create separate accounts of the world by disciplines which thereby lose the 'raw material' available from others, and so reinforce their isolation.[76] Michael Polyani and Stanley Jaki are among those who have recognized that particularity and specificity, far from disrupting an assumed homogeneity or undifferentiated sameness, lie at the heart of the cosmos. Complexity and order are no longer to be regarded as mutually exclusive; instead of automatically implying absence of order, complexity may be described in a wide variety of ways as involving subtle relationality and dynamic organization. In particular, there is now a growing tendency towards viewing multi-component systems as possessing collective qualities which for the discrete component are absent or prove meaningless.[77] Characteristic phrases which summarize the rejection of the Western analytical frame of mind and the assumption that matter is not straightforward are 'the whole is greater than the sum of its parts', and 'life is a holistic phenomenon'.[78]

The most recent phase of scientific theory seems to confirm what many had long suspected, that logical-critical analysis is not sufficient:

Historical-hermeneutical reflection is also needed (just as it is called into play in the history of theology and dogma).

What is needed above all is psychological-sociological investigation (hitherto still largely absent from theology). What we have then is an investigation into science that represents a union of the theory, the history, and the sociology of science.[79]

Prigogine and Stengers, researching the irreversible thermo-dynamics of systems far-from-equilibrium, assert that the notion of evolution should be applied not only to the organic sphere but to the whole universe.[80] Refuting Einstein's conviction that time is illusory, they claim that the universe is not only relational and contingent, but has an inherent directional dynamic.[81] They maintain that most phenomena of interest to the modern scientist may be characterized as 'open' systems, exchanging energy or matter with their environment, so that the attempt to understand them in mechanistic terms must be doomed to failure.[82] Most of reality, according to the Brussels school of physicists, instead of being normally orderly, stable and equilibrate, is actually seething and bubbling with change, randomness and process. The indications are that reality is best described in terms of a journey leading from a static state of 'being' to a continually developing condition of 'becoming' as a leading characteristic of reality.[83]

There are parallels to be drawn in recent developments in ecology. Issues which hold a concern for the future destiny of humanity in harmony with the world, are bound up with the conceptualizing of a new world order in which previous understandings of the domination of man and the compart-mentalizing of matter have to be forsaken. A decade ago Prigogine and Stengers were challenging society to abandon a scientific view which led to alienation between humanity and the world. They pointed to the changes that science is undergoing today which offer new opportunities. The pain resulting from sustained misuse of the natural resources has led to increasing attention being given to appropriate ways of relating human life to that of its environment locally and globally. Human sinfulness and the complexity of the issues, together make progress in this area highly problematic. The ecology debate is built on the growing perception that 'nature' is not just a source of neutral resources to be exploited for human benefit. The complexity of the political, sociological and economic debate related to these new concerns, demonstrated notably in Linda Starke's *Signs of Hope, Working Towards our Common Future* (1990), is primary data for the argument that the truth about reality can only be worked in a fragile complexity of relationships.

There is an urgent need for theologians to work with theorists of other disciplines towards imaginative and creative responses. Gunton's Didsbury Lectures (1990) offer a clear invitation for the disciplines concerned with the future of the planet to work in partnership with theologians towards an understanding of the cosmos in relational terms. As a Christian theologian, he proposes that the true end of the whole creation is to be realized by humanity, caring for the perfecting of the non-personal world in co-operation with God. Human sinfulness would make this impossible, but through Christ and in the Spirit, the whole creation can be brought to God's final hope:

> Creation is not merely through Christ, but *to* him: from the beginning, it has an eschatological thrust. Salvation takes place *within* the created and material order with an eye to the perfection of that which was begun.[84]

I am making no claims to be able to understand more than a fraction of developments in other disciplines. It does, however, seem clear that the insights of theology will be limited unless there is a recognition that the interdisciplinary world of theories about being and relating is the proper context for all discourse. As Hardy has summarised: 'The *substance* of science should interact with the *substance* of theology'.[85] We have begun to find ways of understanding the nature of order which are in opposition to the traditional scientific world view. Scientists alone cannot give an adequate understanding of the realities of nature through predictable laws. Just as there are limits to what science can offer to a world-view, so there are questions about the appropriateness of humanity controlling and mastering the cosmos. The present ecological crisis has resulted from human exploitation of the world seen in merely objective terms. It is increasingly recognized that concentration on analysis and subdivision of systems into their constituent parts lead to an inadequate atomistic view of matter and an individualist ethos.

The complex understanding of coherence in modern scientific thought, intrinsically linked with freedom or contingence in unstable conditions, can I believe be understood as having limited but insightful parallels with some recent theological construction, regarding the nature of the triune God and the natural order. As Gunton has expressed it:

> I am arguing for a doctrine of analogy, of an understanding of the being of the created world by analogy with the being of God, which affirms rather than calls in question the reality of the many. The world may be understood as a universe of interrelated substantial particulars, because God its creator may in the first place be so conceived. The advantage of drawing on the concept of hypostasis is, accordingly, that it writes plurality and diversity into the being of the one interrelated world.[86]

Our enquiry, leading eventually to a doctrine of ordained priesthood, by way of an understanding of the Church's role in God's purposes, proceeds from here on the basis that the world is the creation of the triune God. I am assuming a correlation between a universe in which no part exists in isolation from another and the God who, as a differentiated loving communion of Persons, gives it being and purpose.

(b) Some Modern Conceptions of Personhood and Society

Again cautiously, I shall show how the same current theorizing about the nature of human beings and of society is part of the proper context of theology today. It lends support to an ecclesiology rooted in trinitarian concepts and orientated towards God's final hope for all creation—an eschatological-trinitarian ecclesiology.[87]

Descartes' influential bequest to the modern period of an identification of the person primarily with the mind, led to individualism and dualism. So, as the mind was identified wholly with the non-spacial, leaving to the body all that is both spacial and material, the individual was left with a problematic relationship with other individuals. Further, the legacy of Descartes resulted in a philosophical discussion of the person in terms of an ontology that was both dualist and individualist.[88] He believed that human beings are really just minds or thinking things united with bodies, distinct from the true self. The loss of a sense of personhood together with the severe results of isolation have made pervasive individualism a leading characteristic of modern Western society.

Modern industrial society in an age of computerization and consumerism has a tendency towards the building up of a prosperous, capable, and controlling minority of citizens severed from a disadvantaged and dispossessed majority. The lack of human compassion in the modern market economy contrasts with biblical concepts of economy, showing how the former reveals a distorted understanding of God.

Economically efficient countries prosper to the disadvantage of those known euphemistically as 'developing' nations. Moreover, the global warming debate reveals the complexities of living responsibly in a world community. Christian churches, as part of the human dilemma, but also possessed by the diversity of the triune God's final hope (the sense of 'continued becoming' of which Gregory of Nyssa speaks), may have a unique contribution to make. Can they find the tools to communicate with a world in which, for example, the urgent need to maintain an ecological balance is in conflict with the needs of those who without timber now for fuel, will die. In Britain the long-running process of the critique of the Beveridge Welfare State is focused in conditions in prisons, the availability of adequate housing and healthcare, the distribution of opportunities for work, the availability of free and appropriate education for all, maintenance provision after divorce and the position of vulnerable children.[89] In countless ways, the prevailing philosophical and political attitude assumes that individuals have it within them to make isolated choices which determine whether they are on the side of confident survivors able to manipulate systems in their favour, or of the failed, dependent, needy and relatively powerless. A general impression from the

political, sociological and economic point of view would be
that Britain in the 1990s is moving towards a new and more
complex contract between the State and the citizen which
places far more demands and responsibility on the individual
than many are able to bear.[90] Professor Alvin Schorr, in his
recent analysis of the personal social services in Britain gives
warning that the fabric of present systems is malfunctioning
and on the edge of total disorder. In the complex context of
the present situation he recommends urgent radical renegotia-
tion of expectation between central government, local authori-
ties, social services departments, the courts, the media, and
the public.[91]

In addition, there is widespread evidence of cultural,
gender and religious prejudice serving to aggravate an already unequal and divisive social scene where the lives of
individuals, families, companies and communities are becoming increasingly complex, resulting in a failure of many to
discover the inner resources for survival. This is a broad
brush stroke picture, but it represents a way of persons living
together which is far from the concept of redeemed sociality.[92]
Archbishop John Habgood's words continue to find echoes:
'We live in a country at least partially divided into different
regions and cultures; a country conscious of deep social
divisions, divisions made even more apparent by our present
economic strains; a country with many uncertainties about
its aims and values.'[93] Habgood has often required the
Church to perceive its calling as guardian of culture and
carrier of identity. His essay 'The Naked Public Square'
adds support to the conclusion that the Church, facing
rather than avoiding complexity in the world, can hope to
be recognized as sign and foretaste of God's Peace.[94]

It was concluded earlier that, by adopting an ecclesiology
that takes account of God's final purposes for the world, and
is based on a sound doctrine of the Trinity, the Church
could make a unique contribution to the process of redeeming
human relations. Such an ecclesiology would genuinely assist
in the recovery of 'the manysidedness of our humanity in the
undifferentiated unity of the whole.'[95] For too long the
Church has given the impression of being separate from
rather than bound up in society. Uniquely, the Church has

resources for fostering and nurturing communities of freedom and responsibility that testify to personal self-worth and imaginative creativity. Instead of distancing itself from the dilemmas of social institutions, the Church, recognizing itself as an institution, has the potential to demonstrate the beginnings of authentic sociality as 'an imaged response to the sociality of God'.[96] Christians are not separated from society by their particular allegiance to the gospel expressed in church membership. In their capacity as church, and in their vocation as promoters of the kingdom with and through the Trinity, Christians can place themselves at the service of, and in companionship with, humanity. Such a church, never forgetting that it is also part of the problem, should seek to draw out parallels between fruitful present theories concerning society and personal relations, and the trinitarian nature of the creator and redeemer God. Marshall has succinctly summarized the potential for relationship between doctrinal thinking and social issues,

> Doctrinal work can be the thinking through of the experience of the Christian community so that it is made *productive* by articulating its significance for fundamental questions of human relationships. In this way we may hope to arrive at an at least relatively distinctive Christian contribution which has a recognizable theological source and identity.[97]

To demonstrate this contention I will now examine four testimonies.

First, a Christian philosopher of social theory, John Milbank has offered an appraisal of how, since the Enlightenment, the Church has inappropriately permitted social theorists (e.g., Adam Smith, Hume, Locke, and Stewart), to present as the law of the universe an understanding of human society as an artificial construct in which 'possessive individualism' is a vital strand.[98] In marked contrast, Christian theology should be using its resources to offer a distinctive model of rationality rooted in the Trinity. Milbank indicates how the Christian doctrine of the Trinity opens up a vision of human being in true relatedness to God. Such a vision counters the so-called truths of modern secular social science, which assume that human beings choose to construct society from their individuality. A trinitarian ecclesiology, in contrast, belongs to a view of humanity in which community relationships are primary rather than secondary.[99]

As an alternative to the artificial view of human relations, Milbank makes proposals which owe much to mannerist art-theory and Baroque rhetoric. He suggest that as a metaphor of God's mind and activity in the world, 'Idea' does not precede the work in the artist's mind.[100] Instead 'Idea' becomes that which is conveyed as meaning to the receiver from the peculiar constitution of the work itself. There is no meaning that lies beyond or behind the process of historical events. Here is a clear parallel with many of the nuances of relationality observed already, and one also which echoes trinitarian theology in the sense that the Father only has eternal understanding in the 'image' of the Son.[101]

As we noted earlier, the possibilities inherent in trinitarian theology for understanding the person, society and the Church were largely overlooked after the Cappadocians. The present time is offering the Church an opportunity to lead others, with appropriate humility, in pointing the way to an understanding of society that is not, as modern social theory has claimed, an artificial construct, not merely a providential design, but rather 'an aspect of the original divine creation'.[102] Milbank rejects the sociology of recent decades, indeed since the Enlightenment, represented by Durkeim, Kant, and Comte. Instead he suggests that churches offer to society the goal of a differentiation which need not imply individualism and a unity of organic complexity which need not require enforced uniformity. The concern to avoid both individualism and collectivism in Milbank's theory of personhood is capable of being extended to an ecclesiology which refuses to be formed by, or accept the critique of, the dominating secular social philosophies.[103]

Second, *On Being the Church*, the collection of essays edited by Daniel Hardy and Colin Gunton (1989) supports the argument for an eschatological-trinitarian ecclesiology. This group of writers set out to discover what it means to be a human being who avoids individualist liberalism on the one hand and collectivist totalitarianism on the other. Hardy uses the term 'sociality' to pinpoint what he believes to be an essential but largely ignored element of being human, namely: 'that we are what we are by virtue of our membership of one another. We are social beings, and without sociality become less than human.'[104] Hardy's thesis is that the truest account of the reality of being human, not something merely appended by Christian theologians, includes this crucial feature of sociality, whereby humanity must be primarily recognized as a cooperative enterprise.

A third pointer in recent social theory which offers general support for the direction of my argument is to be found in the work of the anthropologist Richard Newbold Adams. With many modern anthropologists, he has forsaken the view of humanity in terms of the possession of an individual substantial soul and has come to recognize human being as a relational structure. Briefly, his understanding of power, principally in terms of freely entered reciprocal relationship, reverberates strongly with the approach of uniqueness-in-relationship to be found in some contemporary scientific and theological thought. In their different ways, Adams and Hardy adopt the basic stance that the corporate aspect of human existence as a built-in condition, is ontologically prior. This further strengthens my own conclusion that it is the particular gift and task of the Church to aim to anticipate in its own life the fullness of sociality which God has in mind for his creation, as well as to recognize and uncover, or point to the existence of, that underlying sociality which the triune God has planted in all creation, and to further bring it to effect in society at large. Adams himself sees as an important implication of his research the need to resolve the conflict-dichotomy between wealthy and struggling nations such as the United States and China. Instead of a spirit of competitiveness for the survival of the strongest, can there be a freely entered dialogue which can lead to mutual enrichment?[105]

Fourth, the work on personhood undertaken by Alistair McFadyen lends further support to the argument that certain trends in theory about the nature of persons in society offer parallels with the concept of redeemed sociality we have been discussing. McFadyen has argued persuasively for an analogous understanding of human personhood which is informed by a 'sedimentation' of interpersonal relations, intrinsically open both to others and to God through time and involving the expenditure of energy. The term 'sedimentation', the process of laying down personal identity through the processes of communication history, has a particular meaning for McFadyen as he summarizes it in his glossary of terms: 'The Process whereby a personal identity is accumulated through a significant history of address and response which has flowed around a particular point location and gathered around it in a unique way, so structuring a uniquely centred personal identity'.[106]

He believes that orthodox trinitarianism depends on the maintenance of a balance between the indivisibility of God and the uniqueness of the three Persons. McFadyen's trinitarian understanding assumes an active interrelationship as the ground of all personhood.[107] His concept of the person is both ideological (formed through social interaction, through address and response) and, significantly for this point in the argument, also as dialectical (never coming to rest in a final unity). It is in openly sharing everything that individuals are constituted in their uniqueness. No one can be personal except in relation to other persons. The determinate sociopolitical structures through which human persons work out their conscious or unconscious response to God's call, are in Christian terms, in need of redemption or distorted.

McFadyen argues for a Christian vision of salvation which goes further than the perfection of the networks of human intercommunication. Rather, it is the eschatological vision of the Kingdom of God established at the end of history by God's act. In the meanwhile, responding to God's call in Jesus, in the power of the Spirit, Christians attempt to create situations in the present in which the transformation of relations may be understood as anticipation or partial fulfilment of that future hope. The 'place' in which we find ourselves living out our human existence, therefore, assumes more than a momentary importance but also a penultimate significance. This is the case, however, not only as the context in which a particular individual transformation may occur—'where we are found and empowered in a new spirit by God'—but in the widest sense of a universe being remade by the God who brings salvation. McFadyen argues for a concept of redemption to be expressed in relational and social, rather than simply individualistic categories. Such an understanding of the Church's hope in the triune God can, therefore, bring about renewed and undistorted forms of relation, community and society.[108]

Undistorted humanity, responding to God's trinitarian call to community, is moving towards an ex-centric orientation. To be 'ex-centric' for McFadyen, is to be structured 'by a movement from a personal centre outward towards the personal centres of others. Through dialogue one moves towards (and therefore recognizes) the independent realities of others and returns to oneself, becoming absorbed in oneself by moving beyond oneself.'[109] As the Persons of the Trinity live beyond their own boundaries, in and through one another, and in all creation, humanity is challenged to live out its potential transcending the boundaries of the self in 'undistorted' communication. This redeemed sociality among persons, for McFadyen, means human interaction which recognizes participants in relationship as autonomous subjects of communication. People are beings who are created as discrete, and capable of being known only through their free, independent self-communication. In this communication is implied a mutual recognition of the independence and mystery of others and the willingness to make space in relating for the free communication of the other.

Identity, therefore, which results from being created in God's trinitarian image, simultaneously in relation and in unique differentiation, is in contrast with the long accepted tradition in Christian thought that the personal image is purely an internal attribute located in the reason or consciousness. McFadyen summarizes:

> The analogy between God and human existence in the image of God is then properly not one of individual substance but of relation. Just as the persons of the Trinity receive and maintain their identities through relation, and relations of a certain quality, then so would human persons only receive and maintain their identities through relation with others and would stand fully in God's image when-

ever these identities and relations achieve a certain quality.[110]

The Christian thesis that personhood is fostered by the process of being addressed, intended, and expected as a person by others, help us to recognize the extent to which recent theories of human being and personality imply change, energy, and movement. The one particular insight for this book that McFadyen inspires can be expressed as follows. The self with its internal structure of communication, may best be understood primarily as a public structure and only secondarily in terms of a private, psychological structure appropriated by individuals. By definition, to be a person is to be-in-relationship. This stands in remarkable contrast with the individualistic tradition inherited from Augustine that persons are constituted through their innate, internal psychological structure out of which they then organize communication, and choose to enter and order corporate structures.[111]

On this argument, to exist as an individual person should not be understood in terms of substance. Rather to be a person is best conceived in terms of an organizational process, practised in mutual communication. Or being a person might be considered as a hypothesis (not unlike the hypothesis of gravitational fields), referring to the organizational properties of an underlying structure for which there is and can be no direct empirical experience. There is a close parallel in the following proposal of Rom Harré, who writes,

> When we learn to organize our organically grounded experience as a structured field and cognitively as a body of beliefs built up of self-predications, we are deploying a concept of 'self' that functions like the deep theoretical concepts of the natural sciences, which serve to organize our experience and knowledge, whether or not they have observable referents in the real world.[112]

Another close parallel may be found in the thought of Daphne Hampson, the feminist theologian. She pleads for a Christianity that, showing the world a more truly divinely-orientated relationship between the genders, searches for a chosen integrity, rather than a dichotomy or complementary polarity where the strong are construed as tyrannical or dominating and the weak as inferior or marginalized. For Hampson, a human person in her own right should be recognized as fulfilling a certain 'place' within a society organically conceived.[113] She longs for the end of the false dichotomy between regarding God as male, complete and strong, whilst humanity is female, contingent and weak. Hampson, I believe, contributes to the discovery of a freedom which arises in human beings created *imago dei*, and as such, be open to communion with others.

In drawing particularly on the work of the trinitarian theologians described above, Hardy, McFadyen, Millbank, and Adams, the anthropologist, I am not proposing an uncritical correlation between human relatedness and a trinitarian inspired theology of personhood. More modestly, my intention is to draw attention to an instructive interplay between a trinitarian understanding of being as relational and the general tenor of some contemporary theories of human relatedness in freedom. The latter depend on the participants recognizing the desirability of allocating power in a manner which enhances free participation rather than exploitation. Instead of recognizing communities—including the Trinity—as mere aggregates of individuals, Christian theology might conceive of a community as interpersonal and greater than the sum of its parts.

In conclusion: I welcome, in the context of multi-disciplinary exploration, the trinitarianism being developed by some modern theologians, as having a radical contribution to make to the understanding of the nature of humanity in practical interrelationship. For Christian theology there is an analogy between the indivisibility of God and the uniqueness of the three Persons of the Trinity and a concept of human personhood which is informed both by a sedimentation of interpersonal relationships and by relatedness to God.[114] So it may be understood both of the Trinity and of the human person, that to be unique is to exist in relationship. Uniqueness is retained only in that it is reciprocally derived from and present through processes of communication and relatedness.[115]

Openness to external as well as to internal relations, which is characteristic of the Trinity, gives the human creature that capacity to be precisely what created him or her, namely, an outpouring and overflowing of the life of God, in intrinsic relationship with God and with others. A significant example of this understanding of the unity of human beings is the new hope in many circles of redeemed relationships between male and female, at all levels, not in terms of subordination one to another, but of mutuality, justice, and a recognition of incompleteness without the other.[116]

In Chapters Two, Three and Four of this enquiry, I have explored the context within which a contemporary doctrine of the Church must be articulated. The evidence clearly points to an intrinsic connection between speaking of God's being and activity primarily in relational terms, and formulating a doctrine of the Church in eschatological-trinitarian terms. The ontology of the Church which I am proposing is rooted in the evidence for a correlation between a doctrine of God (following and developing the apophatic tradition which recognizes the immanent being of God as trinitarian) and a doctrine of the Church. I have described the relation between the latter and the former as an 'echoing.' The being of the Church should echo the dynamic relations between the three Persons who together constitute the triune God.

Within the continuing history of God's trinitarian involvement with his creation, such a Church is called by God to be a sign and foretaste of that wholeness which is God's desire for the diverse ending of all things. I fully recognize the churches' constant failure to offer inspiring models of society and the presence of God's Spirit in the world. This inadequacy only serves to highlight the need for Christians to make their unique contribution to sociality in collaboration with disciplines such as social theory, psychology and political philosophy. If this line of argument is correct, it implies a great need for more research in the complex area of relationships between trinitarian thought and networks of relationship in the Church, in society and in the world at large.

The following chapter will begin to speculate how, at various levels, the future shape of an ecclesiology might be developed as far as the Church of England is concerned.

Chapter Five
CHURCH: A SIGN OF
HOPE IN THE WORLD

During the patristic period, the understanding of the Church in terms of communion with Christ was more pronounced than it has been for many centuries until the twentieth. It was then that the four marks of the Church evolved as a way of stating ecclesiological beliefs. The Apostles' Creed acknowledges the 'one, holy, Catholic Church', whilst the Nicene-Constantinopolitan Creed speaks of 'the one, holy, Catholic and apostolic Church'. These credal attributes have largely been monopolised by Catholics and given a low profile by Protestants. However they are clearly included in the received version of the Apostles' creed included in Anglican liturgy.[1]

Any understanding of the credal marks today can only begin from the assumption that the qualities of unity, holiness, catholicity and apostolicity have rarely been actualized. They are characteristics of faith, anticipatory and full of promise, not only for the Church but for the entire creation. The ecumenical Lima text holds that the Church is one, holy, catholic and apostolic; it lives in continuity with the apostles and their proclamation. A parallel might be drawn between the recognition in Chapter Four of reality in terms of dynamic yet ordered characteristics, and the Church as having the fourfold capacity to unify, to offer the gift of blessing, to encompass many particular physical contexts, and to relate to each other different eras in time. However, to keep the Church in appropriately modest perspective, it should be said both that it stands constantly in need of reformation, and that its existence in God's plans may well be provisional though necessary.[2]

My proposals for an English Anglican ecclesiology arise from the dialogue earlier described with four late twentieth-century systematic theologians for whom various forms of social trinitarianism provide a basis. It might be asked, then, in what sense could this be regarded as an Anglican ecclesiology? Boff is a Catholic liberation theologian, Gunton is an English United Reformed Church minister, Moltmann is of the German Reformed tradition, and Zizioulas is Orthodox. However, to belong to a particular church today is not a matter of defending a single ecclesiology and doctrine of ministry in polemical engagement with others. Rather it is to recognize that the particular self-definition of one church occurs partly and simultaneously through an open and continuing process of learning from others. We are not Anglicans merely by attaching ourselves to a past tradition with a fixed and completed history. Belonging to a particular church is to be in critical interrelationship with all churches and to participate in the process of shaping with others norms and values which reveal God's mission in the contemporary world. Most Christians admittedly, initially find themselves members of a given church for historical, social, or personal reasons, rather than for doctrinal issues.

Today it appears increasingly appropriate that such membership should be recognized as a point of entry into an international conversation. It may well be that if this process be accepted as legitimate it will often have the potential for discovering images of the Church, in turn rooted in experiences of God's presence, that resonate between many people across denominational boundaries, and conversely that raise anxieties among different members of a given denomination. So in the sense that many Anglicans and possibly Roman Catholics or Methodists will find encouragement in what is written here, and equally others will not, this enterprise can pretend to be no more than one contribution to the continuing dialogical process of discovering an Anglican ecclesial identity. What does, I believe, also emerge is that the vision for the ordering of the Christian Church in the late modern period is not the preserve of any one denomination or group. Some elements within the process of mutual communication emerge as contributing to a collective ecclesial ordering that transcends all previously drawn adversarial lines. Such a process of dialogue between differing churches can look towards a future ecclesiology which is tolerant of a high degree

of pluralism without being reduced to an amorphous homogeneity in which the participants have lost their particular
identities.

1. Communion as a Way of Being: Unity

(a) The Local Church

The key concept for unity in an eschatological-trinitarian
ecclesiology is that of *koinonia*. At the heart of *koinonia* lies a
relationship of identification, the mutuality of a deep and
complete connection between unique individuals. Three aspects of *koinonia* can be identified by the use of different
though related English words. '*Communion*' alludes to the
Holy Spirit making possible the Christian relationship of
unity with God; '*community*' describes the Holy Spirit making
possible a mutual Christian relationship within the life of the
church; and '*communication*' refers to the Holy Spirit making
possible a relationship between Christians and the wider
community or society.

Christ in union with the Spirit gathers those who are
baptized into his death and resurrection into the communion
of the Persons that is the interrelating life of the triune God.[3]
Unity as communion with the Trinity is a vital strand in the
work of Zizioulas. He writes of Christ's 'I' as the eternal 'I'
that stems from his eternal filial relationship with the Father.
However, he continues, as the incarnate Christ, he has
introduced into his eternal relationship with the Father
another element, 'us, the many, the Church', even though he
remains the eternal Son. And yet, writes Zizioulas, 'the
"mystery hidden before all ages" in the will of the Father is
nothing else but the incorporation of this other element, of
us, or the many, into the eternal filial relationship between
the Father and the Son'. In this way Zizioulas helps us to
understand how, as the mystery of the Church, Christians
are drawn into communion with the Trinity.[4] The most
significant use of the word *koinonia* by Paul, certainly from
the point of view of this enquiry, occurs when he is discussing
the sharing of the eucharistic meal in response to Christ's
instructions at the Last Supper. Concerning the Eucharist,

Paul writes of an intimate, organic relationship existing between the Risen Christ and all who receive new life through communion with him: 'When we bless the cup of blessing, is it not a means of sharing in (*koinonia*) the body of Christ? When we break the bread, is it not a means of sharing in (*koinonia*) the body of Christ?' (1 Cor. 10.16) The recovery of this insight may be witnessed in the liturgical revisions of the 1960s, when the Series II Holy Communion liturgy, wishing to stress the principle of Christian community, placed great emphasis on this verse.

Christians live in the space between the unity that is already God's gift in Christ's victory through the Spirit, and that total communion which will be in Christ when the whole creation knows fulfilment. Christian community arises by baptized persons being constituted in communion with God and with each other in Christ, through the working of the Spirit. All who share in the sacramental life of the eucharistic community are invited to be made holy together, sharing in the communion Christ gives and without losing their particularity, sharing a common life of suffering and joy, serving and being served, and looking to the final fulfilment of communion when God will be all in all (1 Cor. 15.28, Eph. 1.10 and Col. 1.19–20). The phrase '*koinonia* of the Holy Spirit' occurs only twice in the New Testament, on both occasions in expressions which suggest the Trinity. The first is the Grace from the closing passage of 2 Corinthians (13.13). The second occurs in Paul's letter to the Philippians (2.1) which REB translates, 'If then our common life in Christ yields anything to stir the heart, any consolation of love . . .' Paul continues by invoking the person of the Holy Spirit:

> If there is any *koinonia* of the Spirit, any warmth of affection or compassion, fill up my cup of happiness by thinking and feeling alike, with the same love for one another and a common attitude of mind. Leave no room for selfish ambition and vanity, but humbly reckon others better than yourselves. . . .

Here, *koinonia* is something which the Spirit provides, generating in the community of the Philippians a common under-

standing, a compassion, a sense of being a community—
nothing less, in fact, than the selflessness that was in Christ
who 'emptied himself' (Phil. 2.7). Another important reference to *koinonia* occurs in 2 Cor. 9.13. The people who
receive the aid from the Corinthian Christians will, according
to Paul, be giving 'honour to God' for, among other things,
the liberal disposition of *koinonia* shown both to them and
towards everyone:

> For with the proof which this aid affords, those who
> receive it will give honour to God when they see how
> humbly you obey him and how faithfully you confess the
> gospel of Christ; and they will thank him for your liberal
> contribution to their need and to the general good.

This community of diversity and mutual enrichment has the
God-given potential to begin the process of overriding barriers of class, gender, race, and hierarchical status, and of
creating a relational unity between local confessional
churches in a particular neighbourhood. Christ through the
Spirit, empowers Christians to discover a new and differentiated way of being with, and accountable to, God and their
fellow human beings. The notion of 'having things in
common' runs through 1 John where *koinonia* almost becomes
the technical term for being '*in communion*' with other Christians (1.3 and 7), and with the Father and his Son Jesus
Christ (1.3 and 6), 'a new way of being with and responsible
to God and others'.[5]

The unity which Christ gives through the Spirit to the
Church cannot, however, be guaranteed from sin or error or
organized purely in terms of law or institution. In freedom
such unity is only created through the willingness of the
Church to hear and respond to the Spirit's encouragement
and judgement. It is a unity which should gradually be
recognized as having no need of the self-protection which
separates itself from its non-Christian neighbours. In this
sense it may be recognized as a pluralism which is the first-
fruits of that order of peace which is God's passionate hope
for the fulfilment of all things. Zizioulas has shown that
koinonia, community, (for which 'sociality' may be an adequate translation) assists in making the gospel link between

the interrelation of the trinitarian Persons and the role of the finite Church in the project of the promised perfection of creation.[6]

No aspect of *koinonia* can properly be enjoyed in isolation from another. Receiving the gift of communion with the Trinity; sharing in the life of Christ through the Spirit; and being equally associated with God in joyfully communicating the truth about life; are three interrelated elements of the freedom and creativity of the triune God, and of the Church that is sign and foretaste of God's longing for the consummation of all creation.[7] Maintaining all three aspects of connectedness, with God, within the Christian community, and with the wider world, proves as history frequently demonstrates, an elusive balance to attain. Empirically, all church communities should admit to only an imperfect harmonization of the three aspects of *koinonia*. There are those who emphasize collaborative church life and service in the world but place little emphasis on direct experience of communion with God; there are those again who emphasize corporate worship and a deep knowledge of God, but largely in separation from the broader community; and thirdly, there are those with a passionate care for the health of society arising from their love of God, for whom the corporate Christian life holds little significance.[8]

From here on I shall be making repeated use of the phrase 'the local church' and it is important that I make a clear statement of my use of the expression. My proposal is that, within English Anglicanism, a genuine catholicity challenges isolated parishes to recognize the local church as existing as an appropriate network of interdependent eucharistic assemblies in a natural geographical area. There may well be bitter disputes about what is the truly 'natural' area, and differing perceptions of this will take some time to resolve. It is a task with which pastoral committees are already familiar. Over a period of years, with changing circumstances, the most appropriate answer to the question may well change.

The intermediate deanery level of responsibility seems in theory ideally suited to drawing together local and central concerns. There are enthusiasts for the future of the deanery, even with full-time rural deans with training responsibilities.

In my own view, however, the deanery is frequently perceived in parishes as an imposed and inadequate construct
which proves on the whole ineffective and a drain on resources. Some existing deaneries are either too large or to
small to be effective in synodical government or as clergy
chapters. The future will be likely to witness the close of
many churches in present use by tiny groups of people. The
work of many Church of England dioceses at the present
time to arrive at appropriate clusterings of smaller territories
in which previously clergy ministered often in isolation, will
hopefully begin to identify 'local churches' within which
parish priests of the future will have new responsibilities in
collaboration with many others, both lay and ordained. A
particular local church as I am defining it may at present
only be aware of itself as a number of parishes (or in some
cases still, a single large parish). This development has a
long way to travel from the nostalgic memory of each parish
being staffed by its own parson. Rather than attempting to
justify existing deaneries or to force local churches today into
the shape of inherited geographical patterns, energy should
be channelled into exploring the ways in which clusters of
probably large 'local church' territories can interrelate and
be mutually supportive within the diocese.

My aim now is to demonstrate how any church, in its
liturgy, especially but not exclusively in the Eucharist, and
in its emphasis on the process of baptism, can grow in unity.
The theme will be developed in terms of the definition of
unity as participation in *koinonia* as communion, community
and communication.

Through worship and prayer in the name of its crucified
and risen Lord, the Church receives the gift of free and open
relatedness with the Trinity. The act of praying is an expression of *perichoresis* (see page 82). The participants in worship
caught up into the interior divine dialogue, constitute each
other as the faithful members of the Church just as the
Persons of the Trinity in their relations constitute one another. The caveat should be added that of course church
worshippers have no monopoly on receiving God's gift of
relatedness. Rather, baptism conveys a specific and challenging vocation, supported by grace in the fellowship of the

Holy Spirit, to engage with God's mission to achieve fulfilment and unity for all creation.[9] In this sense the Church should never claim to contain religious experience but rather to offer tools to all humanity for reflecting upon their everyday and mystical experiences of God. This is not the place to expound comprehensively the ecumenical eucharistic doctrine increasingly accepted and contributed to by Anglicans, but it is an integral part of my ecclesiology that the unity of the local church is, in particular, constituted through participation in the eucharistic liturgy. The Eucharistc celebration is essentially the sacrament of the gift of the triune life that God gives as *koinonia* to the Church through the power of the Spirit. In the eating and drinking of the eucharistic bread and wine, Christ through the Spirit, grants communion with himself and with the community of those who, however faintly, have begun to echo the corporate and diverse life of the Trinity in working for the future of creation.

The complex unity of a local community of Christians need not depend on agreement in every respect of an understanding of the Eucharist. This has particular relevance in rural areas where all denominations but the Church of England have often closed their churches or discontinued deploying clergy. Many Anglican churches have, by default, become home to Methodists, Baptists and others. Rather than stripping them of the dignity of an acknowledgement of their roots, such a local expression of the Church has the opportunity to pioneer a new sense of ecumenical sensitivity within a single liturgical and ministering community. During the earlier part of the century, Catholic and Evangelical groups within Anglicanism insisted (in the light of the Reformation controversies) on the correctness of a single, confessional, and exclusive interpretation of the meaning of the eucharistic celebration. Now the work of ARCIC, BEM, and scholars and theorists of ritual, have helped to clear away some of the historical controversy and to show that, despite twentieth-century adversial, denominational rhetoric, a variety of interpretations of the Eucharist have always existed within church communities and on different occasions. The Church may just be beginning to come to terms with the received scholarly opinion, which over the past two or three decades especially has been drawing attention to the variety of forms and interpretations given to the Eucharist within the early Church.[10] The emerging picture of the pluriform origins of Christian eucharist practice, far from being problematic, lends support to a portrait of corporate Christian worship pointing more fully to, and nourishing, that rich and diverse communion with the triune God which lies at the heart of all true Christian faith, and ultimately of the being of all that exists. This is not to deny that there are sensitive problems regarding the allowable limits of diversity within Church of England eucharistic (and therefore ecclesiological) theory and practice. However, differences of eucharistic theology and practice should not be regarded as barriers to sharing communion at one altar. A variety of eucharistic interpretations could invite creativity and experimentation with liturgical forms in response to particular local cultural settings.[11]

As I noted earlier, one of the characteristics of the Church today is a deliberate move away from static and stereotyped worship. Acknowledging a debt to the Pentecostalist churches, some Anglicans are now adopting rites that seek a balance between stability and spontaneity, speaking not just of the Father and Jesus Christ but also of the Holy Spirit. This opens up the possibility of the Church of England specifically recognizing the significance of local Churches discovering their inner unity in terms of a trinitarian relationship of *koinonia*. In contrast with the previous tendency within the Church of England earlier this century, a significantly new emphasis on the corporate rather than on the individual has been one of the vital strands of change in ecclesiological speculation during the second half of the twentieth century.

Entering into communion with the Trinity takes on a mature quality when held in creative tension with life in Christian community and a concern for communication with society. I have already drawn attention to a sense of movement, change, energy, hope, and longing, in drawing parallels between trinitarian concepts and theories about reality. This also should be emphasized here with reference to the Christian individually and within the community of faith, growing into communion with the Trinity. The Christian tradition shows that, unlike some modern secular doctrines of a constant curve of progress, this communion with God does not always appear or feel to be moving forward, and certainly not to be resting in equilibrium. Communion with God requires us to be ready to risk the challenge of self-criticism with a view to growing in maturity, and to hearing the invitation to embark on a process of constant reconversion. This will have a fuller treatment in the section of holiness. One of the changes in emphasis between the old liturgy of the 1662 BCP and the ASB Rite 'A' order is the revolution in attitude towards the connection between communion with God and building a sense of community with fellow worshippers.

Earlier in the century, attendance at Holy Communion as an isolated and essentially private discipline was often balanced against attending Morning Prayer in the middle of the morning (or for Anglo-Catholics a non-communicating High Mass). This spirit was often found in close parallel with an emphasis on individual piety, almost to the deliberate exclusion of a more corporate approach. It perpetuated a view of reality and of society which implied a permanent separation of rich from poor, exploitation of the environment by a detached humanity, and a misunderstanding of the possibilities for mutuality at every level of human communication. By the middle of the century, the tendency was towards a corporate eucharistic celebration for all 'church members' who could be persuaded to attend. This was explicitly advocated, as the writings of de Candole, Hebert, Robinson, Southcott and others reveal, in the Parish Communion Movement. It is frequently reinforced by modern scholarship as illustrated clearly in the re-examination of the table texts of the New Testament by Smith and Taussig,

> The clear social contexts for the first-century Christian meals place important additional emphasis on current Christian eucharist being an act of community. The lack of evidence for individualistic interpretation of the Lord's Supper in the first century challenges much individualistic piety of today and suggests a more collective model.[12]

The Anglican tradition earlier this century, of anchoring the unity of the Church simply to validly ordained clergy, is ruled out in an ecclesiology which is rooted in a relational understanding of the Trinity. This eliminates the permanent subordination of one group of Christians to another. A more promising beginning, far from alien to Anglican theology, is to adopt the sacrament of baptism in the threefold formula as the focus for overlapping patterns of interrelatedness within the *koinonia* of the Church.[13] In particular, the act of baptism offers a paradigm of the community's beliefs (however confused) concerning its self-identity. The theologically comprehensive nature of the membership of the Church of England, together with the sociological factor of the huge penumbra of associated membership, inevitably makes for a great deal of confusion regarding appropriate tests for admission to baptism. The 1969 'Ely' Commission controversially declared that baptism is complete sacramental initiation and an adequate basis on which to admit children to Holy Communion prior to confirmation. The subsequent synodical debate reveals the extent to which the Church of England contains a wide cross-section of views on the relationship between baptism and full membership of the community of belief. Increasingly there is ecumenical consensus for taking the sacrament of baptism as the keystone for understanding the rich and closely interwoven strands of the mystery of Christian communion. This was the view of Lambeth 1988 which specifically examined the question, 'What is the communion of the Church?' in terms of the union with Christ and the Church created by baptism, defined as, 'the redemptive gift of incorporation into Christ . . . and with all who belong to Christ'.[14] It was unfortunate that ARCIC I did not explicitly develop the baptismal basis of *koinonia*, especially as, in parallel with *Lumen Gentium* 10, it impedes the development of a proper balance between the lay and ordained priestly ministries of the Church, rooted essentially in a common baptismal communion. There will be no attempt here to summarize the ecumenical discussion of baptism, but briefly to indicate rich connections for the purposes of this enquiry.

From the beginning, Christians have understood the process of initiation into the Church as profoundly connected with the dying of Jesus and his rising to new life. In baptism Christians have a trinitarian experience with God through the work of Jesus on the cross and, through the Spirit, the Father's raising him on the third day. Jesus' life of obedience even to death led to the Father releasing him from death to be exalted in glory, and to be the means of the restoration of human and divine life. Through the new relationship with God that Christ made possible for those who put their faith in him and become united with him, there is hope for a new communion with the Father and the invitation to be open to the direction of the Holy Spirit. These themes are interwoven in the ASB rite of baptism with confirmation, for example in the invitation to make a decision:

> Our Lord Jesus Christ suffered death on the cross and rose again from the dead for the salvation of mankind. Baptism is the outward sign by which we receive for ourselves what he has done for us: we are united with him in his death; we are granted the forgiveness of sins; we are raised with Christ to new life in the Spirit.[15]

The underlying indications of the baptismal process (preparation, rite and induction into discipleship by the local church) emphasize, firstly, that through unity in the Spirit with Christ, the Christian journey is essentially bound up in a certain quality of relatedness between the believer and the trinitarian God. Second, the baptism process indicates that this relationship with the triune God demands a high degree of mutual interrelatedness in specific places and over a consolidated period of time, with fellow Christians. In turn this unity within the Christian community is an essential model of and pointer towards that unity which is God's hope for the world.

To summarize the argument: in the above discussion of the unity of the local church the main thrust of the description of a eucharistic and baptizing community has been along these lines. Although the local church will engage in worship that is neither eucharistic nor baptismal, the centrality of these sacraments focuses the church in its trinitarian understanding of communion, community and communication. Through the cycles of the local church's eucharistic liturgy the community of pilgrims is given new life and strength to grow in holiness through communion with the trinitarian God and in company with others. Such eucharistic life is never to be seen in isolation but always in communication with the wider world as a sign and foretaste of the salvation of all.[16] Using the process and rite of baptismal initiation as a key to the inner life of the local church itself, disciples of the Christ whose life, death, resurrection, and glorification brought God's salvation near, are those who are given the gift of rebirth into communion with God, with one another and the whole creation. Separately and together, the members are invited and equipped by their mutual intending of one another as participants united in God's mission.

(b) A Church Deeply Engaged with the Structures of Society

Pragmatically, the understanding of unity in the local church explored above has to be held in tension with the expectation of the majority of baptised persons that their membership of the Church of England need make very little demand on them and will, if anything, provide consolation in time of trouble. Recent surveys both reveal the complexity of achieving meaningful statistics and of achieving agreed procedures of analysis. They also show the stark reality of churches with a core group of a minority of the nation's population against a background of a high proportion among whom the Christian faith still holds an interest.[17] Despite the recurring pleas for the clarity which some believe would be achieved by disestablishment, my own inclination is to avoid that path This is not to say that I can support in detail the existing arrangements, for example, for crown appointments the role of the Sovereign, or the Church of England's apparent disdain of other churches.

Despite the financial pressures, the confusion, distortion, and mistakes that occur as a result of the Church of England trying to be true to itself and simultaneously acting as chaplain to the whole of society, it is a necessary and crucifying road. It would be all too easy for the Church to define itself quite separately from the State. Certainly that relationship will always need to be under scrutiny and in process of reform, especially in the direction of ecumenical partnership. Divorcing the Church of England from the State would be administratively cleaner and certainly theologically simpler, but there would be profound loss on both sides.

A church more narrowly defined as a sect with responsibility only for those who are members is also likely to be a church in which more power than is appropriate accrues to the clergy over against the laity. And a church that regards itself as having only a particular sphere of interest will tend to reduce its beliefs to a simplistic homogeneity, and overemphasize the bureaucratic management of believers. I favour an almost mystical approach to the relationship between Church and State. There needs to be clarity and definition on both sides as at many levels they have unique responsibilities. But their relationship needs at the same time to recognize that, where people and societies are concerned, the free emergence of complex and interrelating powers forestalls either a sovereign State, or a hierarchical Church.

As I suggested in Chapter Two, it would be easy to reject completely the claims to membership of those who, though baptized and even confirmed, apparently make only the barest contribution to the communal life.[18] My own view is that the term 'member' needs to have more definition that has been common in Anglican circles. This is not in order to reject others but in order to reflect more clearly on the relationship between those for whom articulated Christian discipleship deliberately forms their lives, and others for whom this is not the case. However, given that an eschatological-trinitarian ecclesiology regards the Church as called primarily to be a sign and foretaste of the redeemed sociality of all creation, it seems vital to allow for a complex, coherent comprehensiveness that does not separate a narrow 'spirituality' from the tasks involved in working for God's Kingdom in the world.

As concluded already, it is usual for worshipping communities to fail to hold in tension *koinonia* as communion, community and as communication. For many of the baptized, it is precisely this third element of Christianity to which they adhere. It is also true that many take such an attitude precisely because the inner core of church membership is failing in its task of collaborating with those in society generally who, without allegiance to Christ, are working for the Kingdom. Hardy, warning the Church not to be content with merely offering suggestions in the realm of ideas alone, calls for Christians to develop,

> Social structures in which people may become fully human in interaction with God. In fact they [Christians] must learn to 'manage the affairs of the world' (Peter Baelz) in their relationship with God, not in order to take over the affairs of government, but to give practical form to their life with God, and thus provide a more concrete manifestation of what this might mean for human affairs in general.[19]

As persons in relation, constituting each other from our unique stories, none of us are the owners of our individual stories. Rather, our histories are ours insofar as we are equally members of communities, cultures and societies. Our own stories help to identify our place within the communities to which we belong.[20]

It is precisely because one of the elements of *koinonia* is openness to the entire world, that for every local church there must be a commitment to managing the knife-edge balance between community involvement that has the potential to become either a dominating power but hopefully a humble influence, and detachment that leads either to neurotic isolation or better, hopefully, to a worldly holiness. Such a church daily, through at least some of the members within a spectrum of diverse vocations, has to work out its understanding of being in but not of the world, recognizing its unavoidable vulnerability.

The Church of England today inherits a colourful record of partnership in human communities between the city and the church, the citadel and the temple, between kings and priests, the throne and the altar.[21] That is perhaps another way of saying that community life, civic life, and political life, desperately need to be undergirded with the values of the trinitarian gospel. Or it is another way of saying that those whose interest is in such values need to express their beliefs and convictions not just in church circles, but through risky engagement within the life of the wider human community: in national and local government, in administration of the law, industry and commerce, art and music, sport and entertainment, every mode of communication, education at all levels, and all the processes of caring. The study of theology and religion in the universities without denominational constraints has the potential to nourish the proper connections between the practice of faith in many church communities and a rigorous engagement with the fundamental issues of the contemporary world. A working and dialogical bond between church and city networks of authority can proclaim that the latter is not just a mechanism to be tested on efficiency alone, a piece of apparatus that allows space for rank individuality. Rather, a city or settlement of any size, with all its complex networks of engagement, can have the vision of being a community that finds its unity through certain articulated values and principles to which the local church, committed to being a sign and foretaste, can make a unique contribution.

An eschatological-trinitarian ecclesiology will look for a church that, engaging with pressing issues, lives in responsible and mutual companionship with its surroundings. It will seek not to address the community from the moral high ground nor attempt to impose its wisdom from a position of detachment, but recognizing its high eschatological destiny, will attentively and respectfully promote a sense of shared, intersubjective responsibility for the well-being or sociality of the city.[22]

(c) Unity with the World Church

To explore trinitarian relatedness in terms of church unity is a task upon which I cannot embark here, but merely note its vast potential. Equally it is vital to note that when churches are divided, they lose much of their credibility for their task in the world. The right relationship between the Church of England, the rest of the Anglican Communion, and other churches can most truthfully be expressed in terms of *koinonia*, as both a gift and a destiny arising from relationship initiated

by the triune God. It is in recognizing the role of the gospel
community to be that of a sign and a foretaste of God's
longing, and by witnessing together for those issues that
make for true sociality, that Churches can achieve mutality
and intercommunion. Referring to Rev. 7.9f., the ARCIC II
document describes the churches' relationship of communion
with God and with each other in the Holy Spirit as a present
pledge and a foretaste of God's final purpose for his creatures:
'a great multitude which none could number, from every
nation, from all tribes and peoples and tongues . . . crying
out with a loud voice, "Salvation belongs to our God who
sits upon the throne, and to the Lamb!"'[23] This common
vision of proclaiming Christ's peace is one strand of that
koinonia that arises within eucharistic and baptismal communion with the triune God.

Recent decades have seen the beginnings of a transformation of attitude in respect to Christian unity. The late modern
period is witness to a reduction of confessional polemic and
the adoption of the path of communion and community
across denominational borders. Churches are becoming more
committed locally to working towards a common life that does
not imply uniformity. In revealing the first-fruits of *shalom*
through their own unity in prayer and service, churches
could point to the potential unity of humankind that God
offers and desires. Growing together in unity, churches could
be recognized for their capacity to proclaim and promote
reconciliation and healing, to overcome the divisions based
on race, gender, wealth, culture or status.

In summary, with regard to an eschatological-trinitarian
approach to the unity of the Church, my conclusion is that
the unity of Christians in the local church, between denominations and across the world, should be conceived as a trinitarian *koinonia*. As communion with God, fellowship in Christian
community, and as the proclamation or communication of
God's final peace, in word and deed, the Church both
receives the gift of unity and works for its completion among
all people. Every temptation should be resisted, therefore, for
churches to be satisfied with a unity that ignores complex
realities or which in the end fails to embrace the whole of
creation.

2. Echoing the Life of God: Holiness

To describe the Church as 'holy' is to indicate how the quality of its being in relatedness, internally and externally, can mirror the quality of the relationship between the Persons of the Trinity.

As a sign and foretaste of the wholeness which is the holy order destined by God for the entire creation, the Church is invited to be that community which models for all humanity that style of relatedness which echoes God's threefold being. Through the Spirit, the Church is invited to be provisional and exploratory making present, and contemporary identification, of God's ultimate word.[24]

Although scholarly opinion varies regarding the trustworthiness of the New Testament record of the ministry of Jesus, the Church's life should reflect the attractiveness of the picture of God which uniquely it provides. The community inaugurated by Jesus' career, through sharing his death and resurrection, may enter in the relatedness of loving mutuality which is the life of the Trinity. The Christian presence in the world, therefore, becomes more than a recital of the story of Jesus. It is the continuing story of the Church, already realized in a finally exemplary way by Christ, yet still to be realized universally in harmony with Christ, and yet *differently*, by each new generation of Christians. Through the interaction with the entire work of Jesus and successive generations of Christian responses of faith, God's coming Kingdom already interacts with human endeavour towards transformation and wholeness. In this way the Christian community, in mutuality with many other groups in society, can be said to contribute towards the vision of a new goal or ultimate fulfilment which is central to the quality of holiness.

Earlier this century Christian theology had a tendency to locate the Church's holiness, in terms of substance, with the clergy or with an ideal invisible Church. In contrast, I conclude that holiness is better recognized as the intention of the Trinity for the whole of Christian community practice to be sustained in truthfulness through its communion with God's relational self.[25] Merton made an enquiry, at the personal level, into the dichotomy between the *true* self and

the *false* self. His conclusion was that it is through 'attentive-
ness' that the human person discovers his or her true identity
in unity with 'the hidden ground of Love', the Christian
God.[26] In a directly parallel manner, Hardy and Ford have
written that knowledge of God is to permit him to have the
initiative regarding the way in which we come to know him,
and primarily, therefore, a matter of accepting his initiative.
If the object of our knowing is one who already knows us,
then the main emphasis in our knowing will be on preparing
for, and receiving, his communication with us. The knowledge of God leads to a 'glory and love that evokes all our
astonishment, thanks and praise'.[27] To be known by God
and to respond to his knowing is, from a Christian perspective, to be blessed or to be holy. The Church knows its true
origin and character as 'holy' or 'blessed' by interactive
communion with the Trinity. Through worship especially,
the Church grows in holiness and diminishes in all that
impedes that growth.

Holiness in the Church is not to be equated merely with
the attempt to adhere to a moral programme based on Jesus'
preaching.[28] Rather, holy relatedness is the performance of
the Kingdom that is the direct result of the Church, through
communion in the Trinity, entering in God's saving mission.[29] The Church has the potential for offering more than a
'social gospel', but rather to point to a new projection of
reality in response to God's call to a renewed creation. The
final fulfilment of creation will only come through growth in
and through God's own being as holy. Limouris helpfully
speaks of human beings as 'flowers grown from the depths of
his ineffable mystery' with a future to be realized through
the profound life of the trinitarian God.[30]

In contrast with programmes of ethical improvement,
holiness is concerned less with individual virtue, more with
the Christian's response to the story of Christ in his Church.
It is not a matter of accepting propositions, but of becoming
a new person, and beginning to live towards the future, or
living out the new reality that God has begun in the trinitarian life of the people of God.[31] The importance of the
Church offering a sign and a foretaste of both the way of
God's peace and God's trinitarian relationships, becomes

clear when it is contrasted with secular reason. The cut and thrust of sinful human life, from which church members are inseparable, assumes as basic, not God's initiative of blessing, but rather a context of adversarial violence. Even where a heroic 'virtue' is set up in opposition to evil, it has the quality of rivalry rather than the summons to the new common life in the Trinity. Jesus' performance of the Kingdom ethic, for example in engaging with and pardoning the woman taken in adultery, or the thief on the cross, reveals him breaking the spiral of destruction and virtue, law and virtue.

This is the starting point for discovering how even the most formal elements of the constitutional, legal and financial elements of the Establishment can be invited to reflect the holiness of God. A vision of holy management is desperately required in the Church of England which so often separates an other-worldly holiness from the pragmatic decisions, styled on civil service practice, about investments, budgets and the sale of glebe land. Even though the Church's bureaucratic methods may emulate in only a hesitant and provisional manner the shape of the absolute holiness of God to which its existence and practice is intended as a response, the vision is that there are no situations where merely human regulations or secular criteria are sufficient.[32]

A Church that is *koinonia*, has a vocation to learn a distinguishable mode of action. Constituted by the inner life of the triune God, the Church in its empirical historical existence must in some degree, and without concomitant domination, be a 'reading' of other human societies and institutions. For Boff, the Trinity is not just about the logic of God's hope but also a saving and evangelizing mystery: 'Society is not ultimately set in its unjust and unequal relationships, but summoned to transform itself in the light of the open and egalitarian relationships that obtain in the communion of the Trinity, the goal of social and historical progress.'[33] Every expression and experience of the Church, open to the restoring holiness of God, is summoned in its own administration and affairs to be a demonstration of a continual Pentecost, a moral practice embedded in the historical emergence of a new community with a unique character.

The community whose foundational gift of the victory of Christ is constantly made new by the Spirit acting, in baptism and Eucharist is called to show the world a model of redeemed relationships. It finds its vocation, however tenuously, whenever women and men begin to communicate with one another in a way that is directly informed by the sociality of the trinitarian Persons. In the desire for redeemed sociality, the eucharistic assembly is not just a meeting of people but the corporate, public, tangible, deep, and exhilarating sign and foretaste of that community of difference which will be God's final work.[34]

3. The Call to Comprehensiveness: Catholicity

'Catholicity' is capable of many interpretations. In the terms of this enquiry the Church is Catholic in that membership is open to all, in that only through interrelatedness with others can a particular eucharistic assembly call itself 'church', and in that its interior life is not separate from its shared concern for the wholeness of all creation.

Turning to examine in more detail this understanding of catholicity, local churches must often be challenged over the historically observable pattern of excluding others on grounds of belief, gender, ethics, culture, or race. As Christ invites and empowers any church to be a Catholic community, it is called to share the universal, all-embracing concern for all creation of the triune God. A church is Catholic, not through legislative or institutional pedigree, but because it demonstrates these Christlike qualities and concerns. As I concluded in the discussion on holiness, this is not merely a moral concern. In the fullest trinitarian sense, catholicity arises as that quality of life which allows itself to be defined as permanently relational. Christ invites members of his Body to be drawn into communion with himself (and the entire Trinity) and simultaneously to recognize their interrelatedness with the whole of the universe.

Earlier this century, and still today in some quarters, catholicity was often a term of polemic. Some churches defined themselves as 'Catholic' over against others that were not. To avoid past mistakes surrounding the manipulation of the term 'Catholic' for the purpose of domination, it is vital to abandon the prematurely universalizing emphasis which results from an exclusive linking of ecclesiology with the divine nature of Christ. This can lead to the portrayal of a heavenly, perfect, infallible Church in which the eschatology is already realized.[35] Such a Church can easily fall into complacency instead of living with contingency, make final judgements rather than recognize present incompleteness, and appear arrogant despite glaring occasions of sinfulness and brokenness. Despite the progress of the ecumenical movement, there persists an attitude which is far from the spirit of catholicity, namely the antagonism of confessional churches who deny each other the right to be known as 'Catholic' or to share in the Eucharist together. Further, the often negative Christian understanding of the revelation of God to the Jews and also to the other great faiths could be taken as evidence against any ecclesial claim to be already guaranteed by God in a universal 'Catholic' authority. Moltmann relates dialogue with world religions very explicitly to a trinitarian model in which the uniqueness of the faiths are enriched through their mutuality. He sees dialogue with the world religions as belonging to the broader context of the liberation of the whole creation for the coming kingdom. Dialogue with the other faiths has its place in the same framework as openness to the Jewish faith and the political and social agenda for a world where freedom and justice reign. In trinitarian terms, Christianity, while ever true to her own identity, is essentially committed and never afraid of free and open dialogue. This path, especially when it leads to contrition and reformation, is more likely to be one of enrichment than of destruction.

An appropriate christological foundation of ecclesiology takes with seriousness the true humanity of Christ, in contingency (though not necessarily in sin). These arguments oppose the tendency towards the partisan defining of particular manifestations of the Church as approved, with the reverse implication for others. Some ecclesiologies, in different ways, have claimed catholicity in an exclusive and competitive way on the grounds of being empowered by the transcendent Christ. We saw this strong tendency in the

Anglo-Catholic synthesis adopted by the Church of England of the early twentieth century. A trinitarian approach to catholicity, placing a renewed emphasis on the work of the Spirit (pneumatology), points more helpfully towards a contingent Church through which the Spirit offers potential for the realization in finite particular circumstances of anticipations of the Kingdom.

The catholicity of the church, as also its unity, is the gift and invitation of Christ who, through the Spirit, is present in history within the life of the local eucharistic assembly. Zizioulas, to a greater extent than the other theologians who are dialogue partners in this enquiry, invites acceptance of the identification of the local church with the eucharistic assembly, as a primary development of the Christological core of catholicity. It certainly finds its echoes and has attractiveness for Anglicans, especially in the light of the Parish Communion Movement and the fruits of twentieth-century research into early Christianity.

Catholic Christian communities centre their lives on the gospel and formally enact their faith in baptism and Eucharist. However, in the institutional church of late twentieth-century Britain there are two points particularly to be borne in mind. First, given the long-term prospects of a significantly low ratio of clergy to laity in the Church of England, for an ecclesiology rooted in the eucharistic assembly of the local church to be of value there will probably have to be an adjustment in the expectation of the frequency of the eucharistic celebration. Such a move need not indicate a devaluation of its significance, rather the reverse. The situation also demands a willingness to explore a re-ordering of the parish ministry to include priests locally ordained. I am convinced that both of these strategies should and will be actively pursued, and therefore feel confident in adopting the emphasis on the eucharistic focus of the local church that is central to the approach of Zizioulas. Second, as noted in the earlier summary of the nature of the contemporary Church of England, there is the related fact that many Anglicans normally attend worship frequently, and are not communicants. My immediate response is that eucharistic worship— used imaginatively and with respect to varieties of cultural expression—can legitimately be accepted as at the heart of Anglican liturgical life. However, a renewed understanding of the presence of Christ throughout the ministry of the word, as well as of the sacrament, makes space for much of what is developed here to apply to most forms of Christian worship. Underwriting a basic belief in the relationship between catholicity and Eucharist, is the understanding of Moltmann that to begin to speak of church is inevitably to think in terms of community and, in his own words, 'a community without the common table loses its messianic spirit and its eschatological meaning.'[36]

Catholicity is not the preserve of the clergy, nor can they be said to guarantee it to a local church. Perennially the Church of England in its provincial and diocesan operations needs to search vigilantly for a Catholic integrity. How, instead of mirroring the secular organization's dependence on legislation and protective rules, can the Church reveal a Catholic ordering of the Spirit? How can a diocesan family, through the institutions of Bishop's Council, Board of Finance, Diocesan Synod, bishops, clergy and people together, with overlapping and conflicting theologies and personalities, carry out their responsibilities in such a way as to be a sign and a foretaste of God's hope? How, instead of merely protecting vested interest and fighting tooth and nail, can the operators of the institution be witnesses to mutual trust, freedom of speech, a willingness to listen and to place trust in the decisions and genuine love of others? As Milbank insists, the Church has the gift and the responsibility to transmit, in the name of the trinitarian God, a distinct community life, for which he suggest the analogy of music that differentiates itself without dissonance. 'Christianity is, therefore, (in aspiration and faintly traceable actuality) something like the "peaceful transmission of difference", or "differences in a continuous harmony".'[37]

It is not my intention in this enquiry to make prescriptive pastoral re-organization proposals. However, several factors point to an alternative to parish, deanery or diocese as the classic 'Catholic' points of reference: urgent economic problems, the development of revised strategies for stipendiary and non-stipendiary clergy deployment, and a new willingness among all church members to recognize the equal value of the ministries of all the baptized. As I suggested in discussion of the concept of 'local church', if allowance were to be made for local autonomy regarding geographical groupings of parishes (together with appropriate groups of Christians of other denominations, as already happens in local ecumenical projects) the Church of England could move towards a style of self-ordering which could more truly be described as 'Catholic'.

A presiding ministry of courteous but courageous influence would be needed to support a network of congregations forming a 'local' and yet 'Catholic' embodiment of the Church. Although the concept of presiding in the local church will be examined later, it should be registered that its roots lie here in the indivisibility of the 'catholicity' of the 'local' church.

As the local church is in communion with the triune God, formed in Christ, through the Spirit, and as Christ is the creator and saviour of all, there can be no question, theologically speaking, of excluding anyone on grounds of their belonging to a particular human category. It follows too (certainly in line with Pauline usage and expectation) that there can eventually be no question of the existence of more than one 'Catholic' Church in any particular geographical location. It must be our long-term goal to work towards there being only one congregation in each settlement, though that congregation may have many and varied acts of worship, models of communion, and strategies of mission. In a number of settlements constituting a local church, it must be our hope to reach a state where all Christians admit each other's baptismal existence and eucharistic life. In a large geographical area, one communion will need to have the freedom to express its life and witness under varied but interrelated forms. Attempts to stifle pluriformity will need to be opposed. To define catholicity purely in terms of historical, liturgical, theological or even ministerial purity of pedigree and, therefore, for confessional groupings to deny the legitimacy of others, is a position that has lost all plausibility.

What is always in question is whether any particular manifestation of what claims to be a local church is in fact sufficiently in tune with the apostolic faith as to be effectively 'church'. The catholicity of a supposed local church could be so eroded, distorted or impoverished as to render it 'not a church'. As will be explored later, it is one of the primary prophetic responsibilities of the apostolic ministry to maintain the Church in its apostolicity in order to lay claims to catholicity. The test for a local church's 'catholicity' is more the constant internal agenda of that church rather than an objective external process of audit. It could perhaps be expressed by asking three questions:

1. Does this community believe that when it celebrates the Eucharist, the whole of the faith it holds and proclaims within the shape and order of its community life is an embodiment of the risen life of Christ, present through the Spirit?

2. Does the local church recognize in the eucharistic action the truth that its trinitarian life is related back in time to the creation of all things and to the victory of the work of Christ in Jesus of Nazareth as well as forward to the final consummation of the final peace of creation?

3. Does the local church have a vision of catholicity that envisions and empowers the entire body to be, however provisionally and sporadically, the sign and first-fruits for the world of that true sociality of redeemed relationships which constitute the final unity of all creation in Christ through the Spirit to the glory of the Father?[38]

Some English Anglicans would regard the above points as defining a sect rather than a church that exists for the entire community. My understanding is that a church that does indeed exist for the entire community simultaneously needs to know its own identity. It needs to know the faith by which it lives, in many forms and in rich variety of expression. In having a conscious self-identity, it does not oppose itself to unbelievers, nor set up in rivalry with other churches. Rather it is able to be in respectful and mutual dialogue with those of other faiths and of none.

Through the work of the Spirit, Christ enables the local church to embody his own catholic commitment to the salvation of the whole of creation. In opposing all that leads to the fragmentation rather than the peaceful integration of creation, the embodied Christ, the local church is maintained in its catholicity by the action of the Spirit.[39] It is the work of the Spirit who made possible the victory of the career of Jesus and the birth of the universal Church, to make present and effective the presence of Christ in the community eucharistic celebration. The local church's dependency on the Spirit for its association with Christ's work for the redemption of all relationships is a further reminder that neither the structures of its own life nor of its mission can be brought to fruition by purely human progressive programming. The Eucharist as the centre of the church's life both demands and guarantees that the Christian body of believers keeps open to *all* God's invitation to *all*, expressed through the entire career of Jesus Christ. The Eucharist and the church fail to be a Catholic event when they become hedged about by ecclesiastical restrictive practice. Catholicity, therefore, allows no room for human distinctions between the holy or the profane, which is physical or spiritual, ecclesial or worldly.[40]

To summarize this chapter so far: first, the unity of the local church has been described as a positive acceptance of the invitation to be in communion with God, in community with other Christians and in communication with the whole world. Second, holiness is the quality of that interrelatedness because it mirrors the mutual relationships of the love between the Persons of God who is holy. Third, catholicity is the recognition that only in relatedness can the truth of God in Christ be known. The Gospel of the triune God does not allow for individualism nor for communities to define themselves in isolation.

4. Proclaiming God's Activity, Past, Present and Future: Apostolicity

My proposal is that apostolicity is the manner in which the Church is relational through time, in parallel to the way in which catholicity describes its relationality in space. Although in God's eschatological vision, space and time are inseparable dimensions of reality, apostolicity is through the latter what catholicity is through the former.[41] To be apostolic, the Church proclaims the Gospel in the present time in a conscious relationship, through the Spirit, with the apostolic Church in other ages. In word and deed an apostolic Church will be attempting to make connections in the present time between the career of Jesus (together with the significant apostolic era of the Church's birth) and the eschatological desire of God. In a provisional manner, through its dynamically ordered trinitarian shape, the apostolic Church both remembers and anticipates the given and promised fulfilment of all creation. Uniquely in Christ's earthly career and in his final destiny the apostolic hope is portrayed.[42]

Apostolicity is a quality of the Church that relates historically, both backwards and forwards. Like a language it is constantly in dialogue with new ideas and new pressures. Whilst it may in many ways have discernible links with what it was once, but is ever drawn into new and unimagined futures, equally it will collapse completely and lose its identity if too many new words are coined in frequent succession when all sense of its roots in history are denied. A Church is not guaranteed in apostolicity simply by looking backwards and attempting to relive an ancient tradition in the present. Nor is a church apostolic by cutting loose from the past and being willing to change at random with no relatedness to other Christian experiences in different historical contexts. The living presence of Christ, made present through the Spirit, in the eucharistic community, is the gift of God for joining Christ's past and future with the local church's present situation.

Within the worship and life of the eucharistic community, the apostolic message transmitted through history becomes simultaneously the loving invitation of God to create the eschatological future. It follows from this that, truly understood, the apostolic tradition is ever renewed, through the recognizably continuous stream of inspired life in which, by the Spirit and especially through worship, the local church is continually constituted. From the early Fathers, Zizioulas concludes that dogmas should be understood 'as the "faith transmitted *to the saints*", constantly received and re-received by the consciousness of the "community of the saints" in new forms of experience and with a constant openness to the future'.[43] Hardy and Ford commend the analogy of the 'jazz factor' by which they mean the character of Pentecostal worship and life:

> This is a threat to much of the tradition, perhaps most of all because it demands trust both in God and in the worshippers as a group; anything might happen when freedom is granted; but if it is not, some of the most liberating and relevant activity of God is excluded.[44]

The significance of the Eucharist within an eschatological-trinitarian ecclesiology is movingly expressed by Moltmann:

> The glorification of God on earth, which is to lay hold on the whole creation, begins in the feasts of gratitude. Joy in freedom and fellowship anticipates the joy of the new creation and its universal fellowship is the greatest thanksgiving to the Father for everything he has made in creation and has achieved in the reconciliation of the world, and has promised to accomplish in its redemption. In the eucharist the congregation thanks the triune God for all his acts of goodness and sets itself in his trinitarian history with the world.[45]

Much of the twentieth century crisis surrounding the nature of the ordained ministry arises from a lack of understanding of the proper tension between past historical event and the contemporary re-reception, through the Spirit, of this past through the lens of God's eschatological future. The prevailing view for so much of the twentieth century was of apostolicity deriving solely from the career of Jesus (with an emphasis on the God-ward, transcendent side of the incarnation) and a corresponding absence of the work of the Spirit.

For Anglicans, the bishop may be understood as the one who, in his person, always in relationship with the entire eucharistic community of the Church, ensures that the historical and the eschatological dimensions of apostolicity are held together. In writing of bishops here I am not excluding non-episcopal churches. My aim is to produce an ecclesiology which focuses the Church of England's spirit and needs at the present time. It may be that some of what is said here will resonate with other churches and some will not. That is in the nature of a dialogue that does not demand uniformity or homogeneity as a necessary condition of communion.

Moltmann, noting that it was in early conflicts with heretics and schismatics that the early Church fathers, such as Irenaeus, came to think of bishops as legitimators of sound doctrine, finds significance in the characteristic of apostles that they were resurrection eyewitnesses. He begins from the founding of the apostolic mission in the eschatological event of the raising of Christ. He argues that the Church, in looking back to its beginnings in its appeal to the apostles, simultaneously discovers in the risen Christ its eschatological hope. In this process lies the assurance of the Church's messianic mission. Moltmann concludes that it is unsatisfactory merely to focus backwards in time to an 'apostolic age' and its notable apostolic representatives. Apostolic succession is in fact to be understood as nothing less than the continuing and truthful proclamation of the gospel of the risen Christ for which the Scriptures, rather than individual apostles or bishops, are the foundation stones.

The bishop is himself called to be a representative of that unity, holiness, and catholicity that is characteristic of the apostolic Church. It calls for radical changes and discernment for a bishop in today's Church not to be simply overwhelmed by all the expectations of Church and society. However, there is an urgent need for bishops in close collaboration with fellow clergy and laity to discover ways of ministering that are not separate, remote, or dependency creating, but radiant with trinitarian communion.[46]

The Eucharist, as prefigured in the intimate meals of Jesus with his disciples, and particularly the last supper, especially when its physical celebration has been designed with this in mind, portrays that shape of *koinonia* that Christ wanted to give to the world through the Christian community as the first-fruits of God's glory, a dynamic drawing of the Kingdom.

The Church in apostolic terms is that community which chooses to allow itself to be constantly reconstituted in Christ by the Spirit so as to be able to offer to the world an image of trinitarian communion that represents both a criticism of and an inspiration for society.

Such a local church, proclaiming the Good News in word and action will often meet with opposition and suffering. To choose to draw on the humanity of Christ for a new understanding of church is to be prepared to share the mission of the contingent, poor and unprotected crucified Christ. An apostolic church has no share in triumphalism, self-protection, infallibility or strategies of domination. Such a church has the resources to empathize with those who are weak, suffering and relatively powerless in society. To choose to be constituted from Christ's eschatological future is to be a church that allows itself paradoxically both to begin to model and constantly to search for a unity that permits neither divisiveness nor exclusiveness.

In summary, apostolicity refers to the Church's intimate connectedness with its past and its future. As the sign and foretaste of God's peace, it is constituted both by its roots in the events of Jesus' ministry and the rise of the early Church, and also in the eschatological wholeness of the Christ in whose hands the Father has placed the world's final destiny. In any particular context, the church through communion, in community and in interaction with its environment, should be open to hearing God's word, simultaneously from the past and from the future.

Chapter Six
PRIESTHOOD:
THE PRESIDING MINISTRY

No single model of ordained ministry will do justice to every biblical image and theological or practical concern. What follows is just one attempt, among others, to provide an explanation of what is involved in being a parish priest in the Church of England today. In a work that intends primarily to offer a theological vision of the local church and its chief minister, male or female, it is my hope that others will be able to make connections for Christian ministry in chaplaincies and secular organizations. The vast majority of ordinands go through the selection process with a view to becoming priests. This does not prejudice either those women who, with their bishop, discern that their vocation is diaconal, or those who plead for the establishment of a permanent diaconate within English Anglicanism.

Priesthood, whether performed corporately or in dispersion, is integral to the Church. Ecclesiology is always prior to a theology and practice of ministry, whatever the context.

In Chapter Three, I offered an analysis and celebration of the chief elements of the innovative and challenging thinking taking place within the Advisory Board for Ministry (ABM), and the colleges and courses. It is my intention here, finally, to draw conclusions regarding a concept of ordained ministry which supersedes that to be found in those recent official documents.

1. The Priest as Member of the Eucharistic Community

The argument of this book points the way forward to an understanding of all ordained ministry as inseparably interconnected with the life of the whole of the baptized church membership. Whatever unique responsibilities a priest may hold, by God's grace, he is always, at the same time, one of the community of disciples of Jesus Christ. This is the *Communio Sanctorum*, understood not in the medieval technical sense of participants in the sacraments, but in reality as a fellowship of friends, an assembly of believers. There is nothing that could be said of bishop, priest, or deacon that is not in some way true for the Church as a whole. Instead of associating ordained ministry alone with that of Christ, as was commonly the case in the received theology, the assertion here is that the ministry of the entire Church is associated with that of Christ, through the Holy Spirit.[1]

Earlier, in the examination of the unity of the Church from an eschatological-trinitarian stance, we explored how in worship and the shape of its relatedness, the local church is constituted by and mirrors the trinitarian communion. Separately and together, all the members are therefore, 'ministers', invited and equipped by their mutual recognition of each other as equal participants in God's mission. In 1 Corinthians 12 Paul offers a 'definition' of the Body of Christ, the Church *precisely* as the ministry of all. To be a member of the Body is equivalent to having gifts of the Spirit and vice-versa. There can be no proper separation, therefore, between an account of ministry and of the community which the Spirit creates. As Jesus challenged his disciples to find life only by losing it, the baptismal commissioning of church members is certainly for their own salvation, but primarily an invitation to share in the bringing into effect of that wholeness in particularity which is God's purpose for the universe. We have noted earlier how Zizioulas shows that ministry should be understood back from the future, eschatologically, as well as in the present and from the past. Further, he indicates that a ministry associated with that of Christ will have soteriological implications not only for persons but for the whole created universe to be drawn into communion with the triune God.[2] The work of the priest, therefore, in focusing, and helping every church member to recognize their particular contribution to the ministry of the whole church, should be identified primarily as a unique contribution to the building up of the church, whose task is to bring nearer the new economy of God.

Several times already we have noted that one of the Church's greatest problems centres on how to achieve a delicate balance between affirming the laity, without simultaneously undermining the authority and commitment of the ordained ministry. One of the seemingly intractable elements in this problem does of course focus on the fact that, whilst the parish clergy are on the whole paid a stipend or find their dignity as workers through ordination, most laity are usually not remunerated for their church work and find their dignity primarily in other places. It is all too easy to propose an idealistic strategy to engage with equal significance ordained and lay ministries, but in our society it is frequently the case that people are recognized ultimately for the job they are paid to perform. Equally, those who have to find increasing sums of money to pay rising diocesan quotas may well expect to dictate what they wish to receive in return from the authorized and employed parish priest.

There have been many anxieties expressed among clergy in recent years that the development of lay ministry or shared responsibility in the Church is either tantamount to reducing the notion of priesthood to pronouncing absolution and reciting the canon of the eucharistic prayer, or to making redundant the work of priests altogether.[3]

To overcome the polarization of the dual representation of Christ by clergy and laity, some representatives of the catechumenate movement have suggested that churches regard baptism, in spirit if not literally, as an 'ordination' to the order of laity.[4] Such a line of argument could render meaningless the word 'ordination' and challenge the appropriateness of setting aside by ordination any particular group within the interrelated ministries of the Church. The proposal conveys the sense that, on the strength of baptismal relatedness to God and neighbour, all Christians, with differing authorizations, make an equally significant contribution to the right ordering and purposefulness of the Church. *De facto*, the priest is always to be recognized as exercising his unique ministry only in the context of a community of the baptized, including others ordained as deacon or priest. A radical experiment reported of one particular church in Germany emphasizes precisely the basic commitment of the entire membership. The ministerial team each month would nominate a different person to act as pastor, working half-time and supported financially by the earnings of the group. The end result was the request of the community for the ordination of the entire team.[5] In my own view it would be difficult to maintain the catholicity of the Church if such local practice were to become widespread.

Theologically and practically, there is no truth in the assertion that the increase of lay ministry diminishes the role or power of the clergy. Rather, they enhance one another. F. R. Barry urged the clergy to reconsider their work as vital, precisely because of the importance of the Church's entire ministry which they lead. The priest is called upon to excercize a non-dominational power which moves beyond condescension. It is vital that the inherited collusion between clergy and laity should be done to death that results in clerical spirituality and sense of oneness with God being regarded as inherently superior. The power of the priest, *with*, rather than *over against*, the laity, refers to her ability to effect, influence, and sometimes change the direction of community living. The new way of being church requires an ecclesial community that is being created *of* people, rather than provided *for* people. Or looking at the ministry of the committed membership towards the parish, we could say that the need is for the ministry of the entire membership, not the clergy and readers only, to be *for* the people. This new concept is going to take a long while to become accepted by the wider population, and imaginative thought needs to be given to the processes by which new ministerial expectations are commended. When discussing planned changes in pastoral organization with clergy in one diocese, I found it instructive to note how few had thought it important to discuss openly and fully these issues with the parochial church council. The expectation was expressed that 'there will be a minimum of interest' and 'not much response'. What is in question is not so much the quantity or the status of the priest's personal contribution to the whole Church's ministry, but rather, the vision, expectation, direction, and the quality.

There is a need to be realistic about the actual capabilities

of the existing clergy. Observation of the most effective
priests in the presiding role indicates the need for sensitivity
and intelligence. Avis has gone further in demanding 'outstanding intellectual performance' from the clergy.[6] Later I
shall be placing an emphasis on the need for clergy to be
theologically alert and motivated as well as conversant with
theories of related disciplines. In the present context 'doing
theology' should rightly be understood on a variety of complementary models, though it is essential that the ordained
ministry attracts to its ranks many who are capable of
rigorous interdisciplinary thought.

My conclusion is that the relation between clergy and
laity is adequately expressed when the particular responsibilities of the prestbyter are presented in terms of overseeing
amongst the other ministries that constitute the local eucharistic community. This concept will later be explored in terms
of 'presidency'. The international Roman Catholic debate
on ecclesiology and ministry since Vatican II in the 1970s
and 80s made extended use of the term 'presidency' to
denote the leader of the local church. It is the entire church
rather than the priest alone who is said to represent Christ.
Rather than defining the role of the priest in isolation, an
indissoluble link exists between the role of the one who
presides at the Eucharist and the one (or team) presiding
within the Church's mission and ministry.[7] Liturgically, the
necessary dialogue of versicle and response, such as 'And also
with you' or 'Amen', stresses the collaborative and interdependent work of the president with the whole assembly,
which has the corporate responsibility of being a missionary
society. The priest presides at the Eucharist by virtue of
presiding in the Church's life, rather than by virtue of being
a priest *per se*.

The publication of the ASB first brought the word 'president' into common use in the Church of England. For a
more restricted group the concept of 'presidency' was offered
as a central pillar of the 1976 General Synod Faith and
Order Report, *The Theology of the Ordained Ministry*.[8] It is a
concept favoured by Hans Küng.[9] Wesley Carr prefers the
term 'consultancy'.[10] As a diocesan itinerant officer apprais-
ing and encouraging many different churches, I recognize in

my own priestly ministry a consultancy role. However, this hardly seems appropriate as the predominant metaphor to describe clergy who are essentially and primarily baptized members of a local church community before they are in any sense detached observers. My proposal is that the term 'president' is capable of bearing many layers of meaning to express the theology of ministry applicable to a parish priest, whether male or female, in the Church of England today. I shall be articulating what this could mean in the remainder of this chapter.

This concept of president, far from negating the 'place' of priests in a local church that takes the ministries of laity seriously, will be found also to release, enrich and interpret the role of the laity more truly.[11] It is in no way to devalue the particular responsibility of the parish priest to emphasize the reality of the Christian life and apostolic ministry of every other baptized church member and his own place among them. Despite all the optimism and experimenting in collaborative ministry of the past twenty years, what still needs to be stated more clearly is that the ordained have no life or ministry in isolation, nor in a permanently higher status, spiritual or material, over against any other Christian.

At the level of attitude, as well as of theology, it is vital for clergy to reject the inherited burden of clericalism, in particular, the collusion between priest and people, that the clergy, because of their ordination are automatically more attuned to the life of God.[12] There is no difference between clergy and laity in the quality of their Christian authority. As a baptized member of the community, the priest's particular authoritativeness should always be seen as flowing out of an open relatedness to God and to others, rather than as authority guaranteed by the reception of an objective substance, whether by the individual or the entire community.[13]

The key to understanding ordained ministry is no longer the individual reception of objective grace, even when this is tempered and balanced by the requirement of a Spirit-filled faithfulness. This is not to deny the value for all ministry of that openness to the Spirit which makes a person available for the ministry allocated by the Church. Such availability is unavoidably connected with the dedication of the ordained minister to prayer, study, and other means of personal and intellectual development. However, the collusion persists between some clergy and laity that the prayers of the ordained are of greater significance or more effective than other church members. All church members are equally liable to fail to be open to the Spirit, so that the character of relatedness to the Trinity and to humanity, given to the candidate at baptism (through grace not through juridical translation), may be distorted by doubt and sin. But the Christian tradition maintains that God remains faithful to his side of the relationship. This was the implication of the medieval Church abandoning the earlier assumption in both East and West that an ordained person, if proven incompetent or vicious, could be stripped of office. Whereas in the first centuries a person so deposed was no longer regarded as bishop, presbyter, or deacon, late in the twelfth century Augustine's notion of permanent or 'indelible' quality of ordination was developed.[14] Lack of human faithfulness in the case of baptism or of ordination does not constitute grounds for the sacrament to be reversed or declared void. One could argue that in the short-term at least, it could, for the growth of the person concerned and even the well-being of the community, result in some form of discipline, instruction or limitation of influence and responsibility. There is however, a vital strand of Christianity that knows the truth and maturity of personal growth through tragedy, failure and certainty. Such a view reflects the contingent nature of the faith of Jesus of Nazareth without denying his sinlessness, and is expressed most powerfully and convincingly, I believe, in some of the poetry of R. S. Thomas and in the whisky priest of Graham Greene. Many clergy today are facing the vulnerability involved in being a priest who attempts to move from operating in a distant role, towards the relationships involved in being a human being, a friend, a spouse, a parent, a community member, and a voter.

There is a sense in which, on the surface at least, none of the foregoing argument is new to the ecumenical debate about priesthood. In recent decades, critical scholarship has highlighted the universal priesthood of all baptized Christians. It has brought about a revolution in ecclesiology, observable in internationally agreed statements between denominations, by opting for the belief that apostolic succession is transmitted through the entire Christian community as well as through the individual ordained minister. For example, Yves Congar, Hans Küng, Léon-Joseph Cardinal Suenens, and Edward Schillebeeckx stand among those in the Roman Catholic Church who have shown from scriptural and patristic research, the need to move from the concept of an individualistic, Christ-appointed apostolic ministry of clergy, to one in which the Spirit-filled community creates its own leaders, pastors, and prophets in a variety of community frameworks. Congar insists on the need to understand the Spirit, not merely as animator of a Christ-centred Church, but truly as the equally co-instituting 'Principle' of the Church.[15]

This theological revolution has arisen in the context of the recognition of power as a social process where people speak and act together in a climate of mutual respect; further, the richly differentiated giftedness of the entire Church is recognized alongside the contribution of the clergy. Edward Schillebeeckx, in particular, has argued persuasively that the difference between orders in the Church is only at the level of function, in that essentially to be a baptized Christian lies at the root of all membership and ministry.[16] This is not to reject the immense value of the challenge offered to received patterns of ministry by those who have focused on the manner in which ministry is delegated to the ordained by the entire apostolic community.

So at one level, nothing is new. Partly, it is important to celebrate this insight and to point out how far it has allowed many churches to move forward in theology and practice.[17] Equally, however, it may be asked what different ecumenical commissions and agreed statements have made to church practice. Also, even where the ecclesiology that has followed in the wake of Vatican II has been widely influential, significant problems remain. In particular there must be noted an unsatisfactory incoherence in doctrine which, despite wanting to offer the highest dignity to the laity and despite reducing the emphasis on the juridical character of ministerial authority, retains an overdeveloped or disproportionate emphasis on the role of clergy.

In the *Statement on Ministry and Ordination* (1973) of ARCIC I, ministerial priesthood is spoken of as belonging to another realm of the gifts of the Spirit. The *Elucidation* (1979) of the statement adds that the priesthood of the people of God and of the ordained ministry 'are two distinct realities which relate, each in its own way, to the high priesthood of Christ, the unique priesthood of the new covenant, which is their source and model'.[18] The 1986 Report of the Church of England's Board for Mission and Unity's Faith and Order Advisory Group, *The Priesthood of the Ordained Ministry*, chaired by the Bishop of Chichester, Eric Kemp, in dialogue with contemporary ecumenical statements, perpetuates the concept of the priesthood of Christ being mediated to the Church through the parallel but separate avenues of the whole baptized Church on the one hand and the ordained priests on the other.

> The common priesthood of the community and the special priesthood of the ordained ministry are both derived from the priesthood of Christ. Bishops and presbyters do not participate to a greater degree in the priesthood of Christ; they participate in a different way—not, that is, as individual believers, but in the exercise of their office. Thus theirs is not a magnified form of the common priesthood; the difference is this, that their ministry is an appointed means through which Christ makes his priesthood present and effective to his people.[19]

Many who are engaged in the dialogue of modern ecumenical theology long wholeheartedly for a way of drawing into true partnership the ministries of all believers.[20] It is the chief conclusion of this book that without an explicitly eschatological-trinitarian framework, which relates an understanding of ministry to the ontology of God, an adequate solution to the question of the role of the ordained ministry in the Church is not readily available. A trinitarian church in the end, must abolish the linear priority of either the individual minister or the community, and accept the simultaneous uniqueness of both. Even the insight of Vatican II

(LG 31 and AA 2 and 3), much repeated in popular wisdom, that fundamentally the clergy are also laity, carries a double message: the hierarchy are the institutional core of the Church, bearing the essential apostolic mission entrusted by Jesus to the Church, and the laity are the background against which the clergy minister. It remains a form of clericalism, and in particular can usurp the proper contribution of laity in church government.

The earlier discussion of the trinitarian basis of ecclesiology, clearly emphasized that trinitarian thought takes as axiomatic the relational understanding of personal being. God is not to be conceived of in a linear way, first as one and then as three, or primarily as three but then also as one. God is three Persons simultaneously and freely engaging. If this trinitarian principle is related to a doctrine of ministry, it suggests the inappropriateness of attributing a process of causality of any kind. Rather, what is required is the assertion that apostolicity does not come either from a chain of individuals or even through a historically 'guaranteed' line of apostolic communities.[21]

I have argued already that the eucharistic community (the local geographical gathering of the baptized and confirmed) is constituted in mutuality through the Spirit, by its membership. I am aware that there is a danger here of idealizing the Church, and acknowledge that much of the Church's life is in stark contrast with its aspirations. My assertion is that when searching for the root of inspiration for ecclesial life, the starting point should be a church that worships the Trinity. A meditation of the St Andrew Rublev's Icon of the Trinity by an anonymous monk of the Eastern Church suggests that a trinitarian church will live in a 'rhythm of adoption, of out-pouring, of gift, of generosity, and of grace', in which 'generosities are neither opposed or juxtaposed but posed, as it were, each in relation to the other—not posed before the other but in the other, in such a way that it is in this relationship of love that each Person experiences self-discovery as distinct Person . . .'[22] If all Christian life may be understood in terms of a complexity of ministries, as Paul suggests (1 Cor. 12), each Christian as minister in relationship to Christ and to the other ministers, creates the Church as a relational entity. This is especially relevant to the question of the exercise of power and authority. There is an expectation that the leader of the Christian community is steeped in the gospel in such a way that she can expect a response from the other members as to one who clearly lives in the gospel. Paradoxically, she is also called to live under the yoke of the gospel. Like all baptized members of the Church she should only expect to inspire agreement as one who shares obedience to Christ in the Spirit.[23]

All Christians make a varied contribution to the Church's ministry. To be a priest is a calling to a unique vocation, but one which is of no greater value than any other. It is helpful here to consider vocation in terms of three levels of call. First, a general vocation to be 'in Christ' through baptism and confirmation; second, through the Church each baptized person is summoned in particular moments or phases of life, to a role best described as 'ministry'. This ministry is the privilege and responsibility of all church members and is largely given to one and defined by others. Third, there is the uniqueness of each person's call which to some extent will be a task engaged in for the love of God and for the love of the work. Whether the work is paid employment or voluntary, it will be seen as a vocation fulfilled to the extent that through it others will find enrichment, release, and a sense of their wholeness through their relatedness to God. Ministry, reflecting the ontology of the triune God, and open to God's eschatological future for the sake of the world's salvation, may vary in direction, particular purpose, or area of responsibility, but never in significance.

In summary, each member of the Church, whatever their particular ministry, is at heart a disciple of Jesus Christ through the work of the Spirit. Alert to the significance of their baptismal commitment and gift, church members share a common responsibility and commissioning to witness to God's love. To root a conceptuality of ordination in an eschatological-trinitarian ecclesiology, mirroring the ontology and the passionate cause of God, provides a coherent path towards the goal of the modern Church of recognizing all ministries as equally representative of that of Christ in the character and task of the Church. Ordained ministers should be encouraged to understand the nature of their vital and unique authority in terms of relatedness. They have no existence outside of a relationship with their fellow members of the baptized community; their own uniqueness is created and sustained within relationships of mutuality with their fellow ordained ministers.

A relational view of ministry presumes that authority establishes itself as a demand of the relationship itself. In these terms the Church becomes hierarchical only in the sense in which the Holy Trinity itself is hierarchical. The ordered relationship between clergy, and between clergy and laity, will not be one of domination when informed by mutual indwelling. In the writing of Gregory Nazienzen the fundamental notion of 'specificity' indicates how the Son has everything in common with the Father and the Spirit except being Father or Spirit, and the Spirit possesses everything the Father and the Son possess except being Father or Son.[24] Hierarchy and power in the Church are, therefore, to be modelled on the being of the triune God, rather than on secular notions of precedence or the removal of freedom.

In a trinitarian ecclesiology, order is not provided or imposed by a single group, permanently over against another, but by the fluctuating movement in relationship of the personal participants.[25] An eschatological ecclesiology reads back from God's desire for final unity of all things, a contemporary agenda for the hope of salvation for every part of creation. This cannot be constituted in terms of freedom for some but not for others.[26] A church which introduces permanent subordinations within its life reveals its lack of understanding of the mystery of the Trinity and its unwillingness to relate it directly to ecclesiological concepts. In a perichoretic community of love, a self-ordering process takes place in which, although individual persons will fulfil unique and necessary roles, the total ordering is achieved without any one being in a permanently subordinate position to another.

It is my contention that such a relational view of ministry outflanks previous disputes as to whether the individual priest possesses an indelible character or whether the character of ordination is functional or ontological.[27] The only ministry in the Church is that which Christ, through the Spirit, shares with his Body, the Church. Apart from a local church community, the ordained minister is nothing and possesses nothing.[28] Bishops, archdeacons, and specialist ministers need to have a special care that their ministry to the diocese, in the service of many local churches, is balanced by close encounters with specific experiences of the local church. It is stretching a relational understanding of priesthood to recognize that a small minority of clergy, for a while, will know 'local church' only as a succession of temporary gatherings of church members, for particular purposes of education or training. It must always be healthier when those with a roving ministry also have a base with lay and clerical colleagues in a particular local church.

In the discussion on the contemporary trinitarian context of theorizing about ecclesiology, personhood and the nature of creation, I drew the conclusion that all being, truly interpreted, is relational. There is every indication here that a notion of church may be identified which bypasses the need for the permanent dependency or inferiority of any constituent part. A church which is defined as a local missionary society will always need to have room for those in need of support and loving care. This is the work of all the baptized and no one should be regarded (especially on grounds of age, health, intelligence, or competence) as permanently assigned to the group in need of care. Temporary dependency may be associated for example with bereavement, loss of work, or the end of a relationship, but should not in the church turn into a permanent dependency.

Within a particular eucharistic community, the ordained minister may be spoken of as having an assigned 'place', though not in a rigid or juridical manner to represent God, as though God were himself absent. In using the word 'place' (which resonates with the tradition of the resident not unconnected with the idea of 'parson' or *persona*, despite the different literal meaning) there is a risk of too much rigidity or individuality. As I shall explore later, the task of presiding may also be one that invites all members of the church to be fluid in their appreciation of each other and their preparedness at different times to be flexible in the use of their gifts.

The priestly work of focusing and distributing needs at once to be precise and also to be in dialogue with the immediate context. By relating himself both to God and the church in the context of the particularities of a given eucharistic community, the priest becomes the person who can be the vehicle of mediation between humanity and God. With and on behalf of the community, he offers to God the eucharistic gifts. If the entire Christian community is described as 'priestly', it is not a derivation from the priesthood of the ordained ministry but is recognized rather as the interdependence of the orders of ministry within the church.[29] To say otherwise is to denigrate the laity as having no special responsibility and to see ordained priesthood as the essence of the Church, a promotion or superior 'place' in the community. It has often been the case that when laity have taken important steps forward in disciplined faith, they have themselves become a prey to a neo-clericalism.[30] In a parallel manner, laity and clergy, desperate for the depth of faith parishes have failed to provide, have created renewal movements and the Franciscan Third Order. Laity, in other words have had to belong to other networks in order to be that to which their baptism intrinsically calls them.

It is the whole community, the Body of Christ, which is priestly because all ministry is integrated and related to him in his incarnational career and in his eschatological consummation.[31] The ministry of the whole Church is the vehicle by which the saving power of Christ, through his own life and that of the Trinity, is made available to the whole world. The traditional liturgical practices of never ordaining a priest in the abstract but always to a title, and of always ordaining at the eucharistic assembly rather than in private, continue to bear enormous significance as a demonstration of the corporate, rather than individualistic, nature of all ministry.

The clergy, therefore, do not create or order a church for the non-clergy, but each in their respective and particular ministries, collaboratively order the church in communion. Unless a new understanding of the word 'laity' is sought, apart from to mean 'not a clergyperson' it would be better left out of use. A positive theology for laity to understand themselves as as much integrally church as the clergy is a vital and urgent necessity. At heart, all orders of church members are called in word and action to know and to respond to the triune God through the saving act of Christ in the Spirit in his earthly career, now and in the final consummation.

We come now to an examination of the priest's role specifically in terms of presiding. It is essential to recognize that she has a particular significance in exactly the same way as everyone else, and that in a community based on trinitarian relations, this will be open to constant interpretation and revision. This is not to suggest a uniform manner for the carrying out of the presiding role. Each priest's particular gifts, insights, and opportunities should lead to the exercizing of the presidency in appropriate and changing ways. A priest may have musical talents, an ability to teach, gifts of communication with the young, the elderly and so on. He can exercise his presiding ministry through any particular skill, without necessarily having to be 'in charge' of every meeting or in the seat of administration. This concept will be explored in the later section on 'blessing'. To assist in keeping the local church true to its calling, both in its message and the form of its own life, the priest needs to be invested with just sufficient authority to exercise disciplinary regulations and laws with a sensitive and discerning touch.[32]

2. The Priest as President of the Eucharistic Community

I have already established that the priest is never to be regarded as defined separately from fellow Christians in the local church. The unique priestly ministry exists within and is created by the continuing communion of relatedness within the church and with the triune God. The stress involved for both clergy and laity while this process of adaptation is taking place, makes heavy demands on spirituality, maturity, capacity to negotiate, and courage in the face of disappointment. The most powerful metaphors of *ACCM 22* are those which speak of the priest 'focusing' and 'distributing' the ministry of the entire church. The priest focuses with particular clarity and representativeness what is (or ought to be) true of the life and work of the whole church. This is a key reason for removing all issues of gender as qualification for ordination. The catholic systematic theologian, Legrand, having argued that neither Scripture nor tradition offer barriers to the ordination of women as priests, expresses the belief that, by virtue of being qualified to preside within the church's life, women may theologically speaking preside at the Eucharist. He observes that in whatever sense priests represent Christ it is never purely in the literal individual sense that could exclude anyone on grounds of gender but always at the level of mystery. His vision of collaboration between men and women is checked however, by his greater personal commitment to the unity of the Church: in the face of strong objections, he approves the bishops' refusal to consider women's ordination, 'because the ministry of communion must not exacerbate divisions'.[33]

The priest's work, expressed in terms of 'presiding' within the eucharistic community, baptizing and preaching, certainly can be conceptualized as a ministry of focusing and distributing. The key issue must be to ask how it is possible to be 'in charge' of a community in the sense of the bishop's invitation at the moment of a priest's institution ('Take this charge which is both mine and thine'), and simultaneously to be a member. In other words, is it possible to avoid the dichotomy between the representative nature of the ministry of the ordained and the laity?

Theologically, the role of the Father among the Persons of the Trinity can offer the necessary insight. Earlier analysis of the contribution of the Cappadocians showed that God's being reveals how the nature of all being is only truly understood in relational terms. To exist and to exist in relation are one and the same. So even though the Father is said to be the origin of all creation, he is simultaneously in a mutual relationship (*perichoresis*) with the Son and, therefore, can never be in a position of domination. Rather, his Fatherhood is expressed only in terms of interrelation to the Son to whom he is Father. The understanding of God as a communion of personal relations in which none is ever in a permanently dominating role, offers a vision for a concept of priesthood that is *primus inter pares* without being separate or superior.

The quality of relation between priest and people may be expressed as an unwritten mandate. The priest, in a spirit of vulnerability, is saying: 'Although I believe I have been called simultaneously by you, the bishop and God, to be your parish priest, please never forget that I am also, like you, a baptized member of this congregation.' On their part, it is as though the people were saying, in a spirit of openness: 'Yes, we are glad to hear you acknowledge that at heart you are one of us by baptism, but we also ask you, for as long as it seems right from both sides, to be president of this local community in a spirit of persuasive and courteous leadership.'[34]

The following sections will explore the roles and qualities of priestly relationship required in one who presides in terms of discernment, blessing and witnessing.[35]

(i) Discernment

Discernment must come first because, unless the priest herself and with the community within which she presides, hopes to be maintained in the gift of right judgement, she will probably be in danger of reducing the work of ministry to the mechanical operation of function or office. If the priest is to be more than a maintenance officer or decision-maker for the institution, he not only needs to be committed to growing in discernment for himself, but also to be able to stimulate and recognize the facility of discerning gifts of the Spirit within the local church.

Discernment, by its very nature, is harder to describe than it is to recognize. Earlier in the century English Anglican priests had a lonely vocation, with both the joys and heavy responsibilities of 'a man of God', taking as his role model Jesus Christ, with an emphasis on the God-ward side of the incarnation. As I noted earlier, signs of such a monarchic priesthood were usually taken to be a lack of 'worldliness', a disciplined concentration on a semi-monastic style of spirituality, a stability of belief and behaviour, and intrinsically a clear sense of individual calling and communion with God to which a layperson would not be expected to aspire. One of the triggers that set in motion a search for a new way of being church and, therefore, the attempt to reflect on and articulate it, is the cluster of difficulties that many clergy now have with the received model. A growing number of clergy and laity are looking for a church in which to share their capacity to love and live in openness: to experience church as a place to experiment with trust, immediacy, spontaneity, courage, generosity, and wonder. A church that concentrates merely on formality and certainty inhibits the often painful and alarming search for living and redeemed relatedness.

An understanding of priestly discernment may be expressed in terms of contextual awareness, theological vision, and a commitment to spiritual development and growth.

(a) Contextual Awareness

As a body, the Church that is pledged to collaboration with the Trinity for the realization of God's plan will need to be acutely aware of the complex pressures, burdens and joys of differing sections of contemporary society. For individual persons, the priest must be recognized as one who can enable them to grapple with fears of many kinds: of growth, of living, and of suffering and death. The priest also has the task of helping the whole Church to determine its response to its environment. A positive attitude towards growing in familiarity with the constituent elements of the political and community context in which the local church is set, will work deliberately to avoid an attitude of isolation from 'the world'. It will make it feasible for the church to become a companion with all who are willing to work in the cause of hope, peace and unity for humanity and the world.[36] The unity, holiness and catholicity that the eucharistic assembly seeks to foster, is not for its own sake but to enable the church to be a pointer to the final consummation of all in Christ.[37]

There is a sense in which the vital element of the church's mission is the continuing and never finished attempt to become a community that in its own life so mirrors and articulates the final destiny of all, that outsiders will be led to ask, 'What is the secret of the new reality, this life of praise, of justice, and of peace?'[38] The church that knows and loves its particular cultural context can work, precisely in that place, to reveal God's presence in Christ and to help to realize the coming Kingdom.[39] In other words, there is no invisible, perfect church to protect the contingent local community in the truth. A church that is a sign and foretaste of God's *shalom* will be created intentionally by members making space for each other's unique contribution to a complex network of interrelation.

It is the priest's responsibility to ensure that the local church examines the effects of its policies and strategies and responds to its findings. A severe test of the presiding gift comes when the priest is required to enable the church to wrestle with conflict and make a decision which will inevitably leave some members feeling angry or powerless. The temptation can be great in such circumstances to reach for an automatic clerical right of authority. I am recalling here examples of parishes where the priest was theoretically in favour of collaborative ministry but in practice reverted to exercising power alone. This can be true, say, when planning forms of worship not provided in the ASB. If a group is commissioned to produce a liturgy, it is vital that ground rules of authority are agreed at the beginning of the process, rather than when the planning is at a mature stage. It is too late then for the priest to regress to former models of authority and say, 'This will not do'. Either from the beginning the priest or another member of the staff team needs to be part of the group, or else those planning the event need to negotiate an agreed strategy and adhere to it. It is perfectly possible for the laity concerned to break an agreement, just as much as the clergy.

The implications of this enquiry are that such situations are extremely complex and that a church and priest committed to growing in maturity will recognize this. The parish priest focuses and distributes, rather than bears alone, the leadership of the church community. A maturing church will be struggling to share responsibility, including both the pain and the pleasure, for the overseeing of the missionary task and of the internal relationships of the local church.

The catholicity of the church ought to mean that Christians formed by one culture should be able and willing sometimes to hear criticism from society and from churches in other parts of the world. Catholic eucharistic communities, inherently incomplete by nature, do not close themselves off in isolation. In liturgy, education, membership, contact with other churches in many parts of the world, social concern and community involvement, the importance of interaction between gospel and context will be on the agenda of the presiding priest.

(b) Theological Vision

Chapter One portrayed the expectation within the Church of England of great pastors who maintained a lifelong and wide-ranging academic discipline. Michael Ramsey expected clergy and laity to exchange their dedicated learning from various disciplines.[40] When in the 1960s Bishop John Moorman affectionately addressed his collective clergy as 'we theologians', however, he may not have had in mind the model of reflective practitioner advocated here.[41]

In order to grapple with the context of ministry today, as well as to develop their personal insight, it is essential that those who preside within the local church community should engage vigorously with a wide variety of appropriate styles of reflection. Diocesan strategies for Ministerial Review and continuing ministerial education are known to be encouraging clergy and laity to regard disciplined reflection by the former, not as a personal luxury, but as an essential and imaginative element in the regular work of all ordained ministry.[42]

In particular, fully recognizing the differences which personality, background, and present context will determine, the following points must be made regarding the essential study and reflection that need to be built in to the working diary of a parish priest. First, the priest is one who must ensure that the local church, in its internal and external relations, is stimulated by an awareness of and excitement about God's being and activity. The priest may not himself be the most obvious focus for this work; he may prefer to encourage others to stimulate the church in this way. As president of the community, it is her task to ensure that this perspective of the life of the church is developed. Precisely because her place or role is to preside, she does not need to aspire to be omnicompetent, nor to feel guilty or jealous if someone else in the local church overshadows her in terms of discernment. The test is more about the spiritual maturity of the entire community. Second, an honest engagement with movements of contemporary theology by the priest, at whatever level is accessible, should prevent three things from happening. One is the fossilizing of the church in the ambience of a particular age, as though that were the final wisdom for all time. This is not the same as never forming any policy or taking a decision because future generations might disagree, but honestly recognizing the limits of every time and place. Second is the possibility that liturgies are planned, strategies created for evangelism, and issues of power resolved with only scant reference to the Scriptures, theological thinking, or knowledge and skills adapted from specific relevant fields. Third is that the church may be limited by having as a priest one whose understanding of his task is merely routine maintenance or who does not engage (at an appropriate level) with the contemporary theological and intellectual debate.

A third and vital ingredient for the local church, which owes much for example, to the liberation theology of South America, the pioneering work of Alan Ecclestone in Sheffield, and the Urban Theology Unit, is the collaborative reflection of a eucharistic community. Priest and people, together with representatives of neighbouring churches, local community agencies and Christians from other places may discover through prayer, meditation, praise, Bible reading, discussion and silence, a new sense of vocation for themselves in the local context. The purpose of everyone doing reflective theology together is so that it will become clear that the Christian faith has the potential to give a vision to a community to work without certainty of success for unity and hope for all. This style of theological reflection raises most clearly the issues of an eschatological-trinitarian ecclesiology. Therefore, it calls for a courageous and adventurous personality, and a secure and widely read ordained minister, to release for the local church this style of group thinking, resolution and action. This seems not to be acknowledged by many zealous pioneers of parish ministry. There is a danger of offering an expectation of ordained ministry which is simply unachievable for the average priest. To do so would be to produce a recipe for a new clericalism with its attendant dependency. The need has already been referred to for presidency not to be understood as a lonely, managerial task in which everyone else slots into place.

In fact, the Church often recognizes that through the Spirit, a deepening Christian maturity simultaneously grows alongside a co-responsibility for ministry. The experience of missioners and lay training advisers certainly indicates that church members who are invited to share in collaborative ministry begin to make demands to be nourished by learning the processes of theological reflection and a deeper life of prayer. Mistakes will be made as well as right judgement exercised, so that upheld by grace, but with no ultimate protection of indefectibility, clergy and people together move forward in the complexity of certainty and doubt.

The question of how far the priest should expect to promote his own ideas and how far to listen to local viewpoints in matters of parish strategy is related to his own developing spiritual maturity and theological vision. The corporate decisions and mission-focused agenda of a eucharistic community should be made out of the reflection and prayer of a community that is prepared to give sufficient time to arriving at a consensus, so that neither the priest nor some anarchic lobby within the local church seeks to introduce a dominating authority by which to impose their views. The emphasis on the priest building up the confidence of the church to take responsibility—which will be stressed later—impinges considerably here also. At the institutional level, dioceses and patrons, when making appointments, have a responsibility to keep faith with local church members so that the confidence to reflect theologically which they have begun, slowly and painfully to learn with one priest, is not demolished on principle or through ignorance by her successor.

(c) A Developing and Growing Spirituality

We earlier concluded that the Church ministers in the world through being, by the Spirit, in communion with Christ and the Trinity. Although every act of worship may not be a celebration of the Eucharist, there is at the heart of the Church a life which is best characterized as eucharistic. Zizioulas writes:

> The Church must be conceived as the place where man can get a taste of his eternal eschatological destiny which is communion in God's very life. If we accept the Eucharist as the sacrament intended to offer this taste, then we must recognize it in it, or otherwise adjust it to the requirements of the Trinitarian way of existence.[43]

Instead of the Church having a programme for bringing close the Kingdom of God, in Christ, it claims to know in its deepest layers of intimacy as well as institution, the loving relationship that constitutes the Trinity. A church that lives thankfully in communion with Christ, the true foretaste of the Kingdom, continually through baptism and Eucharist remembers and praises God for the story of salvation, particularly as stated in the incarnational career of Jesus. At the same time, imperfectly, but already in the existential presence of Christ through the Spirit, the eucharistic community knows, reveals, and acts out that peace which is God's final hope.

Essentially, the priest, as a baptized disciple, is a part of this being and activity of making Christ's presence known. His role is to set the conditions for all to engage in a spiritual journey. She cannot exercise a ministry of presiding, preaching, baptizing, pronouncing absolution and blessing, unless she is herself committed to the life of discipleship rooted in praise, penitence, communion, and service. In practice, one of the chief functions of the priest is to spend a large proportion of energy on preparing (alone and with others) acts of public worship, both for committed Christians and the wider public. Through giving time and concentration to being open to the Spirit, after the example of Jesus Christ, he will need to be continually discovering resources that prevent him from becoming merely a taker of services.[44] Further, her observable commitment to matters of faith in no way reduces or absorbs the responsibility of others. Rather, there should be seen in him the offering of a type or paradigm of how all Christians can give themselves to a communion with God in worship. Here is an example of what the Advisory Board of Ministry describes as a ministry of focusing and distributing.

The eucharistic community, foreshadowing the final unity of all things in Christ, has a responsibility to eradicate from its internal relationships wilful disunity, and also to collaborate with others for the healing of divisions within the neighbourhood, institutions and nation. As a celebration of Christ's own uniting presence, the Church requires an ordained ministry that models interdependence and mutuality with the laity and between all the ordained. Needless to say many who attend churches seem to have little desire to 'become' the church but are seeking a dependent relationship with a professional figure. Clergy often experience defensiveness and embarassment when they attempt to promote a vision of interdependence and translate the insight into action. Also part of the process may well be the lack of confidence or sense of isolation of the clergy who then find a theology to justify their desire for mutuality. The appropriate balance of intimacy and remoteness between clergy and laity is complex and necessarily flexible. It will be discovered from both sides in situations both formal and informal, in liturgy, meetings, and conversations. There has to be sufficient separation for some objectivity in decision-taking but this should be grounded in an assumption that the priest is first and foremost one of the community. The priest may sometimes be led to confront others with the contribution they are making towards division within the church. Also, for the sake of the health of the gospel community, he must be able to hear from others their criticisms of himself. As a sign and a foretaste of that unity which is God's will, there is no place for a ministry that deliberately perpetuates the institutional divisions constituted by hierarchical domination or the debarring of individual persons from holding office on grounds of culture or gender.

An important element in the priest's contribution is to demonstrate how to tie the search for God with the joys and frustrations of the enterprise of living. At the personal level, the priest needs to know and accept himself as partly redeemed and partly still broken, as having human strengths and weaknesses, all of which will inevitably be the resource for his ministry. Deep seated insecurity among clergy, especially with relation to the feelings that accompany talk of new ministerial arrangements, inevitably hamper the mature development of a church. This is especially the case for the Church of England, which is structured so that the laity are permanently dominated and always under the control of the clergy. There are clergy who find a collaborative style of presidency extremely threatening, with the consequence that those laity who remain in the Church are often self-selecting as people who prefer a passive or dependent role.[45] The pastoral element within the whole of the Church's task must allow for the fact that at some stages in the human journey everyone needs a healthy dependency. What is at issue is the problem created when a local church remains permanently in a dependency role. Anxiety flows in both directions when a priest deliberately decides to adopt a ministerial style radically at variance with what has gone before. An integral part of the process of change should be frequent genuine opportunities for explanation, discussion and feedback.

In a time when the high rate of marriage break-down in society is increasingly present also in the Church of England, and when stress levels connected with work are high, priests need to find the confidence to decide for themselves and to advise others regarding what constitutes an appropriate commitment to public ministry. In order to be a personal embodiment of the link between the 'spiritual' and the 'practical' elements of human living, the priest needs to be in a position to attempt to model not only priesthood, but a marriage partner, parent, friend, and member of the local and world communities. Again it may be commented that this is to ask too much. One alternative is not to ask enough, or to put it another way, to ask for too much of what is inappropriate. A sizeable proportion of clergy becomes entrenched in a narrow field of vision and activity in which most other relations are abandoned 'for the sake of the church'. In those called to witness in the public office of president within the local church and wider community, some evidence of a new balance is required, towards participation in the untidy relations of family, community and society. Questions surrounding the priest's suitability to hold the position of president in a community must surely include her observable capacity to communicate and to negotiate, to assess and adjust her own performance, as well as to handle alcohol, anger, money, sexuality, and time. However, it needs to be said very forcefully that some of the most effective priests have been those whose idiosyncrasies and areas of brokenness have been clear for all to see. I have known this to be the case for example with a number of clergy who were often themselves depressed. They were particularly helpful to others in similar situations. I can think of incumbents who have monopolized all power, dominated all services, and expected others to listen to them for excessive periods of time, who have enriched the lives of others, and drawn many into God's Kingdom. Sadly, negative examples are easily brought to mind also.

The insights of modern concepts of personality types and basic insight into the pyschology of human relationships, would also appear valuable in the recognition and sometimes redirection of the dynamics of the local church. The rudiments of counselling methods can also prove a valuable tool for the priest's growing capacity for understanding both parishioners and himself. All these relatively new areas of knowledge feature to some extent in training courses before and after ordination, although clergy have great freedom in deciding on their value for ministry. There is certainly no need for all clergy to be qualified in every field of knowledge. There are at least two possible ways forward, both collaborative: one is to share the specialist gifts of particular clergy across a much wider geographical area than is now the custom. Assuming that most clergy could offer a specialist concern, a new sense of mutuality and shared team ministry can result. The second is to discover the wisdom of the laity (personally and in the wider community) and, in freedom persuade them to share it in the service of the Church's mission.

The conclusion was drawn above that in an eschatological-trinitarian church, in which ministry is exercized in a co-responsible manner, there are no positions of permanent subordination. The whole Church represents and is for the world the ministry of Christ. Therefore, being a layperson, whether or not with a particular role such as reader, or being deacon or priest, is never to be interpreted as being set apart from the community. The public worship of this community in its characteristic Sunday expression should offer a clear indication of that truth that in Christ there are no divisions. No one has power to delegate to others and no one is merely called 'to help' another, because there is only a Spirit-possessed community. There are no individuals who 'possess' spirit authority. The evidence points to the conclusion that the president of the church community (or one of his ordained colleagues), should normally be the eucharistic president. The priest as president of the local community is the natural one to preside when the Eucharist is celebrated, in that there has been given to her the ministry of ensuring that the eucharistic community remains true to its apostolic calling. Since this is classically defined as a eucharistic community, and since it has been established that there is no status or privilege properly implied, it would seem the most natural thing for those chosen, and ordained, to preside at the eucharistic celebration.

There should be many voices and gestures other than his involved at the liturgical celebration. Indeed, it could be argued that precisely to choose a different person to preside at the Eucharist, or to leave it to chance, would be to overstate the significance of presiding. Presiding in itself is nothing (though it may give great pleasure to the individual). Priest and church community should ensure that many other opportunities exist for different people with different gifts to come to the fore in leadership roles for appropriate occasions in the church's life and work. It is a corollary that any community which is normally focused in its ministry by a local layperson (or persons) should not be left in the position of importing a priest from elsewhere for the celebration of the Eucharist. In such cases the bishop, with the people's consent and advice, should ordain as eucharistic president such persons as are focusing and distributing the ministry of the local church.[46] There is room for much reinterpretation and redeployment within most churches' ministerial lives at the present time.

A eucharistic community is nurtured by growing into communion with the triune life. It is called to demonstrate to the world the shape of that unity and peace described by Jesus in his words and works of the Kingdom. A priest who presides plausibly within such a church community will be someone who gives time to prayer in many forms and who attempts to conform his inner and personal relationships to the law of Christ. Even here, however she is not merely alone. Growth and wholeness can be found in the honest sharing of pilgrimage with other members of the community. As a matter of course the priest should be encouraged and enabled by the local church and the diocese to regard a continuing programme of education and training as a vital ingredient, and not an addition to time given to ministry. In honesty and acceptance, each ministry is responsible for recognizing and fostering the potential humanity and godliness of the other.

(ii) Blessing

At the heart of the relationship with God is openness to hearing good things spoken of ourselves. The church's eucharistic celebration lies at the centre of the local community receiving in word and sacrament the highest divine affirmation. From the many ways in which churches receive the blessing of God, comes the responsive 'amen', by which they accept the task of collaborating in his work; renewing the goodness of persons and the whole of creation; beginning now and being completed at the end of all things. The profoundest evidence of a church rooted in such holiness is the presence at its Sunday Eucharist of the widest cross-section of different people, including those often marginalized or regarded as difficult. It is telling that congregations so often find it a struggle to cross cultural boundaries in worship or genuinely to include a variety of age groups or those with a mental handicap.

Although this book does not include a developed doctrine of the Eucharist, it has assumed that the highest and deepest aspirations of the doctrine of the Church developed here find their normative roots in the celebration of the eucharistic community. In the discussion of the holiness of the local church, it was emphasized in particular how blessedness results from communion with the triune God, makes no distinction between sacred and secular or between ordained and lay, and is nourished by God's action in Christ through the Spirit in the past, the present and the future. Recent biblical research helps to rescue blessing from being thought of as a priestly, sacral act. Blessing should also be recognized as a point of focusing and distributing engagement with God in the infinite ways in which he encourages the furthering of his final purposes. This, notably, is the meaning of the blessing at the close of an act of worship.

At his or her ordination, which is itself a rite of blessing, the priest has been set aside by God and the Church to lead the transforming work of the Church in the context of God's desire for Creation. Specifically, as parish priest in a given community, he or she is one who focuses and distributes blessing, whether of the triune God by the whole church, or of the church by God. The concept of blessing God should not be understood in terms of the Church conferring on God a quality he did not have already. Rather it is an acknowledgement and returning of thanks to God as the source of all blessedness.

God's blessing is not an individual possession; it is not even the prerogative of the Church, but has the function of being a sign and a foretaste of the quality of all redeemed relatedness.[47] The priest, in pronouncing God's blessing, is focusing and distributing the task of the entire Church in recognizing, naming, embodying, and encouraging co-operation with and dependence on the active, saving presence of the triune God.

The parish priest has a particular role in enabling the liturgical performance of sacramental acts that are blessings. Through the Spirit, and within the body of the local church, they make real what they intend: baptism, Eucharist, or reconciliation. In the eucharistic assembly and in worship, preaching, prayer and study generally, the triune God is blessed. There are also para-sacramental blessings, such as might be given to children by their parents, or mutually between spouses, partners, or friends; there are many healing and intercession ministries; and there are pastoral, evangelical and serving ministries which for the eucharistic community are known as blessings from God. Mutual blessings come between God and his people when there is work undertaken for wholeness in the created order. All blessings now are a promise of that final state of blessedness when all things come together in Christ to be given, through the Spirit, into the hands of the Father.

The Jewish origins of the idea of blessing discourage the belief that it is the preserve of an élite. The Christian priest should not be regarded as having a monopoly on pronouncing blessings, as some mistaken theology may once have suggested. In contemporary liturgy, the point is clear that the president offers a ministry that speaks of the local church as a community of hospitality, engagement and involvement. However, within the church as president, he has a particular role of blessing liturgically that is a mirror of his more general role of blessing. This is about encouraging (or inversely, discouraging), or as it were 'giving permission' (or not), to a step forward in mission or ministry. This concept of the priest's role as blessing and encouraging the community in its apostolic tasks is intended also to reduce the expectation of his own insight or skills. She is merely the one who blesses; this is not to encourage the collusion that the ordained are expected to be the church's primary resource. A discerning presiding priest, unburdened by the suggestion that she is personally responsible for all that happens in the local church, need have no fear of her shortcomings, provided she has the humility and courage to let others take initiatives. It is so vital that the priest takes delight in drawing out the understanding, the skills, the commitment and the hope of every church member. The ministry of blessing is about praising, encouraging, and expecting the growth in ministry of the whole of the body of the church.

Further, the everyday ministry of laity at work and in the community goes largely unsupported. The local church, in order to be a sign and foretaste of God's hope, needs to hold a number of aspects in creative tension. In its visible eucharistic, gathered life it allows its members to grow into Christ through the Spirit as conspicuous examples of those who are taking steps to find liberation from patterns of distortion. In relation to the world, the Church, through the scattering of its members, often secretly and anonymously, should engage with contemporary events as agents of God's *shalom*. In order to be able to fulfil this vocation with awareness, the scattered church members need an ordained ministry that recognizes the value of their task and actively promotes an internal church life that sustains them as agents of the world's potential in God's name. Every effort should be made to assist church members, at differing levels of liturgical commitment, to reflect together and alone on their daily responsibilities in the light of the communion with the Trinity to which they are invited. The Church should offer structures that enable the laity to share with others the problems and achievements of their working or community life. The focus of such dialogue should be the question, 'If this is God's vision for the present and the future of his universe, what contribution can I make given my circumstances and gifts?' A similar process should be taking place regarding the role of the local church in the community and the institutional church in a global society. The presiding non-stipendiary priest should have a particularly strong contribution to make in this area. A stipendiary priest may be wise to encourage others to lead in this aspect of the community's life.

So, while rejoicing at the strides forward made possible by the new ecumenical ecclesiologies that take *koinonia* seriously, I am urging here a speedy acceptance of an ecclesiology based upon trinitarian relations and the future fulfilment of God's plan for creation. It will enable the Church to move beyond the uneasy dualism that presently exists between the commitment to a sharing in the ministry of Christ of every church member, and the received understanding of the separateness of the ordained minister. Such a dualism exists, despite the innovative ecclesiology of Küng, Suenens, Ramsey, and many more recent works on clergy and laity in collaboration. Schillebeeckx most poignantly holds the tension between a concept of an authoritarian separate ministry and a concept of the whole Church as priestly and apostolic, wanting to deny a dualism between clerical and lay ministries, but even he is confessionally restricted by the limits of the documents of Vatican II, the pronouncements of subsequent popes, and the Synod of Bishops on the ministerial priesthood, *Ultimus temporibus* (1967). The latter declared the 'priestly ministry' to be 'distinct from the common priesthood of all the faithful', 'in essence and not merely in degree'. Cardinal Hume insists that laity, especially since Vatican II, are not seen as second class citizens of the Church, yet this is the direct implication of official Catholic teaching regarding the hierarchy to which he inevitably also refers.

The conclusion has been reached that apostolic succession should not be understood objectively as a power handed on either between individuals or even between communities that delegate to individuals. Further, it has been established that there is no ministry at all that can plausibily be understood out of the context of the Christian community. Priests represent to the local church only what is true for the entire community, namely, that they are together as one body, the presence of Christ, and as such share fully in communion with the life of the triune God.

If we listen to discussions at synods and conferences, one conclusion could be that the Church of England has no problem with collaborative ministry or redefining priesthood. Another, and one which seems more realistic, is that during a long period of transition from one paradigm of church to another, at the levels of thought, practice, and feelings, there are many difficulties. What would be a possible step for the Church of England towards grasping the truth that the whole Church, through its equal but differentiated ministries, in a relation of communion that echoes the trinitarian perichoresis, shares the apostolic ministry and mission? A strategy will be required that removes the clergy from the supposed position of standing over against the laity, however gently, in an attitude of superiority of faith, knowledge, wisdom or love.[48] It means denying that clergy alone are called to provide all inspiration, motivation, and direction. The priest is charged to give time so that all members of a local church may be reminded through liturgy, preaching, teaching and the courtesy of the common life that they are equally members of Christ and called to the apostolic life. In this way the priest assists at the birth of the common priesthood of all the baptized. He misuses his opportunity and may appropriately be accused of clericalism when he lacks the discernment to choose how to spend time wisely. If she needlessly engages in the ministry that others could be fulfilling, she is robbing them of their priesthood.

A presiding ministry consists largely in encouraging others to see what they are called to and have the gifts for, and then sustaining them as they grow into their ministries. Equally, a way is needed for denying the received truth that clergy have the sole, personal responsibility to keep order and to prevent the laity from making errors in doctrine and practice. A significant answer to this question, which flows out of a trinitarian eschatology, is to conclude that within the whole priestly Church of Christ, the ordained minister, perpetually in a relationship of mutuality, presides by exercising a ministry of blessing. Dioceses are aware of parishes where the priest is able to offer little more than the leading of a basic minimum of services. Perhaps this limitation is linked with choosing to remain isolated, with ill health, a broken personal relationship, or by an unwillingness to live with given realities. In the new context of financial stringency and expectations that clergy will lead local churches in mission, it is not surprising to hear voices of complaint among the laity more stridently than in years gone by. In such circumstances, however, I have observed that, willing or not, the priest often learns graciously to bless the ministry of the whole local church as it comes to birth around and almost in spite of his own lack of insight.

In the first place, a local church should together plan to focus its share in Christ's ministry by prayer and discussion so aiming through the distribution of tasks to discover a way of implementing its agenda for life and mission that accepts the talents and ministries of all its members. The parish priest needs to be one who has such a vision and can be instrumental in facilitating this process. A particularly significant opportunity for developing such a ministry is presented in strategies for developing local ministry teams. Clergy (stipendiary and non-stipendiary), readers and laity, chosen and commissioned, act as a corporate focus and distributor of ministries. The element of blessing comes through in that the priest makes room for the scheme in the first place by abdicating his solo ministry role. This is by no means a foregone conclusion. At a synodical on the subject, one priest met with approving applause when he suggested that local ministry may be ideal in theory but 'whether it works in practice will remain to be seen'. Another priest threatened that if ever he became vicar of a parish with a local ministry scheme he would close it down within weeks. Such illustrations are a salutary reminder that new theories for ministerial arrangements do not everywhere meet with understanding or approval.

Second, the priest blesses the process for selection of suitable lay pastors, evangelists or teachers, and thirdly, he or the bishop will bless the team. Hopefully, they will also bless her and it will not be taken for granted that she will chair all meetings, lead all worship, or offer all teaching, merely on account of her position as ordained minister. Reflection on the various diocesan schemes for local ministry shows the need for great flexibility and mutuality. One of the dioceses, for example, who were early in this field, now recognize that, rather than imposing a single model on every parish, the diocese should show commitment to a vision and invite many local variations with the overall checks and balances of diocesan life. Another diocese created a scheme of enormous complexity, but with only one permitted way of operating for local churches. Not surprisingly, the most recently devised schemes are attempting to learn from such experience. Given the restrictions imposed by the lack of finance and personnel to encourage and educate local ministry teams, it will be difficult for a right balance to be established between diocesan and national guidelines and local need and initiative. Given freedom and a high expectation of growing in maturity, there is every reason to expect local Anglican ministry teams (eventually with ecumenical co-operation) to demonstrate both a steadfast commitment and a high degree of competence. Working in freedom, contingency, and trust will produce profound results but not without the problems that arise whenever a group of human beings begin to work together in unfamiliar ways.

It is the parish priest's function both to remind the community of their apostolic responsibilities and to be a focus of blessing for initiatives and ministries. The phrase 'management of change' occurs frequently now in invitations to clergy training courses. Part of the ministry of blessing requires the priest to perceive with the church community a distinction between specific strategies, and a governing framework or imaginative idea that guides the choice of such strategies. The priest should not be expected, simply because of his ordination, to exercise this function alone, but rather to ensure that in appropriate ways, it does take place. Where a church is moribund or far from considering these matters, the ordained priest, without intending to build up a sense of guilt, may have to give time and loving energy to showing the people as best he may, the acceptance, delight, and longing that God has already invested in them. Their response will hopefully arise from becoming aware of their destiny and resources in a new way. He may also be able to bear with the people when they make a new beginning and yet seem to be making little progress. Although her own depth of prayer and dependence on the strength of the crucified Christ will then be tested, her ministry is never separate and therefore, there will be a mutual expectation of the discernment of the entire community. As has been suggested already, there will often be times when it is the priest who needs to receive loving encouragement from others, both those loyal to and those far from the worshipping community. In humility, the president will need to recognize the wisdom and resources of others.

Sheer practicality demands that all Christians cannot be clergy and certainly the Church as institution needs to be rigorously selective concerning those whom it entrusts with the task. It is vital, however, as has already been stressed, to make the concept of presiding sufficiently flexible to be accessible to a wide range of ordination candidates, whilst out of respect for both candidates and Church, exercise a rigorous process of selection.

In the matter of presiding at the celebration of the Eucharist, the author is confident that for the Church of England in the forseeable future this will be a role reserved to the clergy. There are those who contrast this orderly view of presiding with the freshness and spontaneity of basic Christian communities. The variety of types of membership, finely balanced within most Church of England congregations, may be particularly well placed to hold together presidency by the priest and a degree of variation in the liturgy as a whole. The gathered community of kindred spirits, such as described by Amrein in Switzerland, can more easily keep order when the presence of clergy 'does not mean that they always preside'. Those Anglican churches that do press for lay presidency tend to reflect the gathered church model.[49] Eucharistic presidency is not merely gathering people in a building and leading an act of worship. The one who is recognized as focusing the ministry of all the baptized, in so many areas, who holds such confidences, and is privileged to be with people in times of joy and tragedy, is the one who should preside at the liturgy. This is because the eucharistic event itself classically sums up the threads of Catholic Christian significance and makes Christ present for the Church and the world. The same principle extends to other priests working together as a team within a local church, even though one of them will act as the central focus of all their ministries. However, there are immense dangers for a priest and the community if such celebration becomes merely mechanical. His way of presiding should aim to be simultaneously confident and self-effacing in the spirit of Paul's own ministry:

> I came to you, without any pretensions to eloquence or wisdom in declaring the truth about God. I resolved that while I was with you I would not claim to know anything but Jesus Christ—Christ nailed to the cross. I came before you in weakness, in fear, in great trepidation . . . so that your faith might be built not on human wisdom but on the power of God (1 Cor 2. 1–5).

Finally, by way of summary, the ministry of blessing requires the parish priest to recognize her primary task, not as being personally on the frontline of mission but, more humbly assisting others to recognize their own ministries and then to be available as a resource, challenge, and support.

(iii) Witnessing

When it comes to witnessing, the Church fails. She is called by God to witness to what she knows. That is an essential part of her task. Yet, it is precisely in the act of witnessing that the Church vulnerably declares to the world how little of God she has really absorbed. Yet, fortunately through God's graciousness, all is not lost.

As president, the parish priest is called to witness generally in two ways. First, the local church has given him the time, experience and privilege of relating to the wider Church (ecumenically) the insight and needs of the local church. This also works the other way round. Partly because of his itinerant ministry and partly because he reads books, attends conferences and synods, he is able to bring back to the local church catholic insights from the wider Church for reflection and perhaps action. She relates personally, though not without the lay representatives, to the diocese, bishop and the world wide Church.

Second, the priest is required personally to be the representative of all the other members of the local church within which he presides to the wider community. So at baptisms, weddings and funerals, although he shares much of the ministry with others, he in particular is expected to be the interface with the public. He is expected to have given time and effort to pondering issues of life and death and general concern, in dialogue with the gospel tradition of the church, and the local context. From this wisdom he can communicate with others for their strengthening or towards common plans for the neighbourhood and all human conditions in the world. In showing solidarity with urgent movement towards sociality she does not take the place of the other members of the local church but speaks in this regard from a privileged position of awareness and experience. On the surface this may appear very similar to the old expectation of the 'parson', and at one level it is. However, at a profound level it is very different because the priest of today should be aware of entering a radically different relationship with the whole of the local church and this awareness will communicate itself in new ways. It is her unique responsibility to

witness to the fact that no minister, indeed no person or
community, can recognize their true significance except
through a commitment to the search for redeemed
relationships.

The priest in the wider community beyond the church's
eucharistic gathering has great evangelistic opportunities,
but this does not discount the disparate ministries of the
whole local church. His special opportunity is to articulate
and face people with that which they may know only uncon-
sciously. This ministry concerns the network of relationships
in families, communities and indeed throughout creation.
Her task is to speak and act prophetically in order to assist
others to reflect on, come to know, and consummate a
higher quality of relatedness. He knows from his special
study and reflection on the Scriptures and of theology related
to human experience something about communal joy, celebration and grief. She can hold and say for the community what
no one else can because of the godly wisdom being focused
in her by the Spirit. Yet because his ministry can never be
separated from that of the church all will recognize that no
one will have a monopoly on wisdom and therefore on
decision-making. This ministry will also be limited by the
extent to which the priest is devoted to the gospel and
opens himself in honesty and self-giving to both God and
humanity.

Given the complex networks between a communal local
church and its context, it is important not to draw unnecessary boundary lines in the priest's work. Indeed her involvement with some people may well make nonsense of all
boundaries so that the central focus of Christ in the Eucharist
is the only point of stability. Priestly witness will certainly
meet some of that rejection of which St John spoke of as the
world's hatred (John 15.18), and just as Christ's own crucifixion is portrayed in the eucharistic offering, breaking and
sharing, ministerial witness to the gospel today is a hymn of
praise to the trinitarian God.

It would be unwise to attempt here to draw up a complete
set of guidelines for parish ministry. The aim has been
to offer a hint of the wisdom that derives from an eschatological-trinitarian ecclesiology which would assist a priest

and local church together to begin to ask questions about their corporate ministry in Christ, through the Spirit, in their own particular and constantly evolving context. The church that embraces this kind of ecclesiology, echoing the being of the triune God, accepts a demanding but unique vocation. Sharing in God's mission, its task is to offer a fragmentary and partial sign and foretaste of the final destiny of all created life, personal and impersonal. God invites his Church to participate in creating a redeemed world of freely differentiated persons in relation. The priest in her own person and relationships is called particularly to be a sign and first-fruit of that vocation which in the Spirit, the Father offers to all who call on his Son in faith and hope.

CONCLUSION

The urgent question for the Church of England which has been the subject of this theological enquiry was 'What is now required of a parish priest?' As I have shown, there is powerful commitment at many levels in contemporary English Anglican life to increased co-operation between clergy and laity in ministry. The particular contribution of this enquiry has been first, in the context of a transitional period in the Church of England, involving many experiments and strategies for making shared ministry a reality, to offer a rationale for the presence and work of the parish priest. Second, I have demonstrated that ordained priesthood can only satisfactorily be defined in the overall context of an ecclesiology. The potential for such an English Anglican doctrine of the Church, rooted in a trinitarian understanding of God, is to recognize that diversity is a fruitful resource rather than a problem. A church that adopts an eschato-logical-trinitarian ecclesiology may understand itself as echoing, albeit faintly, God's own being and so be available for the salvation of the whole creation.

In order to reach the point where the central question could be addressed, I have worked through logically prior questions regarding the concepts for understanding Godself in relation with creation, God's final hopes for all creation, the Church's invitation to be an agent of God's project, and the quality of internal relationships within the Church. Only then has it been possible to make a statement about the particular role of the ordained priest in the local church.

One of the basic premises of the book has been that the present situation in the Church of England should be re-garded as one of transition from a set of criteria for church and ministry increasingly acknowledged as implausible, to another set rooted in an eschatological-trinitarian ecclesiol-

ogy. This is not to deny that some of the characteristics of
the received tradition will be discovered and welcomed in
the new paradigm. I have acknowledged that such a leap of
faith and understanding will require two elements to be
worked on in parallel, both locally and institutionally. From
the outset I recognized three pressures which simultaneously
are bringing to birth a new way of being church: a financial
crisis, the continuing reduction in the numbers of deployable
clergy, and a renewed theological understanding of baptism
and the relationship between laity and clergy in mission
and ministry. To the extent that this complex of factors is
shared by churches other than the Church of England, my
hope is that some of the vision spelled out in this enquiry will
be of value ecumenically. So in conclusion I make five
points.

First, the Church of England must find the security finally
to distance itself from the polemical agenda set by early
twentieth-century Catholic Anglicanism. In daring to work
towards a commitment to an ecclesiology appropriate to the
contemporary theological and social context, not without
controversy and dialogue, English Anglicans should celebrate
the particular insights they receive from and bring to the
ecumenical international Church. A theology rooted in a
triune God who links the Good News of the person and story
of Jesus with the God whose creation in every sense and at
every level, is personal and freely relational in intent. My
argument has been that the Church can be instrumental in
calling intelligent creation to respond to God's invitation to
be filled with his own relational life and to work with God
towards the drawing together of all things in a kaleidoscopic
unity of difference. It is commonplace to scorn and disown
the Church of England for its slow and complex delibera-
tions, emphasis on the pastoral rather than on the prophetic
and disciplinary, and for attempting to function across a
wide spectrum of cultures, beliefs, and activities. As an
institutional manifestation of part of the Catholic Church,
the Church of England, with all its faults and anomalies,
especially in its ambivalent links with the structures of society,
is well placed to bring hope to a complex world created by
the triune God. We should, therefore, be glad to celebrate an

attitude and ecclesial framework which, though often problematic, is well suited not so much to defending faith as to exploring and knowing salvation within the dynamic and interrelated differentiation which is the hallmark of creation.

Second, both locally and within the Church institutionally, especially in the selection and training of ordinands, care must be taken gradually but determinedly to work towards new images and practices. In particular I advocate an understanding of priestly ministry in terms of sharing the task of overseeing with the bishop as one who presides through discernment, blessing and witnessing. It is my hope that this framework, widely interpreted in differing situations, will provide an interpretive tool for working out more clearly in a collaborative church what is the confident and specific purpose of the parish priest, recognizing that each one will also have particular personal gifts to offer to the community. Then, as increasing collaboration between clergy, readers, and laity develops a redefined understanding of all ministry, a new generation of presiding ministry will be raised up which will significantly redefine the role of the parish priest.

An example of how this can be achieved relates to the selection and training of candidates for ordination. In this connection everyone needs to realize the context of priesthood in the Church of England today and the call to a collaborative ministry. Selectors, educators and assessors need to be assured of the potential of ordination candidates in group work and relationship skills. It is encouraging to see that *Integration and Assessment*, the 1991 Report of an ABM Working Party on Educational Practice, makes perceptive demands on those being trained for ordination. In particular, skills in communication, self-expression, listening, empathy, leadership, group co-ordination, initiative-taking, encouragement, and management are highlighted. It could be argued that this is to expect too much of the average clergyperson. In response, the conclusion must be pressed that the Church today requires priests deliberately to adopt a new role. Given the voluntary nature of the Church, the priest's authority requires that he understands and knows how to promote a spirit of reciprocity with the laity about the work of the local church and the framework of expectation in which both can work in mutuality. This is consistent with and draws out further implications of *ACCM Paper 22* which expects ordinands to be prepared to work in a collaborative manner, to achieve appropriate networks of communication, and be personally capable of building up interrelations. The chief test, however, will be whether the Church of England, through its bishops, synods, selectors, colleges, and courses takes seriously the need and the opportunity provided by the contemporary debate and critical circumstances.

A second example of how this study could be implemented is in a review of the principles that inform the methods of training ordinands. In particular it should be borne in mind that the form and content of ordination training is probably the most significant factor in the formation of the Church's life. Apart from commending the explicit consideration of the doctrine of the Trinity as the key to theological enquiry, it is the author's hope that the theological implications of this for understanding the mission of the Church, its worship, its ministry, its ecumenical relations and its relationship with society would be a high priority for ordinands in training. Further, it follows that theology should be studied in dialogue (rather than in parallel) with other disciplines, and that the implications for understanding freedom, personhood, society, and reality in terms of relationships should be urgently explored. The extent to which education for ordained ministry has built into it the spirit and method of dialogue and collaboration will be highly influential in role-modelling to the student the desired pattern of church and ministry. The process of education for ministry, apart from being collaborative and dialogical in vision and method, needs to be promoted as continuous, self-motivating and rooted in a trinitarian ontology.

First, this means that signals are given from the start that college and course work is only the beginning of a life of study, reflection and prayer. In a two or three year course, students can be introduced to goals which ministers will hopefully be motivated to pursue throughout their lives. This process will again be seen partly as the necessary work to equip priests more effectively for tasks which are unique to their calling, and partly as focusing the constant development and questioning which is the work of the entire Church. Second, rather than being offered in a spirit of compulsion or of necessity such education of ordinands and working clergy needs to be offered persuasively in order to encourage self-motivation in this area. The reason for clergy to pursue continuing ministerial education is so that they may be best able to serve the mission of the Church in a particular place and time. Third, a check needs to be made on the increasing tendency for college and course training to be extremely pressurized. A model of integration is required between working for deadlines and having leisure to read widely, between attempting to cover many subjects briefly and finding opportunity to be drawn into a given area in some detail, between the conflicting pressures of family, college life, academic work, placement, seeking an appointment, and time for a vision and practice of spirituality. A trinitarian ontology implies that clergy will be people, who for the sake of the health of the church, themselves model a tension between putting down deep roots of identity, through study, prayer and self-knowledge, and relating to God, their colleagues, family, and the wider Church and world. In a co-responsible Church, in which *koinonia* is recognized as communion with God, community, and communication with many diverse people, there is no room for presiding clergy who are, already by their training conditioned to be stressed, to work in isolation because of strictures of time, or to have no desire or space to focus their ministry on knowing God.

My third main concluding point is to note the urgent need for revising the Ordination Service. It is part of the perennial question of how simultaneously to give value to all orders in the Church. To avoid an unnecessary limitation on the development of ideas in this book, I have deliberately avoided a close link with the text of the Ordinal, either in the Book of Common Prayer or The Alternative Service Book. However, it is vital that those charged with revising the ASB for the year 2000 should critically examine both the text and performance of the Ordination Service with regard to priests.

At the moment when certain persons are being solemnly placed in a new relationship to God, Church, family, and society by ordination, it would be churlish to suggest that they do not need great encouragement and an atmosphere of celebration. Much sacrifice, hard work, forethought and courage has led up to this day. A social trinitarianism would nevertheless look for such a great occasion to express in its liturgical shape as well as in specific phrases the sense of a collaborative church within which many differing ministries interrelate and mutually support each other in their specific responsibilities. Although it is the particular task of those who share in the task of overseeing to focus the church's vocation, it is the entire church membership, corporately and personally that shares in God's mission and for holding the meanings and values of that calling. Briefly, I shall outline a few of the many revisions to the Ordinal which may be considered both desirable and possible in order to allow the service to present this truth more clearly.

These include sometimes ordaining priests in the parish church or part of the diocese where they already are ministers, arranging for lay representatives to present candidates to the bishop, involving a small group of laity and clergy in the laying on of hands with the bishop, enabling children and others in the wider community to present the Bible and stole, considering the place of the priest's marriage partner, and to increase the dialogical voice of the congregation in the liturgy.

There is also the question of how to spell out liturgically the relationship between the ordaining bishop and the priest with a ministry to preside in the local church. If at the ordination the bishop concentrates on doing only that which is essentially his public ministry, this could leave many openings for liturgical reformers to give lines, prayers and actions to others. How often does he need to put on the mitre? Does he need to be involved with the administration of communion? Here the newly ordained and local clergy and laity can have a key role. At the close of the service, the new priest, rather than the bishop, should take pride of place. In such simple ways, a renewed theology of ministry could be not only acted out but learned and developed by all.

The text of the Ordinal must be completely overhauled

both to articulate a new model of priesthood and specifically at this time in the light of women's ordination. Individual dioceses will work on this as part of the process of preparing for the first women's ordinations. The various suggested modifications, especially after reflection on their use, will provide strong material for revisers to consider for the future. Certainly the ordination of women provides an immense opportunity for bishops, directors of ordinands, and liturgical committees to engage in radical rethinking.

Fourth, I have come to recognize that a fundamentally eschatological approach to ecclesiology is of vital significance. This work has, therefore, been able to outflank many previous considerations of priesthood by being released from a purely historically informed theological approach. Instead of merely recapitulating supposed New Testament and early Church practices and transposing them into the present, I have approached apostolicity in three ways. There has been no denial of the importance of all church practice finding resonances with the character and content of the ministry of Jesus and the first apostles, together with those of the earliest generations of Christians. However, taking the view that every generation is equally close to Christ, loved by the Father and inspired by the Spirit, I have attempted to discover a theology of church and ministry that is also immediate, in that it responds to the present critical moment in English Anglicanism. It is contextualized.

Lastly, I have recognized the significance for ecclesiology of God's final vision of the coming together of all people and all creation in a differentiated reconciled unity. Every local Catholic and apostolic church is best described as a missionary society. Those who by baptism, confirmation, and regular participation in Eucharist and the life of the Christian community define themselves as God's People, have equal though differing parts to play in the internal and external mission of God. Such a church that wants in the present and in that particular context, to be a sign and foretaste of the triune God's *shalom* will model itself not just in the light of past and venerable tradition, not just on the urgent needs of the present place and moment, but also with a view to making real, even to the tiniest extent, something of the dominical prayer 'your Kingdom come on earth as in heaven'. To the extent that a local church is making a contribution to God's final passionate hope, there will be signs of true apostolicity and a fruitful understanding of all ministries and specifically that of the ordained priest.

In offering this vision to the Church, which at various times I both love and mistrust, it is not my intention to create burdens impossible to bear. There might be a danger that even on our best days few of us could aspire to the presiding ministry I have portrayed. My hope is that always recalling that we live by grace, in the churches we can learn to be gentler with one another, less exacting in our mutual demands of time and omnicompetence. Our faith is rooted in God whose Son's victory lay in lonely execution as a condemned criminal; it is a continual invitation to be redirected and rebirthed through the Spirit leading us into deeper communion with the God who is a vulnerable community of self-emptying love.

The renewal of the understanding of mission and ministry in the light of a trinitarian God will profoundly influence the development of the Church's internal ministerial relationships, worship, evangelism, service of the neighbourhood, and the encouragement and critique of society. There are no easy answers to the deepest questions with which humanity is presently confronted. One of the greatest resources for the world lies in the continuing pursuit of the Christian understanding of what it means to be created, redeemed, and longed for by a God who is three Persons in one. Avoiding all false triumphalism, it is no exaggeration to claim that the Anglican Communion now has a particularly exciting contribution to make to this development. This is because of its inherited wisdom, present experience, and comprehensive theological resourcefulness. To be called to the Anglican priesthood today, is to become part of the leading edge of this theological and pragmatic exploration of communion with the trinitarian God. The confident attention to this ministry of discerning, blessing, and witnessing, will be a vitally-creative element in the proclaiming of Good News at the beginning of the third millennium.

NOTES

Chapter One

1. Until its influence faded with World War I, the Idealist school of philosophy represented by Green, Caird, Bradley and Bosanquet, showed sympathy towards an unhistorical form of Christianity. cf. Macquarrie, 1988, pp. 23ff; Card, 1988, p. 36; and Wilkinson 1992, pp. 5ff. The need for the creation of specific colleges at Oxford and Cambridge, for those who were preparing for ordination provides further evidence of the growing divide between church and society. cf. Towler and Coxon, 1979, p. 19.
2. cf. Lloyd, 1966, p. 90 and Hastings, 1986, p. 231.
3. Newman and others had abandoned the Church of England in the belief that it was inescapably dominated by the State. For those who accepted Prayer Book Catholicism this struggle for the freedom of the Church remained an underlying issue throughout the period. cf. Cornwell, 1983 and Hastings, 1986.
4. Advice given to urban clergy by the Bishop of Truro at the close of the nineteenth century gives a glimpse of this missionary vision of the Church from a position of separateness and strength. He urges them to become, 'the living, lifegiving, soul of our great towns. It will develop a new phase of manifold life, some new spiritual colour and form will bear witness to new divine energy, some prophecy will be fulfilled, some Christian grace will illumine the world, which at present we know not, or now very slightly.' Gott, 1895, p. 8.
5. The decline in the number of active clergy between 1851 and 1976 took this shape: 1851 (16,194); 1901 (23,670); 1921 (22,579); 1951 (18,196); 1961 (13,660); 1966 (13,724); 1971 (13,182); 1976 (12,156). cf. Towler and Coxon, 1979, pp. 28ff. Davies, Watkins and Winter, however make the telling point that, despite the decline in numbers throughout this century, in rural areas at least, clergy are still in the 1990s statistically likely to be more available to people in need than social

workers, solicitors or the Citizens' Advice Bureau (1991, pp. 2ff.).

6. Towler and Coxon, 1979, pp. 9 and 24.
7. Russell, 1980, p. 262.
8. cf. Gore, 1900.
9. Moberly, finding support in Gore's *The Church and the Ministry* (1886 and reprinted throughout the first half of the present century), speaks of the Church divinely conceived as a corporate body by contrast with Hatch's 'tendency towards the formation of associations' and 'coalescing into societies' (1905, p. 9).
10. ibid. 1905, pp. 58ff.
11. Here Moberly, 1905, p. 68, is prepared to accept Hatch's interpretation.
12. Moberly, 1905, p. 71, quoting Gore, 1886, pp. 85ff.
13. cf. the evangelical critique of the Anglo-Catholic ecclesiological synthesis in Bradshaw, 1992, p. 70.
14. Moberly joins Hatch in protesting against any suggestion of an essential inequality between clergy and laity. Gore too opposed the notion of vicarious priesthood as it seemed to suggest that a priest has a closer relationship with God (Gore, 1886, p. 84).
15. Moberly, 1905, p. 102.
16. Moberly, 1905, p. 106. This is the substance of Article 23 of the Church of England. Moberly shows awareness of the history of the Article as clear enough in 1538 to exclude Anabaptist acceptance of a personal call to ministry alone, but not strong enough to exclude a presbyterian understanding of the nature of ordination. cf. Bicknell Carpenter, 1935, pp. 404ff.
17. Modern New Testament and historical scholarship undermines the accepted method of Moberly and his contemporaries of arguing back from the second century to the first. Professor A. T. Hanson, for example, claimed of Moberly that, 'His treatment of Clement in particular relies very much on the argument, "it must have been thus, therefore it was thus"' (Hanson, 1975, p. 12). Darwell Stone, (Principal of Pusey House 1909–34) followed the same path as Moberly of moving from selected biblical texts and literature of the early Church, to a universal understanding of priesthood in every age in terms of the reception of the direct and distinctive commission of Christ first given to the apostles (Stone, 1900, pp. 207ff. and 1905). In an extreme form, A. R. Whitham, Principal of Culham Training College, emphasizes with reference to the Scriptures and church tradition, that ordination, no less than baptism, marks the soul with an indelible character. Whitham, 1903.

18. See Hylson-Smith, 1989, p. 230.
19. Thomas, 1905, pp. 375ff.
20. Allen, 1912, pp. 3ff.
21. ibid., pp. 95ff.
22. Lambeth 1930, pp. 175ff.
23. Allen, 1912, pp. 126ff. cf. Donovan, (1978) 1982.
24. 'Fellowship in the church of Christ is Fellowship with the Father, which we have in Jesus Christ as the Son'. Doctrine Commission of the Church of England, 1938, pp. 105ff.
25. 'And we believe that, whenever the church is loyal to its mission, it will retain or seek to recover outward unity both in order and in the expression of its faith. We hold, therefore, that the Church of England is entirely right in attempting to combine retention of the historical creeds and ministry of the church with recognition, within that framework, of various types of Christian teaching and devotion'. ibid. p. 107.
26. ibid., pp. 113ff.
27. 'From the first there was the fellowship of believers finding its unity in the Twelve, the Apostolate as an element within the church. Thus the New Testament bears witness to the principle of a distinctive Ministry, as an original element, but not the sole constitutive element, in the life of the church.' ibid., p. 115.
28. ibid., pp. 115ff.
29. They claim the support of Hooker who opposed the Puritan argument that, 'Nothing ought to be established in the church, but that which is commanded in the word of God'. ibid., pp. 117ff.
30. 'We do not doubt that God has accepted and used other Ministries which through breach of continuity in the past are deficient in outward authorization; but we are convinced that the Anglican Communion has been right to regard the historic Episcopate as in a special sense the organ of unity and continuity'. ibid., p. 122. cf. Lambeth 1930, p. 119: 'But while we thus make a stand for the Historic Episcopate as a necessary element in any union in which the Anglican Communion can take part, and have given our reasons for so doing, we do not require of others acceptance of those reasons, or of any one particular theory or interpretation of the Episcopate as a condition of union.'
31. Doctrine Commission of the Church of England, 1938, pp. 156ff.
32. Ramsey, 1936, p. 7.
33. 'The two traditions puzzle each other. The one seems legalistic;

the other seems individualistic. To the one "intercommunion" is meaningless without unity of outward order; to the other "intercommunion" seems the one sensible and Christian way towards unity. And thus the debates between the two traditions are often wearisome and fruitless.' Ramsey, 1936, p. 8.

34. ibid., 1936, pp. 10ff.
35. ibid., pp. 26ff.
36. 'To burrow in the New Testament for forms of ministry and imitate them is archaeological religion: to seek that form of ministry which the whole New Testament creates is the more evangelical way. And our view of the ministry had better be evangelical than archaeological.' ibid., pp. 68ff.
37. ibid., p. 84.
38. ibid., p. 85.
39. ibid., p. 117.
40. ibid., p. 176.
41. Robinson, 1952, p. 51.
42. ibid., 1960, p. 22.
43. cf. Hammond, 1960, pp. 168ff. cited in Robinson, 1960, p. vi.
44. Robinson, 1960, p. 31.
45. ibid., 1963, pp. 22–23.
46. This is a significant theme in James, 1988.
47. Barry, 1945, p. 64.
48. ibid., p. 77.
49. Barry, 1958, p. xii.
50. Mayfield, 1963, p. 56.
51. Barry, 1958, p. xiii.
52. cf. Hendrik Kraemer, former Director of the Ecumenical Institute at Bossey, Switzerland, Kraemer, 1958, pp. 136ff. and Aidan Nichols OP, in Ford, 1989 (I) pp. 229ff.
53. Barry, 1958, p. 13.
54. ibid., p. 43.
55. ibid., p. 42.
56. ibid., p. 50.
57. cf. Garbett, 1950, pp. 68ff.
58. Barry, 1958, p. 159.
59. Hanson, (1961) 1975.
60. J. H. Bernard in his commentary on the Pastorals seems to Hanson to be presenting Paul as 'an old-fashioned Anglo-Catholic' while R. F. Horton reveals 'a Paul who was a Congregationalist with a leaning towards Liberal theology'. Hanson, 1975, p. 11.
61. Hanson, 1975, p. 13. Fourteen years after its first publication

Hanson was not convinced that this theological message had been heard.

62. Holtby, 1967, pp. 48ff.
63. ibid., p. 22.
64. 'The Principal embodies the whole ethos of the college and exemplifies its ideals'. Holtby, 1967, p. 28.
65. Moorman, 1947, p. 105.
66. ibid., p. 125.
67. Chadwick, in Holtby, 1967, p. vii.
68. Moorman, 1947, pp. 106 and 114.
69. Swain, 1939, p. 28.
70. Holtby, 1967, p. 29.
71. cf. the spirit of the remark made in 1864 by Bishop Wilberforce of Oxford, founder of Cuddesdon: 'The best ministers of the church are gentlemen by breeding and education; not only are they on equal terms with the leaders of thought; the poor also prefer them.' Cited in Wilkinson, 1992, p. 276.
72. Holtby, 1967, p. 45.
73. ibid., p. 76.
74. ibid., p. 84.
75. Moorman, 1947, p. 102.
76. ibid., p. 108.
77. Hopkins, 1939, p. 37.
78. Holtby, 1967, pp. 33ff.
79. ibid., pp. 47ff.
80. ibid., p. 82.
81. Moorman, 1947, p. 135.
82. Hopkins, 1939, p. 36.
83. Pickering, 1989, p. 122.
84. cf. McGrath, 1990, p. ix, quoting Foucault, 1990, p. ix, and p. 383, quoting Milbank. The contrast with the usage of New Testament material to make a case for ministerial patterns is illustrated in Schillebeeckx, 1985 and Young and Ford, 1987, pp. 221ff. On the necessity of taking context with great seriousness, see Gunton in Gunton and Hardy, 1989, p. 59.

Chapter Two

1. cf. Sykes, 1978 and McAdoo, 1991.
2. cf. Hastings, 1992 and Greenwood, 1993.
3. cf. Appendix to Sykes, 1987, pp. 284ff.
4. cf. Frend, 1989, p. 387.

5. cf. Henson's anxiety in 1947 regarding the extreme views of Kirk and Barnes, both regarding themselves as Anglicans, in Braley, 1951, p. 204.

6. Sykes, in Rowell, 1992, p. 230.

7. Milbank, 1990, p. 380.

8. cf. Sykes, in Rowell, 1992, pp. 227ff.

9. cf. Russell, 1993, pp. 168ff.

10. For a discussion of the demographic, economic and structural factors behind the reality of emptying churches cf. Gill, 1993.

11. cf. Sykes, in Rowell, 1992, p. 229.

12. Evans and Wright, 1991, §596, pp. 585ff. Approximately 1.2 million Anglicans in Britain attend worship regularly, according to a Central Office of Information survey, HMSO, 1992.

13. cf. Willmer, 1992, pp. 74ff.

14. cf. Ecclestone, 1988, and Gill, 1988.

15. Collins and Power, 1982. cf. Santer, 1984, Fiorenza and Carr, 1987, and Sedgwick on the experience of women in parish roles, 1990.

16. Substantial examples across a wide spectrum include Herzel, 1981; Hebblethwaite, 1984; Chittister, 1986; Moltmann-Wendel, 1986; Loades, 1990.

17. cf. The Reports of the Windsor Consultations 1991 and 1993.

18. cf. Field-Bibb, 1991, pp. 67ff.; Furlong, 1984 and 1991, pp. 96ff.; Howard, 1984; Stephenson, 1978; Moore, 1978.

19. Evans and Wright, 1991, §544, p. 517.

20. cf. Uhr, 1992 and Byrne, 1992, pp. 97ff.

21. Hardy and Ford, 1984.

22. Ramsey, Terwilleger and Allchin, 1974, pp. 68 and 71. cf. testimonies to the power of this movement in Banks, 1986. David Martin, Professor of Sociology, and Peter Mullen, parish priest edited a collection of diverse responses to the movement. Martin and Mullen, 1984.

23. Perham, 1978.

24. cf. the Episcopal church in Brazil, Confelider 1988. Statement of meeting of bishops with sixty priests and about eighty lay persons, in Porto Alegre, October 1988, Evans and Wright, 1991, §599, p. 590.

25. *ACCM 22*, 1987, 31.

26. ARCIC I, 1976, §5 and §6.

27. Here Anglicans are quite open to such widely varying influences as the essays on ministry by an ecumenical group of scholars, Franz Schnider, Werner Stenger, André Lemaire, Alexandre Ganoczy, Stephen Neill, Piet Fransen and others (Schnider,

1972). cf. Lucas Grollenberg, Jan Kerkhofs, Anton Houtepen, J. J. A. Vollebergh, and Edward Schillebeeckx (Grollenberg 1980); Schillebeeckx, 1981; Thurian (1970) 1983; Tavard, 1983; Lienhard 1984; Macquarrie, 1986. Also Tiller and Birchall, 1987; Hill, 1988. cf. Marsh (Professor of Dogmatic Theology, St. Patrick's College, Ireland), 1984, and Mitchell (lecturer, St Meirad School of Theology and associate ed. *Worship*), 1982.
28. Eastman, 1982; Burnish, 1985.
29. In an unpublished pamphlet, *A Vision of the Rural Future*, one of the commissioners, Andrew Bowden, writes, 'Wherever they went people said that they wanted "their own vicar". This enthusiasm for the minister is a tribute to the hard work of his predecessors in carrying out a role which is universally respected. Most of all people seem to appreciate a pastoral ministry—"knowing that someone cares about them and appreciates them". They see a role for a person who is committed to "enhancing community life"—particularly in our fast changing society. They respect someone who has the time to reflect on the direction (rural) society is taking, who can see over the horizon and help plan intelligently for the future. They respect someone who is dedicated to the things of the spirit and who is available to help them to see the troubles of the present in the context of eternity.'
30. For the broader perspective cf. Schillebeeckx and Metz, 1980.
31. cf. Greenwood, 1988, and Stokes and Shilling, 1980.
32. cf. *ACCM 22* McFadyen's analysis of the relationship between church and mission holds that, 'It is in this externally directed and eschatologically orientated mission towards the redemption of its situation that the church achieves its identity'. McFadyen, 1990, p. 246.
33. cf. Saris, 1980.
34. cf. Ball, 1986 and 1992.
35. On the relation between the worship of the Christian community and the life of society, cf. Balasuriya, 1977, Swayne, 1981, Mick, 1984. Some encouragement to this process has been offered: Bleakley, 1981; Davis and Gosling, 1986, *Instrumentorum Laboris* E. T. 1987 and Grundy, 1992. On world ecological matters, cf. Fox, 1983.
36. cf. Boff, 1986; Gutierrez, 1984; England, 1981; and Paget-Wilkes, 1981.
37. Sheppard, 1983, p. 225. cf. Vanstone, 1977, p. 97 and de Gruchy, 1987.
38. cf. an unpublished parish educational project in the Diocese of

Gloucester, *Together in Mission and Ministry*, Greenwood, 1987; Newbigin, 1989, p. 149; and Hocken, 1989, a, b, and c.

39. Educational and training material is increasingly available to local churches, much of it produced at a regional level and backed up by diocesan or regional church appointments. cf. the national survey conducted by Graham Hendy in 1990. On Adult learning cf. especially Hull, 1985. On the spiritual dimension especially, cf. the work of David Adam, Christopher Bryant SSJE, Ruth Burrows, Peter Dodson, Gerard W. Hughes, Anthony de Mello, Br Leonard of Taizé, Kenneth Leech, Gordon Jeff, Robert Llewellyn, Br Ramon SSF, and J. Neville-Ward.

Chapter Three

1. *ACCM 22*, Preface, p. 7.
2. The Faith and Order Advisory Group of the Board for Mission and Unity, in its Report *The Theology of Ordination*, spoke of all three orders of ministry as an 'articulating focus' for the total life of the church. FOAG, 1976, para. 46, p. 17. However, the general tenor of that Report was to assume the dual or distinctive, rather than interrelational representation of clergy and laity.
3. There is rightly a fear of reducing priesthood to what is implied in the metaphor of management. Good management is essential in the church but priesthood requires a cluster of metaphors to be held together in tension. There is no reason why the church in choosing its clergy should not aim to discover those who can integrate the qualities of holiness, good management and pastoral care. Recent studies on 'leadership' are fertile especially where they point to the leader as one whose task it is to share in bearing the community's values. cf. Avis, 1992, pp. 107ff.
4. The colleges which kindly allowed me to read the texts of their submissions as part of research for a University of Birmingham Ph.D. thesis were: Mirfield Theological College (Anglican), The Queen's College, Birmingham (ecumenical), St John's Nottingham (Anglican), Westcott House, Cambridge (Anglican).
5. pp. 12ff.
6. p. 19.
7. The legalities of belonging to the Church of England are duly noted but interpreted in a moral framework.

Chapter Four

1. cf. McGrath, 1990.
2. cf. the conclusion to Chapter One and Toulmin in Küng, 1991. p. 153.
3. cf. Boff, 1988, p. 112.
4. Mackey, 1983, pp. 7ff.
5. Rahner has shown how already in the New Testament, the Greek expression *ho theos*, used originally only of the Father, was 'slowly, as it were shyly and cautiously . . . detached from him', and also used of Christ and, later, of the Spirit. Lash, 1992, pp. 27ff.
6. cf. Moltmann, 1981, p. 60 and Gunton, 1991, pp. 31ff.
7. Interpreters of the early development of trinitarian theology include Langdon Gilkey in Hodgson and King, 1983, Anthony Kelly, 1989, and the British Council of Churches Study Commission, 1989.
8. Moltmann, 1981, p. 1.
9. cf. Hill, 1982, p. 83. Zizioulas shows how Augustine makes the Trinity ontologically secondary in God. British Council of Churches, 1991, p. 25, n. 22. For a discussion of the inadequacy of Augustine's trinitarian argument cf. Torrance, 1985, pp. 167ff.
10. Jenson, Professor of Systematic Theology in St Olaf College, Minnesota and an acknowledged interpreter of Barth's writings, in Ford, 1989, I, p. 42. cf. Barth, 1975, I.i, pp. 295ff.
11. The BCC Report, 1989, stressing the significance of Barth's trinitarianism notes its indebtedness to Augustine and to the Eastern tradition §4.2.3. 'The *Church Dogmatics* is in fact a huge doctrine of being, which offends against the previous tradition of Western thought by putting an individual, the risen Jesus Christ, at the Ground of reality. One need not approve this system in its entirety to find it exemplary' (Jenson, in Ford, 1989, I, p. 46).
12. Moltmann, 1981, p. 3. cf. Küng, 1991, pp. 197ff.
13. Hill, 1982, pp. 114ff. cf. *Church Dogmatics* 1936, I, 1, p. 297.
14. Barth, 1936, I, 1, p. 417. 'God reveals, he reveals himself, and reveals through himself, therefore, Trinity is the structural form of that event we name God'. 1936, I, 1, p. 382.
15. ibid., I, 1, p. 431.
16. cf. Jenson, in Ford, 1989, I, p. 47. For an account and critique of Jenson's own development of Barth's thought, see Hill 1982, pp. 124ff. Assessing Barth's significance, Hill writes,

'Barth has recouped the truth of the centrality of the Trinity to Christian faith, its indispensability to the question of the meaning of human existence and salvation.' (1982, p. 116).

17. cf. Tripp, in British Council of Churches, 1991, p. 65.
18. Gunton commends the ecclesiology of the Puritan John Owen in which, 'The Holy Spirit . . . is the *immediate, peculiar cause*, of all external divine operations; for God worketh by his Spirit, or in him immediately applies the power and efficacy of the divine excellencies . . . unto their operation', quoting Owen in Gunton and Hardy, 1989, p. 64.
19. Moltmann, 1981, pp. 31ff.
20. 'The triune God is the God who is open to man, open to the world, and open to time'. Moltmann, 1977, p. 56. cf. Torrance, 1985, pp. 184ff.
21. cf. Gunton, 1988, p. 145. Similarly Zizioulas, 'By referring to Christ as the Alpha and Omega of history, the New Testament has transformed radically the linear historicism of Hebrew thought, since in a certain way the end of history in Christ becomes *already* present here and now'. 1985, p. 71.
22. This has been described as 'less a futurist eschatology than a true *eschatologia crucis*, whose inner structure is trinitarian'; 'The Son comes to his glory in the joy of redeemed creation'. Hill, 1982, p. 167.
23. 'The key word of trinitarian doctrine, *homoousia* (one single nature) was taken from the Gnostics, Ptolemy, Theodotus and Heraclion'. Boff, 1988, p. 46.
24. Denzinger and Schönmetzer (eds.), *Enchiridion Symbolorum* 1967 §125.
25. 'Can we not conclude almost inevitably, that given the ultimate character of God's being for all ontology, substance inasmuch as it signifies the ultimate character of being, can be conceived only as communion?' Zizioulas, 1985, p. 84.
26. cf. Johnston, 1092. With many references to the patristic texts, Torrance provides an illuminating summary of the Cappadocian doctrine of the Holy Spirit (1965, pp. 219ff). Supported by the earlier work of H. B. Swete on the Holy Spirit in the early Church, Torrance helps to mitigate the criticism that engagement with Cappadocian trinitarianism is a contemporary enthusiasm. cf. Clapsis, 1992, p. 109 and Basil of Caesarea, *Letters*, 7, 44.
27. cf. the accounts in Prestige, 1952, pp. 259ff., Hanson, 1988, pp. 676ff. and La Cugna, 1992, pp. 53ff.
28. Gregory of Nazianzus, cited in Gunton, 1993, p. 149.

29. Basil of Caesarea, *Letters* 38.4.
30. cf. Prestige, 1952, pp. 276ff. 'They took not the unity of the divine nature but the three divine Persons as their starting point, seeing them as the basic reality' (Boff, 1988, p. 54). Note that Nicholas Lash does not share this enthusiasm for adopting the term 'person' in trinitarian theology. Lash, 1992, p. 31.
31. 'The substance of God, "God", has no ontological content, no true being, apart from communion.' Zizioulas, 1985, pp. 17 and 40ff. cf. Boff, 1988, pp. 54ff.
32. See the discussion in McGinn, Meyendorff and Leclerq, 1989, pp. 26off.
33. cf. Boff, 1988, pp. 101ff.
34. Boff, 1988, p. 146.
35. 'The fact that God exists because of the Father shows that His existence, His being is the consequence of a free person; which means, in the last analysis, that not only communion but also *freedom*, the free person, constitutes true being.' Zizioulas, 1985, p. 18.
36. Boff, 1988, p. 93.
37. Moltmann, 1981, p. 151. cf. Gunton, 1991, p. 149.
38. Begbie, 1990 and also 1992, p. 60.
39. Boff, 1988, p. 3.
40. Hardy has pointed to the fundamental relationship of created nature to God, 'since, by reason of the primacy of God, there can be no other source for the ordered cosmos, the fundamental relation is seen as causative, e.g., derivation from God's action'. Gunton and Hardy, 1989, p. 31. In this respect Gunton, whose line of argument I am affirming here, offers the conceptual link of the obedience of Jesus, enabled by the Spirit to obey the Father. If the life of the incarnate Son is to be understood in terms of free relationship with the Father, it could be argued that there is in the Divine eternity a corresponding freedom, so that to that freedom of God in creation and redemption (as Barth argued) there corresponds freedom in the relation of the Father and the Son and the Spirit. Gunton, 1991, p. 149.
41. 'Indeed, to translate the tenets of classic trinitarianism into modern personalist language may very well be one of the major tasks of modern theology'. Walker, in British Council of Churches, 1991, pp. 153ff.
42. Gunton, in Schwöbel and Gunton, 1991, p. 61.
43. 'The two, ontology and relation, stand or fall together rather

than are opposed approaches to the way we understand things'. Gunton, 1993, p. 8.

44. Zizioulas, 1985, pp. 123ff. Gunton writes, 'If God is as truly three as he is one, should we not expect that in some way or other plurality will be as transcendental, as deeply written into the order of things, as unity?' Gunton, 1993, p. 5.

45. Gunton and Hardy, 1989, pp. 52ff. and Gunton, 1993, p. 52 n. 17.

46. 'The church participates in the uniting of men with one another, in the uniting of society with nature and in the uniting of creation with God. Wherever unions like this take place, however fragmentary and fragile they may be, there is the church. The true church is the fellowship of love.' Hill, 1982, p. 65. cf. Gunton's emphasis on pneumatology to make room in the church for the freedom, particularity and contingency of Jesus '*enabled* by the (transcendent) Spirit rather than *determined* by the (immanent) word' (1991, p. 64).

47. cf. Zizioulas, 1985, p. 18. Boff has written, that on the basis of their belief in the triune divinity, Christians 'postulate a society that can be the image and likeness of the Trinity' (1988, p. 11).

48. cf. Gunton, 1992, pp. 11ff.

49. On the difficulties inherent in Christian theology's traditional tendency to a monolithic view of God and truth cf. Boff, 1988, pp. 16ff.

50. cf. Hills, 1993.

51. cf. 'Trinitarian Communion as critic of and inspiration for human society', Boff, 1988, pp. 148ff. and Moltmann, 1985(b), pp. 50ff.

52. A reminder of eminent theories of personhood from the 18th, 19th and 20th centuries is offered in *The Forgotten Trinity*. Walker, in British Council of Churches, 1991, pp. 137ff.

53. Zizioulas argues that communion which does not come from a 'hypostasis', a concrete and free person, and which does not lead to 'hypostases', concrete and free persons, is not an image of the being of God. 1985, p. 18.

54. Zizioulas, 1985, pp. 43 and 53ff.

55. 'Reflecting on the Trinity calls all our human concepts into question. We are dealing with the most radical Absolute, the deepest root, in itself, and total reality'. Boff, 1988, p. 141.

56. McFadyen draws attention to the value of knowing humanity truly through God as well as knowing God through communication and relation with humankind, 1990, p. 24. Moltmann

writing of the parallel, says, 'Love seeks a counterpart who freely responds and independently gives love for love. Love humiliates itself for the sake of the freedom of its counterpart. The freedom towards God of the human being whom God desires and loves is as unbounded as God's capacity for passion and for patience. Love of freedom is the most profound reason for "God's self-differentiation" and for "the divine bipolarity"' (1981, p. 30).

57. See the discussion of 'The Trinitarian Doctrine of Freedom', in Moltmann, 1981, pp. 212ff.

58. cf. McFadyen, 1990, p. 19.

59. Hardy in Gunton and Hardy, 1989, pp. 21ff. cf. McFadyen, quoting Emil Brunner. McFadyen, 1990, p. 20. Torrance also testifies to the concept of person as defined in his openness to God and to others at the same time in obedience to the New Testament teaching that human beings cannot love God with all their heart, soul and mind, without also loving their neighbours as themselves (1985, p. 177).

60. cf. McFadyen, 1990, p. 22.

61. God's ultimate intention for the glorification of all creation is found particularly in Moltmann, 1985(a), but also Schillebeeckx, 1980(b). This eschatological longing of God is expressed in an attractive and compelling manner by Peter Selby, who writes of the Church as the expression in prayer and action of the longing of God. Selby, 1991, p. 2.

62. cf. the work of Hardy, McFadyen, Milbank, Peacocke, Polkinghorne, and Zizioulas.

63. cf. Hardy, 1993, p. 3.

64. cf. Peacocke, 1990.

65. 'God is reduced to a mere archivist turning the pages of a cosmic history book already written'. Ilya Prigogine, quoted by Davies, 1992, 29, n. 1.

66. Casti, 1990 quoted in Hardy, 1993, p. 6.

67. cf. Byrne, 1992.

68. Cupitt, 1990.

69. Gunton, 1991, pp. 24ff.

70. Gunton, 1991, p. 28. Cupitt, 1990, p. ix.

71. Capra, quoted in Kelly, 1989, pp. 11ff.

72. The heart of the *Discourse* consists of four laws to be unfailingly observed: 1. to accept nothing as true which are not clearly recognized to be so. 2. to divide up each of the difficulties to be examined into as many parts as possible. 3. to reflect in an orderly way, beginning with the most simple objects and

moving by degrees to a knowledge of the most complex. 4. always to make calculations so complete and reviews so general that there can be certainty of having omitted nothing. Descartes, 1969 edition, I, p. 92. A helpful background to Descartes is provided by Tom Sorell, 1987.

73. Toulmin, 1990, pp. 150ff.

74. Toulmin, 1990, p. 172.

75. *Determinism:* The future states of a particle's motion can be fully determined by a knowledge of the forces acting on it and its initial position.

Classical Realism: To every parameter used in the equations of physics there corresponds an element of reality.

Infinite Subdivisibility of Energy: Energy which is always constant is transformed from one form to another in a continuous manner and can be infinitely subdivided.

Separability: The results of a measurement in one part of an experiment are not affected by a simultaneous measurement in another part of the experiment.

76. SST paper, 1993.

77. For example, a newspaper photograph composed from myriads of tiny dots conveys a meaning possessed by none of the dots in isolation. Davies, 1983.

78. Davies, 1983. He is an enthusiastic disciple of Capra in the search for parallels between modern concepts in physics and traditional Eastern religious concepts such as 'oneness in the spirit'. Capra, 1975. Davies reveals a wealth of the literature emanating from many disciplines which illustrate richly the revolutionary new approach to mathematics and science, especially in the bibliographical notes accompanying each of his chapters.

79. Küng, 1991, p. 131.

80. Developing the previous work of Eddington, *The Nature of the Physical*, Prigogine and Stengers write, 'We have discovered that far from being an illusion, irreversibility plays an essential role in nature and lies at the origin of most processes of self-organization. We find ourselves in a world in which reversibility and determinism apply only to limiting, simple cases, while irreversibility and randomness are the rules'. Prigogine and Stengers, 1984, p. 104.

81. Prigogine and Stengers, 1984. cf. Gunton, 1991, p. 157. Polkinghorne offers a concise explanation for the novice in these areas, concluding, 'Physics is found to describe process endowed not just with being but also with becoming'. 1991,

pp.38ff. cf. Barbour who summarizes that historicity is now seen as basic to nature and historical conditioning, fundamental to scientific theory, Polkinghorne, 1990, p. 220.

82. It is 'closed' systems if they exist in reality, rather than 'open' that may be the rare or aberrant phenomenon. Prigogine and Stengers, 1984, p. xxi.

83. Polkinghorne, 1988, p. 41. Polkinghorne writes that only when a system behaves in a sufficiently random way may the difference between past and future, and therefore irreversibility, enter into its description, 'The arrow of time is the manifestation of the fact that the future is not given, that as the French poet Paul Valéry emphasized, "time is a construction"'. David Lazyer has argued that the external world described by science today is fundamentally different from the universe of Laplace and Einstein, which is given once and for all in space and time. He emphasizes that he would characterize the world as a place of becoming as well as of being, a world in which order emerges from primordial chaos begetting new forms of order. Polkinghorne, 1990, p. 302.

84. Gunton, 1992, p. 97.

85. Hardy, 1993, p. 15.

86. Gunton, 1993, p. 15.

87. Work in this field of relating trinitarian thought to concepts of priesthood is in its infancy. cf. Zizioulas in Walker, British Council of Churches, 1991, p. 137.

88. An identification of the person with the individual is still maintained by some modern philosophers, e.g. Parfit, 1984, but his position appears egocentric and individualist.

89. cf. Darwen, 1992.

90. cf. Hillyer, 1990, Moltmann, 1989, Brown 1987, Board of Social Responsibility 1987, and Starke, 1990.

91. Schorr, 1992.

92. Moltmann's chapter on the nuclear situation contains valuable references to literature which reveals the gap between a vision for world peace and the ability of individual nations to trigger a climactic catastrophe. The ecological situation, again as noted by Moltmann, reveals a similar fragmentation of human interests. The Church of England Report *Faith in the City*, 1985 is widely recognized as a documentary authority in these matters.

93. 'Public Faith', (enthronement sermon, 18 November 1983), Habgood, 1988.

94. ibid.

95. Gunton, 1991, pp. 88ff.
96. Marshall, 1992, p. 3.
97. ibid., pp. 1ff.
98. 'The conception of society as a human product and therefore "historical" remains one of the basic assumptions of secular social science'. Milbank, 1990, p. 10.
99. The researches of Walker reveal the diminutive quantity of work in the social sciences on theories of personhood. British Council of Churches, 1991, pp. 137ff.
100. Hardy similarly proposes that we should expect dynamic order to be discovered *in* theory, action and expression, rather than as antecedent to them. Hardy, 1993.
101. 'The conceptist 'Idea' is already anticipated by Nicholas of Cusa's view that *factibilitas* is the condition of possibility for human knowing and belongs to a human conjectural *explicatio* of the divine intellectual "comprehension" in the second person of the Trinity.' Milbank, 1990, p. 12.
102. Milbank, 1990, p. 52.
103. cf. Bonhoeffer, taking the example of the church's unconditional acceptance of infants as an illustration of how the Christian community differs from an association of like-minded people, writes, 'The church is a community *sui generis*, a community of spirit and love. In it the basic sociological types, society, community and authority-group, are combined and surmounted' (1963, p. 185).
104. Gunton and Hardy, 1989, p. 4. The close parallels with our previous section on Trinity and non-personal creation are immediately apparent, and Hardy points to future ecclesiological implications.
105. Adams, 1975 and 1988.
106. McFadyen, 1990, p. 318.
107. He shares the vision of Moltmann, 'The three divine persons exist in their particular, unique natures as Father, Son and Spirit in their relationships. It is in these relationships that they are persons. Being a person in this respect means existing-in-relationship'. Moltmann, 1981, pp. 171ff, quoted in McFadyen, 1990, p. 28.
108. cf. McFadyen, 1990, p. 197.
109. ibid., p. 314.
110. ibid., p. 31.
111. ibid., pp. 90ff.
112. Harré', 1976, quoted McFadyen, 1990, p. 100.
113. Hampson, 1991, p. 6.

114. McFadyen describes the pathological consequences for mistaken views about human individuality imaged on the extremes of monotheism and tritheism: 'Both take individual identity to be something presocial removed from the sphere of relations as such. They are, therefore, bound to regard dialogical relations with others which make a difference to individual identity (inform it) as the fracture of an integrated personality or the alienation of identity. The two extremes are the inevitable result of pressing for hard and exclusive definitions (closed boundaries) of personal identity.' McFayden, 1990, p. 25.

115. In agreement with Moltmann, 1981, McFadyen believes that personal identity and individuality are, 'neither asocial nor presocial, but arise out of one's relations and communications with others'. 1990, p. 29.

116. McFadyen, 1990, p. 39.

Chapter Five

1. For Philip Schaff's late nineteenth century work on the history of the creeds, see Hodgson, 1988.

2. cf. Houtepen, 1983, p. 26.

3. cf. the statement on *Communion* by the Second Anglican Roman Catholic International Commission (ARCIC II, 1991). Zizioulas has pointed to the inadequacies of Vatican II ecclesiology, expressed particularly in the Dogmatic Constitution, *Lumen Gentium*, founded on a christology lacking a pneumatology. British Council of Churches, 1991, p. 22.

4. Zizioulas, 1988, p. 300.

5. McFadyen, 1990, p. 241.

6. cf. ARCIC II, 1991, pp. 8–15.

7. cf. ARCIC II, 1991, p. 83, para. 16.

8. cf. the important and careful analysis of Cole, 1990, p. 24.

9. Barth supports this view in Vol IV. 3 which opens with the lines, 'The Word of the living Jesus Christ is the creative call by which He awakens man to an active knowledge of the truth and thus receives him into the new standing of the Christian, namely, into a particular fellowship with Himself, thrusting him as His afflicted but well-equipped witness into the service of His prophetic work'. Barth, 1975, p. 481. cf. ARCIC II, 1991, para. 22.

10. cf. Keirsey and Bates, (1978) 1984.

11. cf. Smith and Taussig, 1990, pp. 70ff.

12. Smith and Taussig, 1990, p. 81.
13. Avis shows how the English Reformers and the chief architect of Anglican ecclesiology, Richard Hooker rejected the popular medieval notion that confirmation was required as a condition to receiving saving grace or as a prelude to full church membership (1990, pp. 31ff).
14. Lambeth 1988 Report, especially the section on ecumenical relations, pp. 123ff.
15. ASB, p. 229.
16. Zizioulas speaks of the Church as the *eikon* of the Kingdom, 1988, p. 300.
17. cf. Brierly, 1991 and Carr (with others), 1992, pp. 7ff.
18. It has been common in recent decades to question the authenticity of Constantine's endorsement of Christianity as the official religion in what was by then a waning empire, cf. Boff, 1985, p. 51. For a recent account of the factors involved, see Hall, 1991, pp. 118ff.
19. Hardy, in Hardy and Sedgwick, 1991, p. 132.
20. Cockerell, 1989, p. 53. Mark Santer has written, 'We must beware of restorationist nostalgia, the kind of spiritual Bourbonism which supposes it to be possible, even if it were desirable, to reinstate the political power and institutional privilege which the church once enjoyed'. Santer, 1991.
21. For a recent discussion of specific questions regarding religion in public life, see the valuable collection of papers edited by Cohn-Sherbok and McLellan, 1992.
22. John Yates, a diocesan bishop for 16 years (for part of that period also a member of the House of Lords and chairman of the General Synod Board of Social Responsibility) has articulated the vision of the Church working in partnership with society to discover a common value system: 'The City needs the Temple to be a focus of people's aspirations, the place of divine presence, a theatre for the expression of corporate repentance, sorrow, thanksgiving or forgiveness. The Temple is the place where ends rather than means are encountered and disclosed. If there is no discussion about ends, what guidance is there for those who have to legislate and administer? But it works the other way round also. What is the use of religion without morals and a community in which those morals can be expressed? What point is there in the cathedral choir singing about the seat of judgement unless in the real world outside the cathedral people are wrestling with the practical problems of justice and equity in society?' Yates, 1991. cf. McFadyen, 1990, p. 269. Yates' vision, despite its Anglican

origins, is capable of an ecumenical broadening to take account of the contemporary pluralist context of Church–State relations.

23. cf. ARCIC II, 1991, para. 23.

24. Moltmann, although he is not using the word 'holiness' speaks of the 'common worth' which the triune God invests in all his creatures as the basis for collaboration together for salvation, in ecological terms (1989, p. 68).

25. 'a story privileged by faith . . . the key to the interpretation and regulation of all other stories' (Milbank, 1990, p. 386). 'Such a perichoretic model of the church would submit all ecclesial functions (episcopate, presbyterate, lay ministries, and so on) to the imperative of communion and participation by all in everything that concerns the good of all.' Boff, 1988, p. 154.

26. cf. Shannon, 1987.

27. Hardy and Ford, 1985, p. 108.

28. The nexus between the ethic and the eschatology of Jesus in his gospel proclamation which critically informs the Church's life, has been the subject of recent reflection. Bruce Chilton and J. I. H. McDonald have shown that the ethical prescriptions of the community of Jesus are secondary or follow as an enactment of the aesthetic underlying perception of God's eschatological activity in the world. cf. Chilton and McDonald, 1987, pp. 114ff. The activity-focused interpretation of Jesus' preaching, advocated by Ritschl, referring to God's will for people and their responsibility for responding to that will, tended, as Johannes Weiss observed, to overlook the transcendental aspect of Jesus' ministry. Disciples of Ritschl, such as Matthews and Rauschenbusch, followed the path of preaching the programmatic demands of the kingdom, whilst Weiss's adherents, notably Albert Schweitzer and Rudolf Bultmann, overlooked immediate ethical issues in favour of God's ultimate concern. cf. Sykes, in Ford, 1989, II, pp. 13 and 16, Hendrickx, 1984, pp. 178ff. and Houtepen, 1983, p. 128.

29. 'The emphasis throughout is on the divine, eschatological action on which ethical response is predicated, so that the fundamental character of performance is transcendent. Jesus' preaching of the Kingdom is in the first place an announcement of God's dynamic rule'. Chilton and McDonald, 1989, p. 118.

30. Limouris, 1986, p. 20.

31. '. . . to perceive a fresh reality. Whoever perceives God ultimately revealing himself in the world must—if he is sincere—behave in that world, for good and all, as a new person. He *is* a new person, whose citizenship has been changed irrevocably.' Chilton and

McDonald, 1987, p. 120. cf. the way in which Hauerwas describes the Church as formed by the truthful story of Jesus Christ (1981).

32. cf. Moltmann's critique of 'political and clerical monotheism', (1981) 1989, pp. 191ff.

33. Boff, 1988, p. 158.

34. The Lima text has the sentence, 'The eucharist is essentially the sacrament of the gift which God makes to us in Christ through the power of the Holy Spirit'. Lima, World Council of Churches, Eucharist 2.

35. 'Even in its comprehensive form, the historical church is particular and not yet *the whole*. Just because it is the people of the coming Kingdom, it is not yet the new humanity itself.' Moltmann, 1977, p. 349.

36. Moltmann, 1977, p. 249.

37. Milbank, 1990, p. 417.

38. cf. Zizioulas, 1985, p. 254, and Boff's understanding of how the community which embodies the life of the Trinity in the eucharistic celebration 'carries out a sort of universal recapitulation' of the faith (1988, p. 103).

39. Moltmann notes the Jewish-Christian tradition of recognizing the Spirit of God as the instrument of the creation of differentiated life in its fullness (1989, p. 59).

40. 'An ecclesiological catholicity in the light of the eucharistic community suggests and presupposes a *catholic anthropology* and a *catholic view of existence* in general.' Zizioulas, 1985, p. 162.

41. 'Apostolicity is the church's special historical designation.' Moltmann, 1977, p. 357.

42. 'The historical church *will be* the one, holy, catholic church through the apostolic witness of Christ, and in carrying out that witness; whereas the church glorified in the kingdom of God *is* the one, holy and catholic church, through the fulfilment of its apostolate.' Moltmann, 1977, p. 358.

43. Zizioulas, 1985, pp. 191ff.

44. Hardy and Ford, 1984, p. 20.

45. Moltmann, 1977, p. 256.

46. Gunton, referring to Cyprian, Augustine and Harnack, shows the substantive absence of trinitarian thought within ecclesiological development, leading to the overlay on the gospel community of a philosophy of hierarchical power, borrowed from secular state and military contexts. cf. Zizioulas, 1985, p. 199 and Milbank, *passim*.

Chapter Six

1. cf. Zizioulas, 1985, p. 212. Third-World churches have much to teach Europeans on this score. With particular reference to the corporate nature of the church in which the whole people are bearers of ecclesial reality and not merely the objects of teaching and administrative clerical authority. cf. Elizondo and Greinacher, 1981.
2. Zizioulas, 1985, p. 211.
3. cf. Küng, 1972. Also see an unattributed article in *Chicago Studies*, Nov. 1983, p. 278, quoted by Flood, 1987, p. 61. For an Anglican discussion of the issues surrounding 'lay presidency' cf. Lloyd, 1977 and Hargrave, 1990.
4. Alan Richardson concluded from his New Testament research that 'Baptism is, as it were, the ordination of a new member of the royal priesthood' (1958, p. 301). cf. '. . . it must be stated emphatically, that there is no such thing as "non-ordained" persons in the church. Baptism and especially confirmation (or chrismation) as an inseparable aspect of the mystery of Christian initiation involves a "laying on of hands".' Zizioulas, 1985, p. 216. He is convinced that Hippolytus regarded the 'place' of a layman in the eucharistic assembly as vital in the sense of necessary. It was only with the private mass of the middle ages that the layperson was regarded as inferior or dispensable. cf. Eastman, for whom baptism alone is 'the keystone sacrament' (1982). It has to be said that the historical research of Faivre into the emergence of the laity in the first five centuries indicates that where the positive significance of the laity was recognized, its membership tended to be severely circumscribed by disciplinary and ethical demands. There are clear parallels here with the inner and outer layers of laity in most parishes today and the willingness of varying groups to recognize the others as members of the church in any real sense. cf. Faivre, 1990.
5. The team aspect of ordained ministry is one which received emphasis in the *BEM* document, Lima 1982, Ministry, para. 26.
6. Avis, 1992, p. 97.
7. cf. Legrand, 1979; Collins and Power, 1982; Greenwood, 1984.
8. VIII, paras. 5off. pp. 19ff.
9. Küng, 1972.
10. Carr, 1985, pp. 14ff.
11. For a powerful expression of the mutuality of ministries inspired by Vatican II, cf. Suenens, 1968.

12. It often seems that the Church, provider of clerical income, is also sustainer of clerical morale to the detriment of mission or lay initiative, cf. Tiller and Birchall, 1987, p. 24. Maggie Ross articulates this collusion as 'the myth of two-level obedience' and points to the early point in the Church's history when the gifts and prayers of all but the clergy came to be treated as second-class. Ross, 1988. Moltmann indirectly supports the argument of this book when he emphasizes that communities are Christian insofar as in their telling of the story of Jesus, the *entire* church combines the story of its sufferings and hopes with those of the story of Jesus. Moltmann, 1978, p. 102.

13. Zizioulas, 1975, pp. 214ff. cf. 'Paul never conceives his authority apart from his conviction that the Corinthians are called by God, share his faith in God, are "in Christ" and have the Spirit (2 Cor. 1.21f.).' Young and Ford, 1987, p. 209.

14. cf. Mitchell, 1982, p. 258.

15. Congar, 1983, pp. 7ff. cf. the work of Grollenberg and others, 1980, and Moltmann ('the congregation from below') 1978, pp. 113ff.

16. cf. Houtepen, in Grollenberg, 1980, pp. 21ff. As noted already, previous discourses on ministry which split clergy and laity into different states within the Church were usually related only to the past and the present, relating to Christology without reference to the Spirit. Zizioulas, however, persuasively outlines an ecclesiology which refers through the Spirit not only to the past and the present experiences of Christ's coming but also to the future eschatological dimension, 1985, p. 211.

17. Carr accepts gratefully that 'it is one of today's theological and practical discoveries that the differentiated ministries of individuals derive from the foundational ministry of the whole church' (1985, p. 9).

18. Cited in Avis, 1990, p. 82.

19. Faith and Order Advisory Group, 1976, pp. 99f. The *BEM* Statement, Lima, 1982, Ministry, simply avoids the contentious issue.

20. The 1988 Lambeth Conference Report avoided a two tier understanding of ministry, stating that, 'baptism carries with it the implied gift of authority for ministry', and, 'the foundation of all ministry is that of a royal priesthood of all God's people with which, by virtue of his or her baptism, every Christian is called to exercise a ministry . . .' Lambeth 1988, pp. 51 and 54.

21. C. K. Barrett's mature understanding of ministry from a New Testament perspective, recognizes the scantiness of the material for much more than 'explanatory borings', emphasizing how

for Paul the whole Church was an interdependent ministering community (1985, p. 31).

22. Quoted by Tripp, in British Council of Churches, 1991, p. 66.

23. cf. Young and Ford, 1987, p. 210.

24. Zizioulas, 1985, p. 223.

25. J. K. McGowan attempts to draw out the potential of Vatican II ecclesiology [now seen to be largely unrealized] for speaking of the laity sharing in Christ's priesthood and ending the permanent domination of laity by clergy. In Liebard, 1978, pp. xivff. Schillebeeckx is unfortunately more correct in his analysis that Vatican II left the laity as 'non-clergy', standing in a subordinate hierarchical relationship to the orders of the sacred ministry (1985, p. 157).

26. The 'freedom in the Kingdom of the Triune God' of which Moltmann writes, 1981, pp. 219ff. This freedom directed towards the future is intended without bounds for all.

27. Küng helpfully summarizes the difficulties some Roman Catholics have with these notions (1972, p. 46). With a foreword by Bishop Graham Leonard, and claiming Roman Catholic support, H. J. M. Turner offers a challenge to what he regards as 'present misunderstandings of vocation' by re-emphasizing the individual nature of ordained ministry as representatives of Christ. Turner, 1990. Note that the Roman Catholic theologian Legrand insists that priests do not act *in persona Christi* on their own account but only by virtue of being *in persona Ecclesiae*. Legrand, 1993, p. 17.

28. cf. Zizioulas who, with reference to the Cappadocians, demonstrates the futility of attempting to objectify the charisma of ordination (1985, pp. 227ff). However, he admits that provided the relational dimension is not lost sight of, there is something positive for the ordained person in that calling (p. 232). Not to accept this would be to fly in the face of experience, though, in context, it raises questions regarding the extremes of certain ordination celebrations and anniversaries. The encouragement of the keeping of anniversaries of baptism, by contrast, requires much attention. cf. official responses to *BEM* on Baptism published by WCC, Thurian (Vol. 1 1986). cf. Doohan, 1984, pp. 24ff.

29. 'By baptism an entire people becomes priestly.' Boff, 1986, p. 69.

30. cf. Jan Grootaers, discussing the Jesuits as originally a lay fellowship, Neill and Weber, 1963.

31. cf. Zizioulas, 1985, p. 211. Ian Fraser, research consultant to *Action of Churches Together in Scotland*, writes in a parallel way of the whole community of Christians acting as 'bishop' in that it will 'see that eucharistic worship is prepared with care'. He

does not, however, see the need to identify particular individuals with specific tasks in the church on a regular basis. Fraser, 1992, pp. 62ff.

32. Paul himself, a vigorous defender of Christian freedom, does not fail to resolve certain conflicts by his authority 'but not to command your faith' (2 Cor. 1.24).

33. cf. Legrand, 1993, p. 22.

34. Avis finds this characteristic of the ministry of Jesus (1992, p. 125). Paul in 2 Corinthians recognizes he has no effective authority without the voluntary consent of church members. Young and Ford, 1987, p. 209.

35. Vollebergh, a Christian psychologist, articulates religious leadership as having the characteristics of helper, prophet, and witness. See Vollebergh, in Grollenberg, 1980, pp. 41ff. Avis indicates some vital issues concerning management, conflict, leadership, and institutions (1992, pp. 107ff).

36. The parish audit process, undertaken at a suitable level of complexity is invaluable here.

37. 'the local eucharistic assembly [according to the *Didache*] understood itself as the revelation of the eschatological unity of all in Christ.' Zizioulas, 1985, p. 155.

38. Newbigin, 1989, p. 134.

39. This has parallels with Carr's conviction (rooted in the primary work of Bruce Reed, *Dynamics of Religion*) that a local church is inescapably invited to work with but, may reject the invested hope, respect and dependency of, the wider community at a deep emotional level. Carr, 1985, pp. 10ff.

40. Ramsey, 1972, p. 7.

41. Unpublished ordination charge, 1970.

42. On this point the author is in agreement with the tenor of Wesley Carr's argument. Carr, 1989.

43. Zizioulas, in British Council of Churches, 1991, p. 28.

44. It is worth remembering that the BCP Ordinal placed high regard on the work of the Spirit in priesthood. At the most solemn moment of ordination, the bishop says, 'Receive the Holy Ghost for the office and work of a priest in the Church of God'. cf. Ramsey, 1972, p. 66.

45. cf. Tiller and Birchall, 1987, pp. 18ff. and Greenwood, 1991.

46. cf. Schillebeeckx and Metz, 1980, and the trend towards Local Ministry schemes apparent in Church of England dioceses.

47. The 1976 General Synod Faith and Order Advisory Group Report, *The Theology of Ordained Ministry* described the act of ordination partially in terms of commendation for a particular

task, 'an act of blessing' para. 26. p. 11. In the ASB liturgy of ordination, the priest's blessing of the people is listed as a central activity (para. 16).

48. 'The core meaning of the word for bishop is not "the one put over" others (as our word "overseer" may suggest), but "the one who gives close and loving attention" to others. In this sense, the whole membership may act as bishop'. Fraser, 1992, p. 62.

49. cf. Fraser, 1992, p. 63.

BIBLIOGRAPHY

ADVISORY BOARD OF MINISTRY 1991 (a)   ABM, *Integration and Assessment: An interim evaluation of college and course responses to ACCM paper No. 22*, London, ABM, 1991.

ADVISORY BOARD OF MINISTRY 1991 (b)   ABM, *Local NSM: The report of a Church of England working party concerned with local non-stipendiary ministry*, ABM Paper No. 1, April 1991, London, ABM, 1991.

ADVISORY COUNCIL FOR THE CHURCH'S MINISTRY 22 1987   ACCM Occasional Paper No. 22, *Education for the Church's Ministry: The report of the working party on assessment*, London, ACCM, 1987.

ADVISORY COUNCIL FOR THE CHURCH'S MINISTRY 1990   ACCM, *Deacons Now: The report of a Church of England working party concerned with women in ordained ministry 1990*, Central Board of Finance of Church of England, for ACCM, 1990.

ADAMS 1975   Adams, Richard Newbold, *Energy and Structure: A theory of social power*, Austin & London, University of Texas Press, 1975.

ADAMS 1988   Adams, Richard Newbold, *The Eighth Day: Social evolution and energy*, Austin & London, University of Texas Press, 1988.

ALLEN AND OTHERS 1993   Allen, Peter, and Others, *The Fire and the Clay: The priest in today's church*, London, SPCK, 1993.

ALLEN 1960   Allen, Roland, (a)   'Pentecost and the World' in *The Ministry of the Spirit: Selected writings of Roland Allen*, ed. David Paton, London, World Dominion Press, 1960.

ALLEN (1912) 1960   Allen, Roland, (b)   *Missionary Methods: St Paul's or ours?* London, World Dominion Press, (1912) 1960.

ANGLO-CATHOLIC PRIESTS' CONVENTION 1921   Anglo-Catholic Priests' Convention, Report: *Priestly Efficiency*, London, Society of SS Peter & Paul, 1921.

ARBUCKLE 1991   Arbuckle, Gerard A., *Grieving for Change: A spirituality for refounding gospel communities*, London, Geoffrey Chapman, 1991.

ARCHBISHOP OF CANTERBURY'S COMMISSION ON URBAN PRIORITY AREAS 1985 *Faith in the City: A call for action by Church and Nation*, London, Church House Publishing, 1985.

ARCHBISHOPS' COMMISSION ON RURAL AREAS 1990 *Faith in the Countryside*, Worthing, Churchman Publishing, 1990.

ARCIC I 1982 *The Final Report*, London, CTS/SPCK, 1982.

ARCIC II 1991 *Statement on Communion: One in Christ*, 1991, 1. pp 82 ff.

AUGUSTINE 1957 *Confessions I*, London, Dent & Sons Ltd, (this edition first published 1907), 1957.

AVIS 1990 Avis, Paul, *Christians in Communion*, London, Geoffrey Chapman, Mowbray, 1990.

AVIS 1992 Avis, Paul, *Authority, Leadership and Conflict in the Church*, London, Mowbray, 1992.

BAELZ AND JACOB 1985 Baelz, Peter and Jacob, William (eds.), *Ministers of the Kingdom: Exploration in non-stipendiary ministry*, London, CIO, 1985.

BALASURIYA 1977 Balasuriya, Tissa, OMI, *The Eucharist and Human Liberation*, London, SCM, 1977.

BALL 1986 Ball, Peter, *Catechumenate Network* 3 June, 1986.

BALL 1992 Ball, Peter, *Adult Way to Faith: Preparing for baptism and confirmation*, London, Mowbray, 1992.

BANKS 1986 Banks, Robert and Julie, *The Home Church: Regrouping the People of God for community and mission*, Australia, Albatross, 1986.

BARBALET 1988 Barbalet, J. M., *Citizenship*, Open University Press, 1988.

BARBOUR 1990 Barbour Ian G., *Religion in an Age of Science, The Gifford Lectures 1989–90 vol. 1*, London, SCM, 1990.

BARRETT 1985 Barrett, C. K., *Church, Ministry and Sacraments in the New Testament*, London, Paternoster Press, 1985.

BARRY (1931) 1932 Barry, F. R., *The Relevance of Christianity: An approach to Christian ethics*, London, Nisbet, (1931) 1932.

BARRY 1945 Barry, F. R., *Church and Leadership*, London, SCM, 1945.

BARRY 1958 Barry, F. R., *Vocation and Ministry*, London, Hodder & Stoughton, 1958.

BARRY 1960 Barry, F. R., *Asking the Right Questions: Church and ministry*, London, Hodder & Stoughton, 1960.

BARTH (1936) ET 1975 Barth, Karl, *Church Dogmatics*, Edinburgh, T. & T. Clarke, (1936) ET 1975.

BAX 1986 Bax, Josephine, *The Good Wine: Spiritual renewal in the Church of England*, London, Church House Publishing, 1986.

BEASLEY-MURRAY 1993   Beasley-Murray, Paul (ed.), *Anyone for Ordination?* Tunbridge Wells, Marc Europe, 1993.
BECKWITH 1964   Beckwith, R. T., *Priesthood and Sacraments: A study in the Anglican–Methodist Report*, Appleford, Marcham, 1964.
BEGBIE 1990   Begbie, Jeremy, Paper given to SST, St Andrews University, 1990.
BEGBIE 1992 Begbie, Jeremy, 'The Gospel, the arts and our culture' in Montefiore, Hugh (ed.), *The Gospel and Contemporary Culture*, pp. 58ff, London, Mowbray, 1992.
BICKNELL AND CARPENTER (1919) 1957   Bicknell, E. J., *A Theological Introduction to the Thirty-nine Articles of the Church of England*, revised by H. J. Carpenter, London, Longmans Green, (1919) third edition 1957.
BLEAKLEY 1981   Bleakley, David, *In Place of Work. The Sufficient Society: A study of technology from the point of view of people*, London, SCM, 1981.
BOARD OF FINANCE 1991   Board of Finance Diocese of Gloucester, *Future Financial Strategy: A vision of the rural future*, Gloucester, DBF, 1991.
BOARD OF SOCIAL RESPONSIBILITY 1987   Board of Social Responsibility, *Goals for Our Future Society—Changing Britain: Social diversity and moral unity*, London, Church House Publishing, 1987.
BOFF 1985   Boff, Leonardo, *Church Charism and Power: Liberation theology and the institutional church*, London, SCM, 1985.
BOFF (1986) 1987   Boff, Leonardo, *Ecclesiogenesis: The base communities reinvent the church*, London, Collins, 1987.
BOFF 1988   Boff, Leonardo, *Trinity and Society*, London, Burns & Oates, 1988.
BONHOEFFER 1963   Bonhoeffer, Dietrich, *Sanctorum Communio*, London, Collins, 1963.
BOX 1937   Box, Hubert S. (ed.), *Priesthood*, London, SPCK, 1937.
BRADSHAW 1992   Bradshaw, Tim, *The Olive Branch: An Evangelical Anglican doctrine of the Church*, Carlisle, Paternoster Press, 1992.
BRALEY 1951   Braley, F. E. (ed.), *Letters of Herbert Hensley Henson*, London, 1951.
BRIERLY 1991   Brierly, Peter, *Christian England: What the 1989 census reveals*, London, Marc Europe, 1991.
BRITISH COUNCIL OF CHURCHES 1989   BCC, *The Forgotten Trinity 1: The report of the BCC Study Commission of Trinitarian Doctrine Today*, London, BCC, 1989.
BRITISH COUNCIL OF CHURCHES 1991   BCC, *The Forgotten Trinity 3: A selection of papers presented to the BCC Study Commission on Trinitarian Doctrine Today*, London, BCC, 1991.

BROOK (1968) 1972 Brook, Peter, *The Empty Space*, London, Penguin, 1972.

BROWN 1987 Brown, R. Lester, *Board of Social Responsibility Report*, General Synod, 1987.

BURNISH 1985 Burnish, Raymond, *The Meaning of Baptism*, London, Alcuin Club, SPCK, 1985.

BYRNE 1988 Byrne, Lavinia, *Women Before God*, London, SPCK, 1988.

BYRNE 1992 Byrne, Peter, *Science and Religion: A review of science and religion: Some historical perspectives*, (CUP, 1991), reviewed by John Hedley Brooke in *Theology*, May/June 1992, p. 230, 1992.

CAPRA 1975 Capra, Fritjof, *The Tao of Physics*, Wildwood House, 1975.

CARD 1988 Card, Terence, *Priesthood and Ministry in Crisis*, London, SCM, 1988.

CARR 1985 Carr, Wesley, *The Priestlike Task: A model for training and developing the Church's ministry*, London, SPCK, 1985.

CARR 1989 Carr, Wesley, *The Pastor as Theologian: The integration of Pastoral Ministry and Discipleship*, London, SPCK, 1989.

CARR 1992 Carr, Wesley (with others), *Say One For Me: The Church of England in the next decade*, London, SPCK, 1992.

CHENU 1981 Chenu, Marie-Dominique, 'The New Awareness of the Trinitarian Basis of the Church', *Concilium* 146, pp. 14ff, 1981.

CHILTON AND McDONALD 1987 Chilton, Bruce, and McDonald J. I. H., *Jesus and the Ethics of the Kingdom*, London, SPCK, 1987.

CHITTISTER 1986 Chittister, Joan OSB, *Winds of Change, Women Challenge the Church*, London, Sheed and Ward, 1986.

CHURCH OF ENGLAND 1980 Church of England, The Alternative Service Book 1980, Services authorized for use in the Church of England in conjunction with the Book of Common Prayer (A.S.B.), London, Hodder & Stoughton, 1980.

CHURCH OF ENGLAND 1986 Board for Mission and Unity (Faith and Order Group), *The Priesthood of the Ordained Ministry* [*GS. 694*], London, Central Board of Finance, Church of England, 1986.

CLAPSIS 1992 Clapsis, Emmanuel, 'NAMING GOD: An Orthodox View', in *The Ecumenical Review*, Vol 44 No 1, pp. 100–112. Jan. 1992.

COCKERELL 1989 Cockerell, David, *Beginning Where We Are: A theology of parish ministry*, London, SCM, 1989.

COHN-SHERBOK AND McLELLAN 1992 Cohn-Sherbok, Dan,

and McLellan, David (eds.), *Religion in Public Life*, New York, St. Martin's Press, 1992.

COLE 1990 Cole, John, *How to be a Local Church*, London, Mayhew, 1990.

COLLINS AND POWER 1982 Collins, Mary, and Power, David (eds.), *Can we Always Celebrate the Eucharist? Concilium*, Edinburgh T. & T. Clark, Feb. 1982.

CONGAR 1983 Congar, Yves, *I Believe in the Holy Trinity, II*, London, Geoffrey Chapman, 1983.

CORNWELL 1983 Cornwell, Peter, *Church and Nation*, Oxford, Basil Blackwell, 1983.

COUNTRYMAN 1992 Countryman, L. W., *The Language of Ordination*, Philadelphia, 1992.

CUPITT 1990 Cupitt, Don, *Creation out of Nothing*, London, SCM, 1990.

DAVIES 1993 Davies, Paul, *God and the New Physics*, London, Penguin, 1983

DARWEN 1992 Darwen, Ron, 'Beveridge and his Giants', *The Month*, June 1992, London.

DAVIES 1983 Davies, Paul, *God and the New Physics*, London, Penguin, 1983.

DAVIES 1992 Davies, Paul, *The Mind of God: Science and the search for ultimate meaning*, London, Simon and Schuster, 1992.

DAVIS AND GOSLING 1986 Davis, Howard, and Gosling, David, *Will the Future Work? Values for energising patterns of work and employment*, Geneva, WCC 1986.

DAVIES, WATKINS, WINTER & OTHERS 1991 Davies, Douglas; Watkins, Charles; Winter, Michael and others, *Church and Religion in Rural England*, Edinburgh, T. & T. Clark, 1991.

de GRUCHY 1987 de Gruchy, John, *Theology and Ministry in Context and Crisis: A South Africa perspective*, London, Collins Flame, 1987.

DESCARTES 1969 Descartes, René, *The Philosophical Works of Descartes*, translated by E. Haldage and G. Ross, Cambridge, CUP, 1969.

DOCTRINE COMMISSION OF THE CHURCH OF ENGLAND 1938 Doctrine Commission of Church of England, *Doctrine in the Church of England*, London, SPCK, 1938.

DOCTRINE COMMISSION OF THE CHURCH OF ENGLAND 1991 Doctrine Commission of the Church of England, *We Believe in the Holy Spirit*, London, Church House Publishing, 1991.

DONOVAN (1978) 1982 Donovan, Vincent J., *Christianity Rediscovered: An Epistle from the Masai*, London, SCM, 1978, 1982.

DOOHAN 1984   Doohan, Leonard, *The Lay-Centred Church: Theology and spirituality*, Minneapolis Minnesota, Winston Press, 1984.

DULLES 1974   Dulles, Avery, *Models of the Church*, New York, Doubleday & Co, 1974.

DUQUOC 1986   Duquoc, Christian, 'The Forgiveness of God', *Concilium* 184, 1986–2.

EASTMAN 1982   Eastman, A. Theodore, *The Baptizing Community: Christian Initiation and the local congregation*, New York, Seabury Press, 1982.

ECCLESTONE 1988   Ecclestone, Giles (ed.), *The Parish Church: Explorations in the relationship of the Church and the world*, London, Mowbray, 1988.

ELIZONDO AND GREINACHER, 1981   Elizondo, Virgil and Greinacher, Norbert (eds.), *Tensions Between the Churches of the First World and the Third World*, *Concilium* 144, April 1981, Edinburgh, T. & T. Clark, 1981.

ENGLAND 1981   England, John C., *Living Theology in Asia*, London, SCM, 1981.

EVANS AND WRIGHT 1991   Evans, G. R. and Wright, J. Robert (eds.), *The Anglican Tradition: A handbook of sources*, London & Minneapolis, SPCK & Fortress, 1991.

FAIVRE 1990   Faivre, Alexandre, *The Emergence of the Laity in the Church*, New York, Paulist Press, 1990.

FARLEY 1975   Farley, Edward, *Ecclesial Man: A social phenomenology of faith and reality*, Philadelphia, Fortress Press, 1975.

FIELD-BIBB 1991   Field-Bibb, Jacqueline, *Women Towards Priesthood: Ministerial politics and feminist praxis*, Cambridge, CUP. 1991.

FINNEY 1989   Finney, John, *Understanding Leadership*, Forward by Bishop George Carey, London, Daybreak, 1989.

FIORENZA AND CARR 1987   Fiorenza, Elisabeth Schüssler, and Carr, Ann (eds.), *Women Work and Poverty*, *Concilium* Vol. 194, December 1987, T. & T. Clark, 1987.

FLANNERY 1975   Flannery, Austin OP (ed.), *Vatican Council II: The Conciliar and Post-Conciliar documents*, Dublin, Costello, 1975.

FLANNERY 1982   Flannery, Austin OP (ed.), *Vatican Council II: More Post-Conciliar documents*, New York, Costello, 1982.

FLINDALL 1972   Flindall, R. P. (ed.), *The Church of England 1815–1948*, London SPCK, 1972.

FLOOD 1987   Flood, Edward OSB, *The Laity Today and Tomorrow: A Report on the new consciousness of lay catholics and how it might change the face of tomorrow's church*, New York, Paulist Press, 1987.

FORD 1989   Ford, D. F., *The Modern Theologians: An introduction to*

Christian theology in the twentieth century, Vol I & II, Oxford, Blackwell, 1989.

FORD 1986   Ford, Stephen H., 'Perichoresis and Interpenetration: Samuel Taylor Coleridge's Trinitarian conception of unity', *Theology*, Jan. 1986, p. 22, London, SPCK, 1986.

FORDER (1947) 1964   Forder, Charles R., *The Parish Priest at Work: An introduction to systematic pastoralic*, London, SPCK, (1947) 1964.

FOX 1983   Fox, Matthew, *Original Blessing*, New Mexico, Bear & Co., 1983.

FRASER 1992   Fraser, Ian, *The Ecumenical Review*, Vol. 44 No 1 Jan. 1992, Geneva, WCC, 1992.

FREND 1989   Frend, W. H. C., 'ARCIC: a New Start Necessary?' *Theology*, Sep. 1989.

FURLONG 1984   Furlong, Monica (ed.), *Feminine in the Church*, London, SPCK, 1984.

FURLONG 1991   Furlong, Monica, *A Dangerous Delight: Women and power in the Church*, London, SPCK, 1991.

GARBETT 1950   Garbett, Cyril, *Church and State in England*, London, Hodder & Stoughton, 1950.

GILL 1988   Gill, Robin, *Beyond Decline: A challenge to the churches*, London, SCM, 1988.

GILL 1993   Gill, Robin, *The Myth of the Empty Church*, London, SPCK, 1993.

GORE (1886) 1949   Gore, Charles, *The Church and the Ministry*, London, SPCK, (1886) New edn revised by C. H. Turner, 1949.

GORE (1900) 1925   Gore, Charles, *Roman Catholic Claims*, London, Longmans Green, (1900) 1925.

GOTT 1895   Gott, John, *The Parish Priest in the Town: Lectures delivered in the Divinity School Cambridge*, London, SPCK, 1895.

GREEN 1987   Green, Laurie, *Power to the Powerless: Theology brought to life*, Basingstoke, Marshall Morgan & Scott, 1987.

GREENWOOD 1984   Greenwood, Robin, 'Presiding: A parish priest's work' in *Theology*, Vol. LXXXVII, No. 720, pp. 412–419, Nov. 1984.

GREENWOOD 1987   Greenwood, Robin, 'Support for the Strong', *Theology* Vol. 90 No. 737, London, SPCK, 1987.

GREENWOOD 1987   Greenwood, Robin, *Together in Mission and Ministry*, Diocese of Gloucester, 1987.

GREENWOOD 1988   Greenwood, Robin, *Reclaiming the Church*, London, Collins Fount, 1988.

GREENWOOD 1991   Greenwood, Robin, 'Towards a Parish Agenda' in *Ministry*, Autumn 1991, Lincoln, Edward King Institute for Ministerial Development, 1991.

GREENWOOD 1993   Greenwood, Robin, 'Vicars, Laity and Holy Management', *Independent*, London, May 1993.

GROLLENBERG 1980   Grollenberg, L. and others, *Minister? Pastor? Prophet? Grass roots leadership in the churches*, London, SCM, 1980.

GRUNDY 1992   Grundy, Malcolm, *Unholy Conspiracy*, Canterbury Press, 1992.

GUIVER 1988   Guiver, George CR, *Company of Voices: Daily Prayer and the People of God*, London, SPCK, 1988.

GUIVER 1990   Guiver, George CR, *Faith in Momentum*, London, SPCK, 1990.

GUNTON 1988   Gunton, Colin, *The Actuality of Atonement*, Edinburgh, T. & T. Clark, 1988.

GUNTON 1991   Gunton, Colin, *The Promise of Trinitarian Theology*, Edinburgh, T. & T. Clark, 1991.

GUNTON 1992   Gunton, Colin, 'Knowledge and Culture: Towards an epistemology of the concrete', in Montefiore, Hugh (ed.) *The Gospel and Contemporary Culture*, London, Mowbray, 1992.

GUNTON 1993   Gunton, Colin, 'Unity and Diversity: God, World, and Society, particularity and the transcendentality of the One. Towards a recovery of the doctrine of substance,' Unpublished SST paper, 1993.

GUNTON AND HARDY 1989   Gunton, Colin and Hardy, Daniel W., (eds.), *On Being the Church: Essays on the Christian community*, Edinburgh, T. & T. Clark, 1989.

GUTIERREZ 1984   Gutierrez, Gustavo, *We Drink from our Own Wells: The spiritual journey of a people*, London, SCM, 1984.

HABERMAS 1987   Habermas, Jürgen, *The Philosophical Discourse of Modernity*, Cambridge, Polity Press, 1987.

HABGOOD 1988   Habgood, John, *Confessions of a Conservative Liberal*, London, SPCK, 1988.

HALL 1985   Hall, Douglas, 'On Contextuality in Christian Theology', *Toronto Journal of Theology*, 1/1 Spring 1985.

HALL 1991   Hall, Stuart G., *Doctrine and Practice in the Early Church*, London, SPCK, 1991.

HAMPSON 1991   Hampson, Daphne, 'Theological Integrity and Human Relationships', Unpublished paper, SST, 1991.

HANSON (1961) 1975   Hanson, A. T., *The Pioneer Ministry*, London, SPCK, (1961) 1975.

HANSON 1988   Hanson, R. P. C., *The Search for the Christian Doctrine of God*, Edinburgh, T. & T. Clark, 1988.

HARDY 1993   Hardy, Daniel W., 'Theology, Cosmology and Change', Unpublished SST paper, 1993.

HARDY AND FORD 1984   Hardy, D. W. and Ford, D. F., *Jubilate: Theology in praise*, London, Darton, Longman & Todd, 1984.

HARDY AND SEDGWICK 1991   Hardy, D. W., and Sedgwick, P. M. (eds.), *The Weight of Glory: A vision and practice for Christian faith: The future of liberal theology*, Edinburgh, T. & T. Clark, 1991.

HARGRAVE 1990   Hargrave, Alan, *But Who Will Preside?* Grove Worship Series No 113, Nottingham, Grove Books, 1990.

HARRÉ 1976   Harré, Rom (ed.), *Personality*, Oxford, Basil Blackwell, 1976.

HASTINGS 1986   Hastings, Adrian, *A History of English Christianity 1920–1985*, London, Collins, 1986.

HASTINGS 1992   Hastings, Adrian, 'Church and State in a Pluralist Society: The Grove lecture, Westminster Abbey, 13 November 1991', *Theology*, May/June 1992 pp. 165 ff. London, SPCK, 1992.

HAUERWAS 1981   Hauerwas, Stanley, *A Community of Character: Toward a constructive Christian social ethic*, Notre Dame, London, University of Notre Dame Press, 1981.

HEBBLETHWAITE 1984   Hebblethwaite, Margaret, *Motherhood and God*, London, Geoffrey Chapman, 1984.

HENDRICKX 1984   Hendrickx, Herman, *The Sermon on the Mount*, London, Geoffrey Chapman, 1984.

HENDY 1990   Hendy, Graham, *Equipping the Saints: Training for lay ministry in the Provinces of Canterbury, York and Wales*, London, The National Society, 1990.

HERZEL 1981   Herzel, Susannah, *A Voice for Women*, Geneva, WCC, 1981.

HILL 1988   Hill, Edmund OP, *Ministry and Authority in the Catholic Church*, London, Geoffrey Chapman, 1988.

HILL 1991   Hill, Edmund OP, *The Trinity Works of Saint Augustine: A translation for the 21st century*, New York, New City Press, 1991.

HILL 1982   Hill, William J., *The Three Personed God: The Trinity as a Mystery of Salvation*, Washington DC, Catholic University of America Press, 1982.

HILLS 1993   Hills, John, with the LSE Welfare State Programme, *The Future of Welfare: A guide to the debate*, York, Joseph Rowntree Foundation, 1993.

HILLYER 1990   Hillyer, Philip (ed.), *On the Threshold of the Third Milennium, Concilium* 1, 1990.

HMSO 1992   HMSO, *Britain 1992: An official handbook*, HMSO, 1992.

HOCKEN 1989   Hocken, Peter, *Covenants for Unity: One in Christ* (a)   Vol XXV 1989–No. 1, pp. 3–13; (b)   1989–No. 2, pp. 153–162; (c)   1989–No. 3, pp. 373–280.

HODGSON AND KING 1983 Hodgson, Peter, and King, Robert (eds.), foreword by Stephen Sykes, *Christian Theology: An introduction to its traditions and tasks*, London, SPCK, 1983.

HODGSON 1988 Hodgson, Peter C., *Revisioning the Church: Ecclesial freedom in the new paradigm*, Philadelphia, Fortress Press, 1988.

HOFFMAN 1990 Hoffman, Lawrence A., 'Rabbinic *BERAKHAH* and Jewish Spirituality,' *Concilium* 1990/3 June, pp. 18ff.

HOLTBY 1967 Holtby, Robert T., *Eric Graham 1888–1964 Dean of Oriel Principal of Cuddesdon Bishop of Brechin*, London, OUP, 1967.

HOPKINS 1939 Hopkins, N. T., 'Dr Seaton as Principal of Cuddesdon' in Swain, E. P. and Hopkins, N. T., *Bishop Seaton of Wakefield 1939*, London, SPCK, 1939.

HOUTEPEN 1983 Houtepen, Anton, *People of God, a Plea for the Church*, London, SCM, 1983.

HOWARD 1984 Howard, Christine, *The Ordination of Women to the Priesthood: Further report; a background paper*, GS MISC. 198, London, CIO, 1984.

HUGHES 1968 Hughes, John Jay, *Absolutely Null and Utterly Void: The papal condemnation of Anglican Orders 1896*, London, Sheed & Ward, 1968.

HULL 1985 Hull, John M., *What Prevents Christian Adults from Learning?* London, SCM, 1985.

HUME 1988 Hume, Cardinal Basil, *Towards a Civilisation of Love: Being church in today's world*, London, Hodder & Stoughton, 1988.

HYLSON-SMITH 1989 Hylson-Smith, Kenneth, *Evangelicals in the Church of England 1734–1984*, Edinburgh, T. & T. Clark, 1989.

JAMES 1988 James, Eric (ed.), *God's Truth: Essays to celebrate the twenty-fifth anniversary of* Honest to God, London, SCM, 1988.

JAMES 1992 James, Eric, *Word Over All*, London, SPCK, 1992.

JENSON 1982 Jenson, Robert W., *The Triune Indentity*, Philadelphia, Fortress, 1982.

JOHN PAUL II *Instrumentorum Laboris*, E. T., C. T. S. 1987.

JOHNSTON 1892 Johnston, C. F. H., *The Book of St Basil the Great on the Holy Spirit: Written to Amphilochius, Bishop of Iconium, against the Pneumatomachi:* Revised text with notes and introduction, Oxford, Clarendon Press, 1892.

KEIFER 1982 Keifer, Ralph A., *Blessed and Broken: Exploration of the contemporary experience of God in eucharistic celebration: Message 1 the Sacraments 3*, Delaware, Michael Glazier, 1982.

KEIRSEY AND BATES (1978) 1984 Keirsey, David, and Bates, Marilyn, *Please Understand Me: Character and temperament types*, Del Mar, Prometheus Nemesis Books Company, (1978) 1984.

KELLY 1989   Kelly, Anthony, CSSR, *The Trinity of Love: A theology of the Christian God*, New Theology Series 4, Wilmington, Delaware, Michael Glazier, 1989.

KIRK 1946   Kirk, K. E., (ed.), *The Apostolic Ministry: Essays in the history and doctrine of episcopacy*, London, Hodder & Stoughton, 1946.

KRAEMER 1958   Kraemer, Hendrick, *A Theology of the Laity*, Cambridge, Lutterworth, 1958.

KÜNG 1972   Küng, Hans, *Why Priests?* London, Collins, 1972.

KÜNG 1988   Küng, Hans, *Theology for the Third Millennium: An ecumenical view*, London, Harper Collins, 1988.

KÜNG 1991   Küng, Hans, *Theology for the Third Millennium*, London, Harper Collins, 1991.

LA CUGNA 1991   La Cugna, C. M., *God For Us*, San Francisco, Harper, 1991.

LAMBETH 1930   Lambeth Conference, *Encyclical Letter from the Bishops: with Resolutions and Reports*, London, SPCK, 1930.

LAMBETH 1988   Lambeth Conference, *The Truth Shall Set You Free: The Reports, Resolutions and Pastoral Letters from the Bishops*. London, Church House Publishing, 1988.

LASH 1992   Lash, Nicholas, *Believing Three Ways in One God: A reading of the Apostles' Creed*, London, SCM, 1992.

LAYZER 1990   Layzer, David, *Cosmogenesis: The growth of order in the universe*, Oxford, OUP, 1990.

LEECH 1977   Leech, Kenneth, *Soul Friend: A study of spirituality*, London, Sheldon, 1977.

LEGRAND 1993   Legrand, Hervé, OP, The 'Non-Ordination of Women', in *One in Christ*, Vol 29, No. 1, pp. 1–23, 1993.

LEGRAND 1979   Legrand, Hervé, 'The Presidency of the Eucharist in the Ancient Church', in *Worship* 27, pp. 413–38, 1979.

LIEBARD 1978   Liebard, Odile M. (ed.), *Official Catholic Teachings: Clergy and Laity*, Dublin, McGrath, 1978.

LIENHARD 1984   Lienhard, Joseph, T. SJ, *Ministry, Message of the Fathers of the Church, 8*, Wilmington Delaware, Michael Glazier, 1984.

LIMA 1982   World Council of Churches, *Baptism, Eucharist and Ministry (BEM)*, World Council of Churches, 1982.

LIMOURIS 1986   Limouris, Gennadios (ed.), 'The Church and Mystery in Ecclesiological Perspectives', in *Church, World, Kingdom*, Faith and Order paper No. 130, Geneva, WCC, 1986.

LINDBECK 1984   Lindbeck, George, *The Nature of Doctrine: Religion and theology in a post liberal age*, London, SPCK, 1984.

LLOYD 1966   Lloyd, Roger, *The Church of England 1900–1965*, London, SCM, 1966.

LLOYD 1977   Lloyd, Trevor (ed.), *Lay Presidency at the Eucharist?* Grove Liturgical Study No. 9, Nottingham, Grove Books, 1977.

LOADES 1990   Loades, Ann (ed.), *Feminist Theology: A Reader*, London, SPCK, 1990.

MACKEY 1983   Mackey, James, P., *The Christian Experience of God as Trinity*, London, SCM, 1983.

MacQUARRIE 1986   MacQuarrie, John, *Theology Church and Ministry*, London, SCM, 1986.

MacQUARRIE (1963) 1988   MacQuarrie, John, *Twentieth Century Religious Thought*, London, SCM, (1963) 4th edition 1988.

MARSH 1984   Marsh, Thomas A., *Gift of Community: Baptism and Confirmation: Message of the Sacraments 2*, Wilmington Delaware, Michael Glazier, 1984.

MARSHALL 1992   Marshall, Brian, 'New Departures in Systematic Theology: The doctrine of the Trinity and social, political and economic questions', Short Paper for the Trinity Seminar 1992, SST Conference, 1992.

MARTIN AND MULLEN 1984   Martin, David, and Mullen, Peter, *Stage Gifts?: A guide to charismatic renewal*, Oxford, Basil Blackwell, 1984.

MAYFIELD 1963   Mayfield, Guy, *The Church of England: Its members and its business*, Oxford, OUP, 1963.

McADOO 1991   McAdoo, H. R., *The Anglican Heritage: Theology and spirituality*, London, SPCK, 1991.

McFADYEN 1990   McFadyen, Alistair I., *The Call to Personhood: A Christian theory of the individual in social relationships*, Cambridge, CUP, 1990.

McFADYEN 1991   McFadyen, Alistair I., 'Theology and Claims to Public Truth': Unpublished paper, SST, Conference, 1991.

McGINN, MEYENDORFF AND LECLERQ 1989   McGinn, Bernard, Meyendorff, John, and Leclerq, Jean, *Christian Spirituality: Origins to the Twelfth Century*, London, SCM, 1989.

McGRATH 1990   McGrath, Alister E., *The Genesis of Doctrine: A study in the foundations of doctrinal criticism*, Oxford, Basil Blackwell, 1990.

McPARTLAN 1993   McPartlan, Paul, *The Eucharist Makes the Church: Henri de Lubac and John Zizioulas in dialogue*, Edinburgh, T. & T. Clark, 1993.

MEEKS 1983   Meeks, Wayne A., *The First Urban Christians: The social world of the Apostle Paul*, Newhaven & London, Yale University Press, 1983.

MEEKS 1989   Meeks, W. D. *God the Economist: The doctrine of God and political economy*, Minneapolis, Fortress, 1989.

METCALFE 1981 Metcalfe, Ronald, *Sharing Christian Ministry*, London, Mowbray, 1981.

METZ 1981 Metz, J. B., *The Emergent Church: The future of Christianity in a post bourgeois world*, London, SCM, 1981.

METZ 1990 Metz, J. B., 'On the Threshold of the Third Millennium, the Foundation', *Concilium* 1/1990, London, SCM, 1990.

MICK 1984 Mick, Lawrence E., *To Live as we Worship*, Minnesota, Liturgical Press, 1984.

MILBANK 1990 Milbank, John, *Theology and Social Theory: Beyond secular reason*, Oxford, Basil Blackwell, 1990.

MITCHELL 1982 Mitchell, Nathan OSB, *Mission and Ministry: History and theology in the Sacrament of Order: Message of the Sacraments 6*, Wilmington Delaware, Michael Glazier, 1982.

 MOBERLY (1897) 1905 Moberly, R. C., *Ministerial Priesthood*, London, John Murray, (1897) new impression 1905.

MOLTMANN 1972 Moltmann, J., *The Crucified God*, London, SCM, 1972.

MOLTMANN 1977 Moltmann, J., *The Church in the Power of the Spirit*, London, SCM, 1977 ET.

MOLTMANN 1978 Moltmann, J., *The Open Church: Invitation to a messianic lifestyle*, London, SCM, 1978.

MOLTMANN 1985 (a) Moltmann, J., *God in Creation: An ecological doctrine of Creation*, Gifford lectures 1984–5, London, SCM, 1985.

MOLTMANN 1985 (b) Moltmann, J., 'Inviting Unity', *Concilium* 177, 1985, pp. 5off.

MOLTMANN (1981) 1989 Moltmann, J., *The Trinity and the Kingdom of God*, (= *Trinity and the Kingdom*, Harper and Row 1981), London, SCM, (1981) 4th impression 1989.

MOLTMANN 1989 Moltmann, J., *Creating a Just Future*, London, SCM, Philadelphia, Trinity Press, 1989.

MOLTMANN 1990 Moltmann, J., *The Way of Jesus Christ: Christology in Messianic dimension*, London, SCM, 1990.

MOLTMANN 1991 Moltmann, J.; *History and the Triune God: Contributions to trinitarian theology*, London, SCM, 1991.

MOLTMANN 1992 Moltmann, J., *The Spirit of Life: A universal affirmation*, London, SCM, 1992.

MOLTMANN-WENDEL 1986 Moltmann-Wendel, Elizabeth, *A Land Flowing with Milk and Honey*, London, SCM, 1986.

MONOD 1972 Monod, Jacques, *Chance and Necessity*, London, Collins, 1972.

MOORE 1978 Moore, Peter (ed.), *Man, Woman, Priesthood*, London, SPCK, 1978.

MOORMAN 1947 Moorman, John R. H., *B. K. Cunningham: A Memoir*, London, SCM, 1947.

NEILL AND WEBER 1963 Neill and Weber (eds.), *The Layman in Christian History*, Geneva, WCC, 1963.

NEWBIGIN 1989 Newbigin, Lesslie, *The Gospel in a Pluralist Society*, London, SPCK, 1989.

NEWBIGIN 1991 Newbigin, Lesslie, *Truth to Tell: The Gospel and public truth*, London, SPCK, 1991.

OPPENHEIMER 1991 Oppenheimer, Helen, 'Belonging and the Individual: I', In *Trust*, A Newsletter of SCM Press Trust, No. 5, Dec. 1991.

PAGET-WILKES 1981 Paget-Wilkes, Michael, *Poverty, Revolution and the Church*, London, Paternoster Press, 1981.

PANNENBERG 1975 Pannenberg, W., *Faith and Reality*, London, Search Press, 1975.

PEACOCKE 1979 Peacocke, A. R., *Creation and the World of Science: Bampton lectures 1978*, Oxford, Clarendon Press, 1979.

PEACOCKE 1990 Peacocke, A. R., Unpublished paper, SST, 1990.

PERHAM 1978 Perham, Michael, *The Eucharist: Alcuin Club Manual 1*, Alcuin Club, SPCK, 1978.

PICKERING 1989 Pickering, W. S. F., *Anglo-Catholicism: A study in religious ambiguity*, London, Routledge, 1989.

POLANYI 1958 Polanyi, Michael, *Personal Knowledge: The freedom of the subjective person to do as he pleases is overruled by the freedom of the responsible person to do as he must*, Chicago, University of Chicago Press, 1958.

POLKINGHORNE (1986) 1987 Polkinghorne, J., *One World: The interaction*, London, SPCK, (1986) 1987.

POLKINGHORNE (1988) 1989 Polkinghorne, J., *Science and Creation: The search for understanding*, London, SPCK, (1988) 1989.

PRESTIGE 1935 Prestige, G. L., *The Life of Charles Gore: A great Englishman*, London, Heinemann, 1935.

PRESTIGE 1952 Prestige, G. L., *God in Patristic Thought*, London, SPCK, 1952.

PRIGOGINE AND STENGERS 1984 Prigogine, Ilya, and Stengers, Isabelle, *Order out of Chaos: Man's new dialogue with nature*, London, Heinemann, 1984.

RAMSEY 1936 Ramsey, A. M., *The Gospel and the Catholic Church*, London, Longmans Green, 1936.

RAMSEY 1972 Ramsey, A. M., *The Christian Priest Today*, London, SPCK, 1972.

RAMSEY, TERWILLIGER, AND ALLCHIN 1974 Ramsey,

Michael; Terwilliger, Robert E.; Allchin, A. M., *The Charismatic Christ*, London, DLT, 1974.

RICHARDSON 1958   Richardson, Alan, *An Introduction to the Theology of the New Testament*, London, SCM, 1958.

RICHARDSON (1957) 1967   Richardson, Alan (ed.), *A Theological Word Book of the Bible*, London, SCM, (1957) 1967.

ROBINSON 1952   Robinson, J. A. T., *The Body: A study in Pauline theology*, London, SCM, 1952.

ROBINSON 1960   Robinson, J. A. T., *Liturgy Coming to Life*, London, Mowbray, 1960.

ROSENBLAT 1990   Rosenblat, Marie-Eloise, 'Surely the Lord is in this Place: Blessing the world', *The Way Review of Contemporary Spirituality*, Jan. 1990 Vol. 30 No 1 pp. 3–15, 1990.

ROSS 1988   Ross, Maggie, *Pillars of Flame: Power, priesthood and spiritual maturity*, London, SCM, 1988.

ROWELL 1992   Rowell, Geoffrey (ed.), *The English Religious Tradition and the Genius of Anglicanism*, Wantage, Ikon, 1992.

RUSSELL 1980   Russell, Anthony, *The Clerical Profession*, London, SPCK, 1980.

RUSSELL 1993   Russell, Anthony, *The Country Parson*, London, SPCK, 1993.

SACHS 1993   Sachs, William L., *The Transformation of Anglicanism: From State Church to Global Communion*, Cambridge, CUP, 1993.

SANFORD 1982   Sanford, John A., *Ministry Burnout*, London, Arthur James, 1982.

SANTER 1984   Santer, Henriette, 'Stereotyping the Sexes in Society and in the Church', in Furlong (ed.), *Feminine in the Church*, London, SPCK, 1984.

SANTER 1991   Santer, Mark, *Ecumenism and Evangelism in the New Europe*, Lecture to the University of Dublin, 26 April 1991.

SARIS 1980   Saris, Wim, *Towards a Living Church Family & Community Catechesis*, London, Collins, 1980.

SCHILLEBEECKX 1981   Schillebeeckx, E., *Ministry: A case for change*, London, SCM, 1981.

SCHILLEBEECKX 1985   Schillebeeckx, E., *The Church with a Human Face: A new and expanded theology of ministry*, London, SCM, 1985.

SCHILLEBEECKX 1990   Schillebeeckx, E., *Church the Human Story of God*, London, SCM, 1990.

SCHILLEBEECKX AND METZ 1980   Schillebeeckx, E. and Metz, J.-B. (eds.), *The Right of the Community to a Priest, Concilium* 133, 1980, Edinburgh T. & T. Clark, New York, The Seabury Press, 1980.

SCHNIDER 1972   Schnider, Franz & others, Ministries in the

Church, *Concilium* Vol. 10/No. 8, Dec. 1972, London, Burns & Oates, 1972.

SCHORR 1992   Schorr, Alvin L., *The Personal Social Services: An outside view*, York, Joseph Rowntree Foundation, 1992.

SCHREITER 1984   Schreiter, Robert (ed.), *A Schillebeeckx Reader*, Edinburgh, T. & T. Clark, 1984.

SCHWÖBEL 1991   Schwöbel, Christopher, 'Human Being and Relational Being: Twelve theses for a Christian anthropology', in Schwöbel, Christopher and Gunton, Colin E. (eds.), *Persons Human and Divine*, Edinburgh, T. & T. Clark, 1991.

SEDGWICK 1990   Sedgwick, P., *Mission Impossible? A theology of the local church*, London, Collins Flame, 1990.

SELBY 1991   Selby, Peter, *Belonging*, London, SPCK, 1991.

SHANNON 1987   Shannon, W. H., 'Thomas Merton and the Quest for Self-identity', *Cistercian Studies* Vol. 22 1987 pp. 172–189, 1987.

SHEILS AND WOOD 1989   Sheils, W., and Wood, Diana (eds.), *The Ministry: Clerical and Lay*, Studies in Church History No 26, Oxford, Basil Blackwell, 1989.

SHEPPARD 1983   Sheppard, David, *Bias to the Poor*, London, Hodder & Stoughton, 1983.

SMITH AND TAUSSIG 1990   Smith, Dennis E., and Taussig, Halx E., *Many Tasks: the Eucharist in the New Testament and Liturgy Today*, London, SCM and Philadelphia, Trinity Press International, 1990.

SORRELL 1987   Sorell, Tom, *Past Masters: Descartes*, Oxford, OUP, 1987.

STARKE 1990   Starke, L., *Signs of Hope: Working towards our common future*, Oxford, OUP, 1990.

STEPHENSON 1978   Stephenson, A. M. G., *Anglicanism and the Lambeth Conferences*, London, SPCK, 1978.

STOKES AND SHILLING 1980   Stokes, Dan, and Shilling, Audrey, *Building an Indigenous Church in East London: The development of a local ministry*, Start, Stepney Action Research Team, 1980.

STONE 1900   Stone, Darwell, *Outlines of Christian Dogma*, London, Longmans Green, 1900.

STONE 1905   Stone, Darwell, *The Christian Church*, London, Rivingtons, 1905.

SUENENS 1968   Suenens, Léon-Joseph, *Co-responsibility in the Church*, London, Burns & Oates, 1968.

SWAIN 1939   Swain, E. Priestley, 'A Memoir', in Swain, E. P., and Hopkins, N. T., *Bishop Seaton of Wakefield*, 1939.

SWAYNE 1981   Swayne, Sean (ed.), *Eucharist for a New World*,

Select addresses, homilies and conferences for 42nd international eucharistic congress, Lourdes 1981, Irish Institute of Pastoral Liturgy, 1981.

SYKES 1978   Sykes, S. W., *The Integrity of Anglicanism*, London, Mowbray, 1978.

SYKES 1987   Sykes, S. W., *Authority in the Anglican Communion: Essays presented to Bishop John Howe*, Toronto, Anglican Book Centre, 1987.

TAVARD 1983   Tavard, George H., *A Theology for Ministry*, Theology & Life Series 6, Delaware, Michael Glazier, 1983.

THEISSEN 1982   Theissen, Gerd, *The Social setting of Pauline Christianity*, Edinburgh, T. & T. Clark, 1982.

THOMAS 1905   Thomas, Griffith W. H., *The Catholic Faith: A manual of instruction for members of the Church of England*, London, Hodder & Stoughton, 1905.

THURIAN 1986   Thurian, Max (ed.), *Churches Respond to BEM: Official Responses to the 'Baptism, Eucharist and Ministry' text*, Vol. 1, Faith and Order Paper 129, Geneva, WCC, 1986.

THURIAN (1970) 1983   Thurian, Max, *Priesthood and Ministry Ecumenical Research*, London, Mowbray, (1970) 1983.

TILLER 1983   Tiller, John, *A Strategy for the Church's Ministry*, London, CIO for ACCM, 1983.

TILLER AND BIRCHALL 1987   Tiller, John, and Birchall, Mark, *The Gospel Community and its Leadership*, London, Marshall Pickering, 1987.

TORRANCE 1965   Torrance, T. F., *Theology in Reconstruction*, London, SCM, 1965.

TORRANCE 1981   Torrance, T. F., *Divine and Contingent Order*, Oxford, OUP, 1981.

TORRANCE 1985   Torrance, T. F., *Reality and Scientific Theology*, Edinburgh, Scottish Academic Press, 1985.

TORRANCE 1988   Torrance, T. F., *The Trinitarian Faith*, Edinburgh, T. & T. Clark, 1988.

TOULMIN 1990   Toulmin, Stephen, *Cosmopolis: The hidden agenda of modernity*, Free Press (Macmillan) N.Y., 1990.

TOWLER AND COXON 1979   Towler, Robert, and Coxon, A. P. M., *The Fate of the Anglican Clergy: A sociological study*, London, Mowbray, 1979.

TREASURE 1991   Treasure, Catherine, *Walking on Glass: Women deacons speak out*, London, SPCK, 1991.

TURNER 1990   Turner, H. J. M., *Ordination and Vocation Yesterday and Today: Current questions about ministries in the light of theology and history*, Foreword by the Bishop of London, Worthing and Folkestone, Churchman, 1990.

UHR 1992 Uhr, Marie Louise (ed.), *Changing Women Changing Church*, Newtown Australia, Millennium, 1992.

VANSTONE 1977 Vanstone, W. H., *Love's Endeavour, Love's Expense*, London, DLT, 1977.

WESTERMANN 1978 Westermann, Claus, *Blessing in the Bible and the Life of the Church*, Philadelphia, Fortress Press, 1978.

WHITHAM 1903 Whitham, A. R., *Holy Orders*, London, Longmans Green, 1903.

WILKEN 1971 Wilken, Robert L., *The Myth of Christian Beginnings*, London, SCM, 1971.

WILKINSON 1992 Wilkinson, Alan, *The Community of the Resurrection: A centenary history*, London, SCM, 1992.

WILLMER 1992 Willmer, Haddon (ed.), *20/20 Visions of the Future of Christianity in Britain*, London, SPCK, 1992.

WINDSOR CONSULTATIONS 1991 Windsor Consultations, *Women in the Ordained Ministry: Final Report* (Unpublished) 1991.

WINDSOR CONSULTATIONS 1993 Windsor Consultations, *Women in Ordained Ministry: Changing perceptions of ministry* (Unpublished), 1993.

YATES 1991 Yates, John, *Address at the Civic Service Commemorating the 450th Anniversary of the Founding of the City and Diocese of Gloucester*, 8th September 1991.

YOUNG AND FORD 1987 Young, Frances, and Ford, David, *Meaning and Truth in 2 Corinthians*, Grand Rapids Michigan, Eerdmans, 1987.

ZIZIOULAS 1985 Zizioulas, John D., *Being as Communion: Studies in personhood and the Church*, Foreword by John Meyendorff, New York, St. Vladimir's Seminary Press, 1985.

ZIZIOULAS 1988 Zizioulas, John, 'The Mystery of the Church': *One in Christ*, Vol. 24-No. 4, pp. 294ff, 1988.

INDEX